KW-360-659

THE COMPLETE BOOK OF
CREATIVE NEEDLECRAFTS

octopus

Contents

First published 1983 by
Octopus Books Limited
59 Grosvenor Street
London W1

© 1983 Octopus Books Limited

ISBN 0 7064 1715 1

Printed in Spain by
Artes Graficas Toledo S.A.
DLTO 1095−83

Introduction

Needlecraft means just what it says, 'the craft of the needle', but there are hundreds of different ways in which the needle can be used and unlimited combinations of design, material, threads and techniques. Most of the methods in this book have been carried out for centuries in one country or another, but nowadays we adapt the old designs, stitches and colour schemes to suit today's décor and fashion.

Fragments of ancient embroidery still exist, including some which are about two thousand years old. The earliest secular example which survives in its entirety, 70 metres long and 50 cm deep (230 feet by 20 inches), is on show at Bayeux in Northern France, and is known as the Bayeux Tapestry. It is not woven on a loom as indicated by its name, but embroidered in wool on linen in laid work, and stem and outline stitch. It depicts the events leading up to the Battle of Hastings in a delightfully simple and explicit manner.

More recently, a series of thirty-four panels were made in England between 1969 and 1975 to record in needlework the events leading up to and including the invasion of Normandy in 1944. This is known as the Overlord Embroidery and is carried out in appliqué and stitchery using traditional techniques. It is now on permanent exhibition at Whitbread's brewery in Chiswell Street, London, E.C.1.

Another famous embroidery, representing a period of time which links the Bayeux Tapestry with the Overlord is the panel designed and worked by Audrey Walker in 1973 to commemorate one thousand years of monarchy. This panel typifies the trend of embroidery in the twentieth century. Interpreted in appliqué and free stitchery, in colouring inspired by its surroundings at the Pump Room in Bath, England, it is a continuous composition of horses, men, armies and flags, starting with the Vikings and ending with the bombing of St. Paul's in World War II.

Clothing and furnishings, both for the church and for the home, have been decorated with stitchery throughout the ages in many parts of the world. In Elizabethan times embroidered head-dresses, for example, and jackets were fashionable. Fine stitchery on canvas, often depicting classical and biblical scenes, was also being done for furnishings at that time. Such scenes became even more prevalent in the seventeenth century, often depicted in raised (stump) work. At the end of that century many coverlets and hangings were boldly embroidered with foliated trees in crewel work.

It is impossible to mention all the sources for inspiration which can be found from historical embroideries around the world, as designs and styles vary from country to country and century to century: the strong counted thread influences of the Scandinavian countries contrasting with the dynamic colouring and richness of work from India; the beauty of embroideries from Turkey and the Greek Islands; the skill of the work from China and Japan with its perfect use of silk and metal threads; and the exciting patchwork quilts made in America.

Wherever embroidery is worked, it reflects something of the style of living of its time. Twentieth-century embroidery reflects the wonderful wealth of tradition, evolved over hundreds of years, from which we get our techniques and inspiration, but today we have the added advantage over our forerunners of a far greater variety of readily available materials and threads. The use of the needle has, not surprisingly, become one of the most versatile of all crafts, and at the same time as being used professionally for embroideries such as the Overlord, it is also a popular hobby. Even the simplest embroidery can greatly enhance dress, accessories, furnishings and small items for the home in an exciting, original and contemporary way.

Right *Details from the Bayeux Tapestry (above) and Audrey Walker's Monarchy Panel (below) worked in 1973, offering an interesting comparison of stitchery and design.*

Equipment and design

General tools

Little equipment is needed for most needlecraft methods but it is helpful to keep sewing things together so that they do not get used for other purposes.

Scissors

It is useful to have some fine-pointed scissors for cutting threads and for some techniques such as cutwork which depends upon very careful cutting of material. Dressmaker's shears or scissors are needed for cutting out material. Paper tends to blunt scissors quickly so it is helpful to have an old pair of scissors for that purpose alone.

Stiletto

This is a sharp-ended tool for piercing holes. It is useful when using metal threads and thick threads in couching, although not essential. The variety with a flat handle is best.

Thimble

A thimble is an aid to speed and efficiency, particularly if you are working on a slate frame when a thimble will be necessary on the second finger of each hand.

Pins

Always use dressmaker's steel pins to avoid marking material. If you find that pins are leaving prick marks when removed from the material, use fine sewing needles instead.

Iron

Press the material, if necessary, before starting an embroidery. An iron will also be needed for pressing some types of work and during making up. The heat of the iron must be suitable for the threads as well as for the background material; always make tests on the material before finally pressing. If stitching cotton fabrics together with synthetic thread in patchwork, do not use too hot an iron.

Drawing board

This is not essential but can be a great help for designing and when producing tracings.

Laminated board or heavy cardboard may be used, but the edges should be straight and the corners accurate.

Fabrics

Materials which are to be embroidered must be suitable for the technique involved and for the use to which the finished work will be put. It is necessary to recognize and understand the construction and properties of material so that your choice is suitable. Materials fall into three categories: woven, knitted, non-woven.

Woven materials

All woven materials consist of warp and weft threads; warp threads run down the length with the weft thread woven across them. The edges where the weft thread turns back on itself are known as selvedges.

As you handle woven material you will find that if you pull it straight down the warp, there is little or no stretch, but if you pull it across the weft there will usually be a certain amount of stretch. It is a good rule to try to have the warp threads running down and the weft running across an item, particularly on a garment so that the fabric will accommodate the natural stretch of the body, and for hangings and curtains to avoid dropping at the lower edge.

Woven materials that are closely woven and firm can be used for many techniques such as surface stitchery, metal thread work, crewel work and cut work. Some conventional embroidery linens are closely woven, as are some types of dress-weight and furnishing fabrics.

Materials may be woven of natural fibres such as linen, cotton, silk or wool, or synthetics which include rayon and polyester. Synthetics are often mixed with natural fibres to give non-crease and minimum-iron properties.

A harsh fabric is generally difficult to handle but a soft one which is too fine can be strengthened with a backing. For most purposes backing should be of a natural fibre such as linen or cotton, in a medium weight and pre-shrunk before starting. Avoid using man-made fabrics for backings.

If materials are loosely woven and have the same number of warp and weft threads in a square, they are known as evenweaves and are used for all counted thread work. Some loosely woven materials such as hessian/burlap, linen and sheer curtain fabrics also suit these methods but, because they are not true evenweave, they may cause some distortion of the stitchery. This is particularly liable to happen in blackwork, pulled work and cross stitch when the stitch patterns will become elongated. For accurate work, use a conventional evenweave linen, cotton, or cotton and polyester. Loosely woven materials tend to fray more than those which are closely woven.

Knitted materials

The stretching properties of these make surface stitchery difficult and counted thread work impossible, but they are very suitable and effective if used for smocking and quilting. Many garments nowadays are made from knitted fabrics and if you plan to decorate one, experiment first on a scrap piece or a hidden part, such as the underside of a hem, to see whether your design is practical.

Non-woven materials

Non-woven materials are those which do not fray when cut and have no grain so they can be used in any direction. These strong characteristics make them suitable for applying without turnings, and for making up an article such as a box or spectacle case where seaming would be difficult. Non-woven materials include felt, vinyl, leather and suede. With modern treatments some leather and suede is washable, making it ideal for fashion garments.

When selecting a material, it is important to consider its washing or dry-cleaning properties as well as whether it will crease or fray. Some materials have a matt surface, others are shiny; some are smooth, while others have a texture or slub finish so make sure that you can get suitable threads to use with your choice of material. Sometimes the wrong side may be what you require, rather than the intended right side so do not be afraid to use it. Colour, too, is important, whether the piece is needed as a match or as a contrast to an outfit or décor.

For most decorative stitchery a plain material is best, but patterned materials such as stripes, checks or dots may be used as a basis for simple decoration and can be helpful for learning new stitches. A few lines of freehand stitches added to a striped material, will immediately make a difference. Sometimes the pattern on a material will spark off an idea for added decoration.

When planning an embroidery, always allow at least 5 cm (2 inches) extra all round beyond the required finished size to allow for stretching.

Threads

Think of threads in relation to the material you are using. Consider the weight or thickness, the texture and whether you need a matt or shiny thread, or both. Remember also that you do not have to use the same thread or the same thickness throughout one piece of work. Sometimes it is more interesting to use a variety of thicknesses.

Man-made fibres may often provide just what you need in colour and texture, and you may even use threads unravelled from woven fabrics. Knitting and crochet yarns, metallic and Lurex threads, as well as some types of string may also be useful.

It is necessary to consider whether the stitching will need to be washed or dry cleaned, depending on the material, and to choose threads accordingly. Most threads which are specially prepared for embroidery are fast-dyed, and the cottons in particular are washable; most woollen embroidery threads are better dry cleaned. It is when using the less conventional threads with unknown qualities that problems occur, and it is important to experiment before starting the main work.

A practice piece of work is always of value as not only will it enable you to test the threads and fabric for washing, but it may help you to calculate the amount of thread that you will need for the full-scale work.

To calculate the amount of thread you will need, measure the length of yarn in a skein. Find out how much stitching you can do with a certain length and then you can work out how much each skein will complete, taking into account the number of strands you will use in the needle. Then work out what proportion of each colour you will need. It is best to buy enough of each colour before you start if a change in dye will spoil the finished result. Sometimes a slight change can be attractive, but in canvas work a slight change on a single coloured ground in a regular stitch will be disappointing. Always keep a record of the type of thread and colour numbers when opening skeins.

When you select a thread, it may seem quite dark in colour when in its skein, but when used singly, it will look much paler.

A thread will tend to wear thin while being drawn through material and canvas, so generally a length of about 50 cm (20 inches) is sufficient.

Conventional threads come in the following categories:

Cottons
Stranded cotton/embroidery floss consists of six strands which may be used complete, but it is usually divided up into two or more strands.
Soft/matte embroidery cotton has a matt finish and makes a contrast to the more glossy mercerized cottons.
Coton perlé (pearl cotton) is twisted and has a sheen. It is available in a variety of thicknesses.
Coton à broder (cotton embroidery floss) is a smooth cotton with a sheen. Many weights are available in white but in colours it only comes in two.

Wools
Tapestry wool is a 4-ply wool specially prepared for canvas work, but it can be used for other purposes such as freehand stitchery.
Persian wool is a three-stranded wool which may be used complete or divided up and used as one or two strands. It is good for canvas work and freehand stitches.
Crewel wool is a fine 2-ply wool which is strong and used extensively for canvas work where hard wear is required. Any number of threads may be used at once.

Silk threads
Filo floss (silk floss) has six strands of loosely plied silk and is generally used by dividing up into one or two strands for fine work.
Twisted silk is a glossy twisted thread.

When working tacking/basting stitches on delicate fabrics which may show marks, it is best to use a pure sewing silk which, when removed, will not show stitch marks.

Linen thread
This is found only in a limited range of colours.

Below *A selection of embroidery threads.*

Frames

Much embroidery can be done in the hand but some methods are easier if the material or canvas is mounted on a frame in order to keep it smooth and taut during working.

There are two types for general use, the ring frame and the slate/scroll frame.

Ring frame

This consists of two simple rings, usually of wood, one fitting inside the other with an adjustable screw on the outer ring. More elaborate versions are made with table fittings, clamps, floor fittings and sitting attachments. Ring frames are available in a variety of sizes, the hand-held variety ranging from 7·5 to 30 cm (3 to 12 inches).

To frame up, place the smaller ring on a table, and lay the material over this so the design to be worked is centred. Place the outer ring over the material and push it over the inner ring, making sure that the material is quite taut. To stop it slipping and to protect the fabric from damage, it is a help to bind the inner ring lightly with bias strips of fine material or lengths of roller bandage. Make sure that the rings still fit together after binding. Any material mounted in a ring frame will gradually slacken in working and will need to be tightened frequently.

Slate/scroll frame

There are many varieties of this but they are all based on the principle of two bars or rollers to which webbing is attached. Each roller has a slot at each end through which flat battens (arms) are passed and which are held in place with pegs or split pins inserted into holes in the arms in order to keep the material taut.

A frame is measured by the length of webbing on the roller. Hand frames are made in various lengths from 30 cm up to about 75 cm (1 foot to 2 feet 6 inches). Floor frames are available in lengths from 60 to 90 cm (2 to 3 feet).

The material to be framed up may be as wide as the webbing on a roller. Its length can be greater than the length of each arm as the surplus may be wound round each roller, leaving exposed a certain area to be embroidered.

As the work is done, remove the pegs in the arms, unroll the area to be worked next and roll up the finished piece – enclosing a piece of soft white flannel-type material to protect any stitchery.

Instead of a roller frame, you can use a strong picture frame or artist's stretcher, to which the material will have to be stapled or attached with string.

To use a hand frame, rest it either on movable trestles or, if you are sitting at a table, on your knees, leaning it against the edge of the table to allow the needle to be passed down and up in two movements. With practice, you will gradually be able to work with one hand on top of the frame and one hand beneath it. Methods for learning embroidery stitches are, however, described using a scooping movement which should be broken into two movements when working on a frame.

Framing up

Turn in 1·5 cm ($\frac{5}{8}$ inch) to the wrong side at the top and lower edges of the material to be framed up. Place the centre of each of these sides to the centre of the webbing on each roller. Pin them outwards from the centre to the outer edges. Again starting from the centre, work oversewing/overcasting stitches through the top of the webbing and fold, using a strong thread.

Tack/baste a length of webbing or strong tape about 2·5 cm (1 inch) wide down the raw edges at the sides of the material. Roll in any surplus material round the rollers. Insert the arms of the frame through the slots at the sides of the rollers. Insert the pegs through the holes in the arms checking that the distance between the rollers at each side is the same, to avoid distortion of the fabric.

Then, using a curved needle, thread a strong twine at 2·5 cm (1 inch) intervals, down through the webbing and up over the arm. To get good results, the material should be really taut. If framing up a fine fabric such as organdie which cannot be laced tightly at the sides, it may be held in place by pinning 1·5 cm ($\frac{5}{8}$ inch) wide tape at intervals, taking it round the arm of the frame between each pin.

Needles

These may be sharp or blunt, and with large or small eyes. Each sewing method needs a particular needle; for example, a tapestry needle with a blunt end and large eye is used for canvas work, whereas a fine sharp sewing needle will be used for patchwork. Always use the correct type and size of needle for the method you are working. A thread should pass easily through the eye of the needle. If the thread frays, use a slightly larger needle. If the material shows holes when working, use a smaller size (the larger the needle's number, the smaller its size).

Tapestry
Blunt; large eye; sizes 18–24. Use for canvas work and counted thread methods.

Crewel
Sharp; long, slim eye. Use sizes 4–10 for most embroidery including freehand stitches.

Chenille
Sharp; large eye; sizes 18–24. Use with thick threads for bold stitching and when taking thick couched threads through to the wrong side.

Sharps
Sharp; small round eye; sizes 4–10. Use for general sewing, making up, patchwork, quilting.

Bodkin *(darning needle)*
Blunt; large eye. Use for threading thick threads, ribbon and thonging.

Beading
Sharp, fine for use with beads.

Above *Embroidery needles from left to right: bodkin, beading, crewel, tapestry, sharp, chenille.*

Binding a ring frame.

Material mounted on a ring frame.

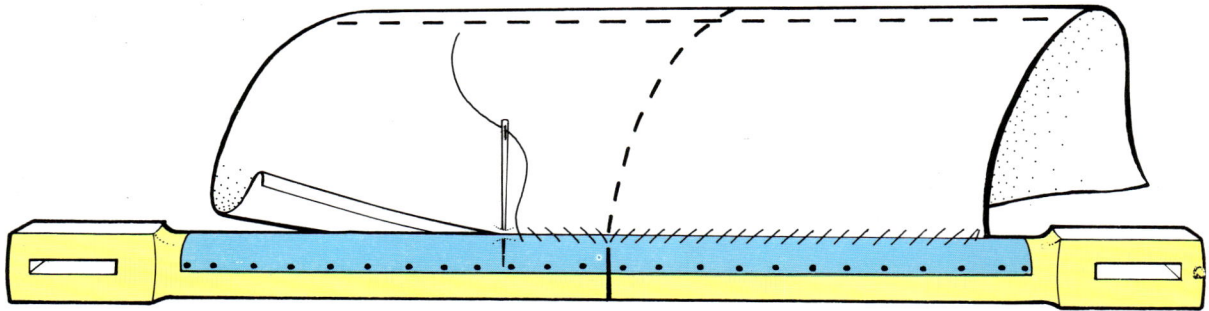

Oversewing material to webbing on the roller of a slate frame.

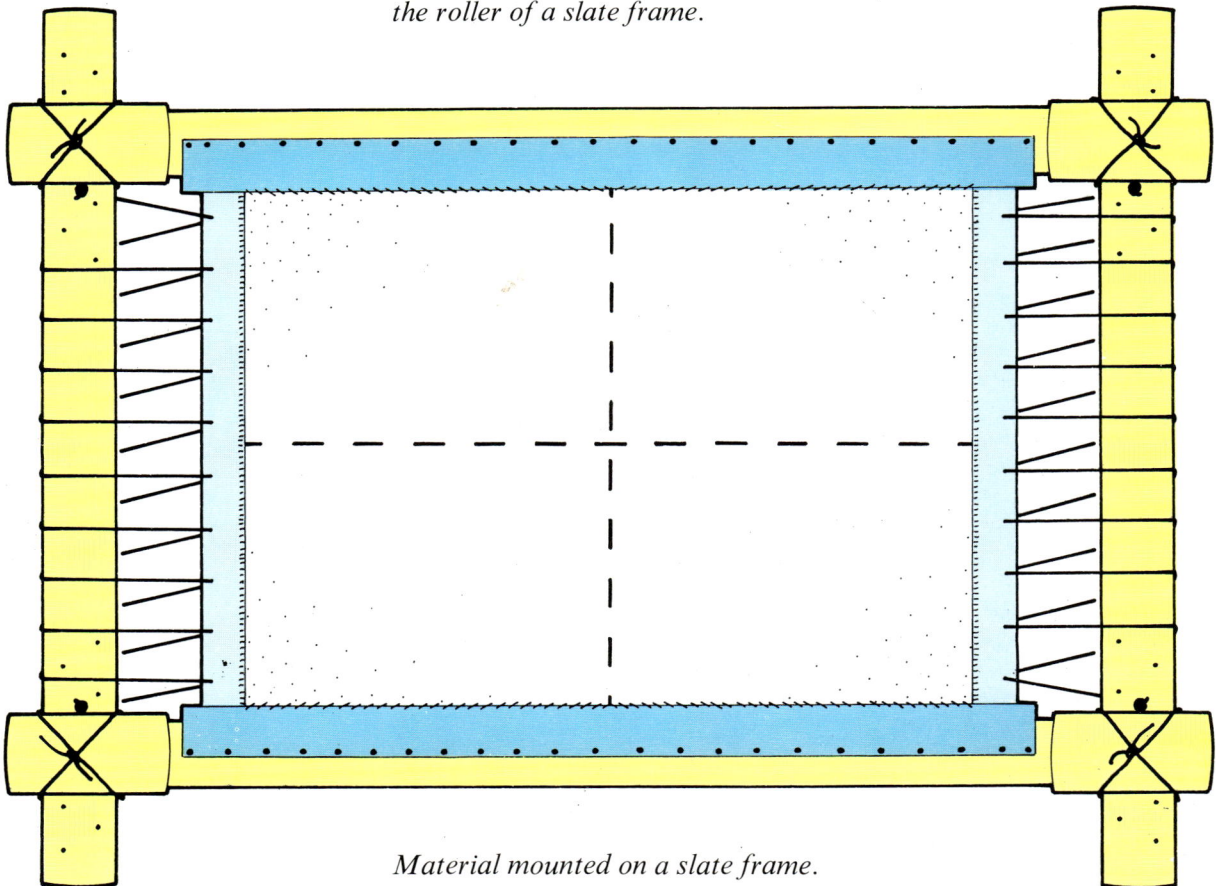

Material mounted on a slate frame.

15

Designing

The thought of making your own design may sound frightening, but although it is a help, it is not necessary to be able to draw in order to create a pattern or design. Designs do not need to be, and in fact should not be, naturalistic, as embroidery is not an attempt to do in stitchery what can be done in paint; it is the interpretation of an idea in fabrics and threads.

Look at all the patterns and shapes which are around you. In the garden, there will probably be flowers, leaves and trees, or a bird flying. Study the pattern of tree bark. Look at the colours and shapes, and those formed by shadows too. As you walk down the street, there may be wrought iron, an elegant house or an interesting old lamp-post. Wood and stone carvings in churches and cathedrals can give inspiration for design. Indoors, patterns may be seen on fabrics or tiles, possibly on wallpaper. As you cut up the vegetables, look at half a cabbage, or the cross section of a tomato or a pepper. A visit to a museum offers a wealth of ideas for patterns from textiles, porcelain and other sources.

If you are able to draw with ease, carry a small sketch book around with you and make quick sketches of things you want to remember. If you find drawing difficult, make notes about shapes and colour; or trace the outlines of leaf shapes and flower shapes to give you a simple shape which you can embroider.

Simple methods of designing

You may like to try out a simple design using initials. A single letter may be repeated, overlapped, turned back to back or upside down, or two or more initials can be built into a pattern.

As you plan a design consider what article it is to be used on, and what method you will use for its interpretation into stitchery. Think also of the scale of the design so that it is suitable for its purpose. A design should fill the area for which it is planned in a well-balanced way. Make sure that the areas left between patterns are pleasing. Some embroidery can be done by using the background between the outlines of the design as the area which is embroidered and this is the principle on which Assisi work, for example, is done (see page 98).

Some people like to work directly onto a fabric, without any preliminary planning but to do this you must be sure of the stitches or the method you will use. It is safer to draw your design on paper first and then transfer it when you are satisfied that it is right.

Using a ruler

The simplest patterns may be made with a ruler and pencil. Experiment with different arrangements of straight lines – evenly spaced, irregularly spaced and of uneven lengths. By crossing lines you will produce diamonds and triangles.

Doodles

A large pad of paper by the telephone may produce some quite dramatic doodles. Doodles are good as patterns for freehand stitches, or for canvas or Florentine work. Use odd scraps of paper or the backs of used envelopes, and scribble away.

A design made by using a ruler.

A pencil is sometimes inhibiting but felt pens of different thicknesses will help you to loosen up. They will also help you make thick and thin lines which will indicate the use of varied thicknesses of threads as part of the design.

Dropped string

Take a piece of string about 1 metre (3 feet) long. Place a piece of paper, the size required for your embroidery on the floor. Get up as high from it as you can. Hold one end of the string high up and drop it onto the paper. It may take up a shape which resembles something – a butterfly, a bird or perhaps an abstract design. If you do not care for the shape, start again. When you are satisfied, lay some tracing paper on the string and trace the shape. Mark in some additional lines if you wish.

If you prefer, you can drop yarn straight onto the material and pin it into position before couching it down. The design can have additional embellishment such as areas of applied material or net, beads or freehand stitchery.

A design made from doodles.

Cut paper

By cutting up paper, quite simple designs can be achieved. Start with a square, rectangle or circle. Using paper-cutting scissors, cut, for example, a circle into five pieces. Spread them out, overlapping some, on a sheet of paper. Pin them into position or stick them on and make a tracing. The design produced will be suitable for most methods where shapes can be used such as counted thread methods, freehand stitchery, appliqué, canvas work and quilting and it is a good method for creating a border. Obviously more elaborate cutting of the paper will lead to designs of more complexity.

Ink blots

A simple form of design can be achieved by dropping ink or paint blobs onto the centre of a piece of strong paper. Fold the paper in half, crease it well and open it out. A pattern will appear. Different effects will emerge if you use more than one colour of paint and it is surprising what interesting patterns you can achieve. As an alternative, blow the blobs gently with a drinking straw to get a spattered effect. Experiment until you have a pattern you like. Try to visualize how you will embroider it: is it suitable for freehand stitches, for whitework, for embroidering in metal threads or any other chosen method?

Using a compass

Circles of different sizes made with a compass can be spaced out, layered, used within one another or used as partial circles. Ideas for circular cushions or small round box tops can be obtained, as well as designs for quilting, counted thread techniques and appliqué. If you are without a compass, draw round coins, cups, saucers and other circular objects and make yourself some round paper or thin cardboard templates.

Landscape

Ideas for landscape designs may be obtained by sketching, from photographs or from colour slides. Simplify the design into one you can carry out in stitchery, appliqué or quilting, considering the methods you will use as you design. A very much simplified landscape may be interpreted in an irregular form of Florentine work if, for example, you take just the lines of sky, hills and foreground.

Using a camera

Use a camera to capture something which fascinates you, and which you would like to carry out in stitchery. Black and white photography is quite adequate as what you see does not have to be interpreted in the original colours. A black and white print will give you an indication of tones in a picture (dark, medium and light areas). If you make two L-shapes of cardboard, you can move them about over a picture until you have picked out an area which you like.

This principle can also be used on a good print in a book or magazine. Even half a wheel, part of a landscape or the centre of a beautiful flower can form the basis of a design.

To use a colour slide for designing, project it onto a white wall or one covered with white paper. Use two L-shapes of cardboard and juggle them about until you find an interesting section on the slide. Lay a piece of tracing paper on the picture and gently trace the outline of the area which you think you would like to use for embroidery. Rarely will you wish to use the whole slide. Avoid getting too many details on the tracing, and simplify it whenever possible.

Sometimes you can get ideas for colour from your slides. A lush herbaceous border may inspire a patchwork quilt or colours for canvas work; lichen will show the beauty of subtle shades of grey-green and off-white.

A design made from an ink blot.

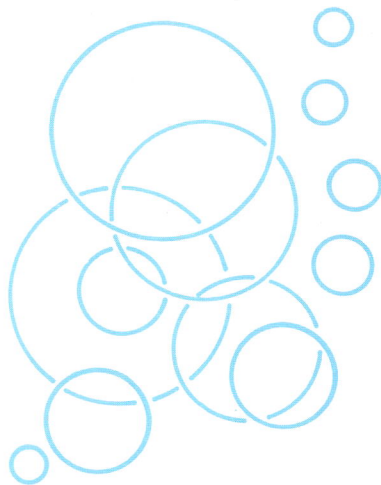

A design made by using a compass.

A design adapted from a landscape drawing or a photograph.

Enlarging and reducing a design

It is quite simple to enlarge or reduce a design. You may have a piece of material which you wish to use as a background but it is just too small for the overall size of your design. Or you may have got an idea for the basis of a design from a book, and it needs to be enlarged for the embroidery on a cushion or hanging. Some greeting cards will spark off an idea but inevitably will need to be enlarged.

Draw a grid of about 2·5 cm (1 inch), or less for smaller designs, on the picture to be enlarged. On a piece of paper the exact size of the planned finished work, mark a grid with the same number of divisions as you have on the picture. Copy the outline of the small design onto the larger grid. Work carefully, square by square. The design will appear in a size proportionately larger than the original.

By reversing the process a design can be reduced in size.

Enlarging a design by copying the outline square by square onto a larger grid.

Designing a corner for a border

You may wish to design a corner so that your border design is continuous, particularly for table linen. Borders in many of the counted thread techniques, such as blackwork, pulled work, cross stitch, pattern darning or Assisi work, may be improved if they are linked by an attractive corner. The method for creating one is not difficult.

Draw the design on paper, flat on a board. Using a small flat-edged pocket mirror, place it diagonally across the border at what appears to be a suitable turning point. If you

1. Decide on the position for the corner using a mirror.

2. Trace the border design up to the mirror position.

3. Fold tracing paper along line of mirror position and continue tracing border design.

4. Unfold tracing paper to reveal corner design.

hold the mirror upright, the reflection of the border will show at right angles. Try several positions before deciding on the corner you like best. Then rule a line diagonally, along the edge of the mirror. Avoid using a framed mirror or one with a bevelled edge, as these will distort the design.

Trace the part of the border up to the diagonal line. Fold the tracing paper along the diagonal line and trace the outline onto the piece of tracing paper directly over the first tracing. This is the adjacent side of the corner. Open up the tracing paper and trace the corner design alongside your border design.

Putting a design onto material

In order to place the design in the required position, work a horizontal and a vertical line of tacking stitches crossing through the centre of the area to be used. Then rule a horizontal and vertical line through the centre of the paper design. Press the background material with an iron so that it is free of creases before attempting to put on the design.

The actual method you use for transferring the design will depend on your fabric and design, but apart from the pencil method for fine materials, you will need to make a tracing of the design on tracing paper.

Running stitches

This is a simple method for designs which do not have fine detail. It is particularly useful for indicating on a background material the position for fabrics in appliqué and it can be used successfully when working freehand stitches, blackwork and other counted thread methods, and quilting. It is the only method which can be used when putting a design on fabrics with a textured surface.

Place the tracing on the right side of the material, matching the centre lines and pin into place. Using a sewing thread which will show up on the material, work running stitches around all the lines of the design through both the paper and material. Take care to keep the shapes, in particular on curved lines and at points, by making quite small stitches. The stitches can be longer on straight lines. Always firmly secure the beginning and end of the stitching with back stitches and avoid using a knot if possible.

Lay the material flat on a table, gently tear the paper away and the design will be marked out in running stitches. Remove these stitches as you work the embroidery.

This method enables you to make changes as you work since there are no fixed lines on the material.

Transfer paper

This is a non-smudge carbon paper, prepared specially for use when dressmaking. It is obtainable from stores selling dress patterns and comes in packages containing an assortment of yellow, red and blue. It is only suitable for materials with smooth surfaces and cannot be used on those with textures or loose weave. Practise on a spare piece of material to see if it is suitable.

The material should be placed right side up on a hard surface. Choose a colour of carbon paper which will show up on the material. Place the carbon, shiny side down, between the material and the tracing (making sure the centres of the material and tracing match). Secure with pins or weights, or drawing pins/thumbtacks if using a drawing board. Use a pencil or ball-point pen to draw all round the outline of the design. Carefully lift off the tracing and carbon paper, and the design is ready to work.

Prick and pounce

This is the most accurate method of transferring a design and should be used for a fine-detailed design such as lettering, a face or a heraldic coat of arms. It produces a fine painted line and is therefore advantageous when embroidering a shape which requires a smooth outline in crewel and laid work, or when working fine satin stitch. Do not try to use this process on velvet or rough textured materials.

This method may be laborious, but the extra time spent before starting to stitch is often worthwhile. It also requires a steady hand.

A few extra pieces of equipment will be required for this process. You should have a pin-vice, or a fine needle with its eye set into a cork, for the actual pricking. A soft pad about 30 cm (1 foot) square is needed: this can be a double thickness of blanket or felt, or a small cork mat. The pounce powder consists of powdered charcoal for use on light-coloured materials and powdered cuttlefish or French chalk for dark materials. Store it in small containers, just big enough to accommodate a roll of material which you will dip into the pounce powder.

To make the roll or pad, use a piece of soft material (flannel is ideal) about 10 cm (4 inches) wide and long enough to roll up into a pad about 3 cm (1¼ inches) in diameter. Stitch the loose end of the strip of fabric into place at the side of the roll. You will also need a fine paint brush and some water-colour paint, blue or white will be adequate for use on most materials. It is necessary to have artist's oil colour and pure turpentine if painting on canvas or a material which you find will not take water colour. Oil colour is more durable and therefore better if you are working on a large project.

Place the traced design over the soft pad with a piece of tissue paper under the tracing. Closely prick along all the lines of the design excluding the centre mark, moving the tracing round as you work. Keep the pricker upright and aim to get about ten little holes to each centimetre (twenty-five to the inch). The holes must be tiny. With care it is possible to work with an unthreaded sewing machine, using a fine needle. Work round the outline on the tracing as though stitching without thread. You cannot afford to make any errors at this stage, as once you have holes in the wrong place you will have difficulty in painting in your design.

When the pricking is ready, place the background material on a hard surface with the right side up. Place the pricking over this, matching the centres. Hold it in place with pins or weights; it must not move or you will get a blurred line.

Dip one end of the rolled pad into pounce powder. Rub it all over the holes of the pricking. Lift off the pricking gently so that the pounce beneath it is not disturbed. Tip any surplus pounce back into the tin and wipe over the tracing with a duster to keep it clean. Check that the whole of the design is visible on the material. If you have missed any areas, use a clean duster and flick off all the pounced outline so that the material is clear before repeating the method.

Then start painting in the outline, working gradually over the pounce powder from the lower edge of the work upwards, covering it with tissue paper as you work to avoid smudging. Use the fine paint brush and mix the water-colour paint with just enough water to give a smooth fine line. If you are using oil colour, mix with a little pure turpentine, again just enough to give a continuous fine line on the material you are using. When the paint is quite dry (only a matter of minutes) use a clean, dry cloth and gently flick away any surplus pounce powder. You should then be left with a clear fine outline of the whole design. If the outline is thick, you have probably used too wet a paint. Practise both the pouncing and the painting processes on a spare piece of similar material before starting your first attempt on an actual piece of work.

Prick holes along the lines of the design.

Rub the pad over the pricking so that the pounce powder outlines the design on the material.

Using a pencil

This method can only be used on fine transparent material such as organdie or lawn. Outline the design in black ink on a piece of strong white paper and place this beneath the well-pressed material. Pin it in place and draw round the outline of the design using a hard pencil.

Colour

Some people have a natural sense of colour, others are colour blind, but most people can develop a colour sense by experimenting. There are colour schemes all around us, in shop windows, in magazines, in gardens and in the countryside, from which to get ideas.

Colours have fashions, and if decorating garments, particularly for children, the current fashionable colours can be used to advantage. Furnishing colours also come and go, and you must decide whether your work should fit the current trend or whether you want a neutral colouring which will always blend with other furnishings.

You may like to embroider a piece of work in a single colour. If you use the same colour as the background, it is called **self colour.** If you do decide to use only one colour, you can get variety by using different types of threads, possibly some matt and some with a sheen. You will find that even if you use all white or all cream there will be a considerable variety of types of thread available.

Monochrome differs from self colour since the decoration will be in tones of one colour on a contrasting background. Tones of a colour vary from light to dark. The choice of tones will depend on the background material: a tone matching the background will tend to be lost when worked in with others. For monochrome the tones used will probably be mainly either light or medium on a dark ground or medium and dark tones on a light ground. If you are working in monochrome over the entire background, as in canvas work or Florentine stitchery, the tones do not need to be from just one range of a colour and often a slight change will give added interest. For example, if you are using a range of sky-blue from light to dark, a small amount of royal blue adds sparkle.

A little of a completely contrasting colour added to monochrome can create a stunning effect. For example, to the range of sky-blues, a small amount of brilliant scarlet will act as a touch of seasoning. The secret of success is to restrict the seasoning to just a dash of colour.

Polychrome refers to the use of many colours. Here, success depends upon the balance of colours.

If you decide to use two or three colours within one piece, it is still important to consider variation of tone. For example, if using blue, green and brown on a light background, one of these colours may be a light tone and one a dark.

Since the darkness of the colour of a thread will lessen as you take it from the massed colour of the skein, you may sometimes need a tone slightly deeper than you expect. The

Left 'Poppies' design in appliqué making use of self-coloured foliage.
Below Using freehand stitches and varied threads for textured effects.

colour of the background may also affect the colour of a thread. Experiment by working stitches on a pale background in one colour scheme and then repeat the same stitches with the same thread on a bright background of a different colour.

It is also interesting to compare the effect of an arrangement of stitches in a dark colour on a light ground with the same stitches in a light colour on a dark ground.

A collection of threads and materials will enable you to play with different arrangements until you feel satisfied. Colour is one of the most exciting facets of needlecraft, and it is well worth making small experiments before starting your main piece of work.

Texture

Texture forms an important function in needlecraft. The various materials, threads and stitches which can be used make it possible to keep one's work flat and smooth, to get chunky relief effects or to get a combination of the two.

To get a smooth surface, choose a material with a flat finish, use fine threads and select stitches which will lie close to the surface of the material. For a textured surface, the decoration may be done in chunky threads, on a textured fabric, and by using raised stitches such as raised chain stitch, French or bullion knots or spider's webs. The incorporation of beads will also add texture to your stitchery.

Finishing touches

Stretching

While working an embroidery or a piece of canvas work, particularly if not using a frame, the threads of the background material or canvas may become distorted. In order to return these to their natural position, and to get the stitchery lying flat, it is necessary to stretch the work, usually in preference to pressing.

Use a square or rectangular wooden table top, a drawing board or a piece of 1·5 cm ($\frac{5}{8}$ inch) plywood. Place three thicknesses of old white cotton sheeting or white blotting paper larger than the area of your work on the board. Over this place the embroidery or canvas work, with the right side down. Hammer tacks along one edge at 2·5 cm (1 inch) intervals so that this first edge is straight (parallel to one edge of the board). Tack down one adjacent side at right angles to the first side, using a T-square if you have one. Continue until all four sides are tacked down and the material is the required size and shape. If it is badly distorted, you will have to pull quite hard. Small pieces of work or fine work may be pinned out with drawing pins/thumbtacks; protect the fabric with tape beneath the pins.

Soak a sponge in cold water, squeeze out any surplus, and press it into the stretched-out material, ensuring that the whole embroidery is thoroughly wet, but not dripping. Do not wet the tacks, as they will rust. Leave the board flat in normal room temperature until the embroidery is dry (usually about forty-eight hours) before removing the tacks. It may be necessary to repeat the process if one stretching is insufficient. Canvas which is badly misshapen may be damped before fastening down.

Only stretch material and threads which are colour-fast. Most conventional embroidery threads are guaranteed colour-fast but you should always test those about which you are not sure. To test material or threads for fastness, press them beneath a damp white cloth with an iron. Any colour which is not fast will appear on the damp cloth.

Pressing

Place the embroidery right side down on a soft blanket or piece of foam rubber covered with a white cotton cloth. Always test the heat of the iron at one corner, using a suitable heat for the threads and use a cloth between the iron and the embroidery being pressed.

Never press canvas work as this will flatten the stitches: always use the stretching method.

The pressing of smocking is done from the wrong side. If you wish to stretch the smocking to the pattern size, it is necessary to have help from a second person. The iron, adjusted to a heat suitable for the fabric, should be held in an upright position by one person. The other person will then draw the wrong side of the smocking backwards and forwards across the iron in the direction of the lines of smocking (across the folds). If the material does not press well, place a damp cloth over the iron.

Quilting and other forms of padded work should not require pressing or stretching. Metal thread work should always be worked on a frame and should not be stretched or pressed.

Making up

The making up of an article is as important as the decoration, whatever method you have used. For making up garments, follow standard dressmaking principles. It is best to do the embroidery before cutting out the pattern piece to save the edges from fraying and to allow for the piece to be stretched if necessary. Mark out the pattern shape with tacking/basting and work the embroidery in the required position. Then cut out and make up the garment in the usual way.

Decorative hem

See page (134) for a method of working a decorative hem by withdrawing a thread from the fabric.

To mitre a corner

When turning down a hem where two adjacent sides meet at a corner, it is necessary to trim away some of the material to reduce the bulk. To mitre a corner, prepare a corner on paper, marking out the position of the turnings (see diagram). The shaded area shown should be cut off and used as a paper pattern for cutting off the corner on the fabric. Mitre one corner of material and tack/baste in place before moving to the next, to avoid fraying. To hold the corner in place, work straight stitches into both sides of the diagonal fold. These should align with the grain of the material.

Material pinned out for stretching.

1. Prepare a mitred corner on paper, marking out the positions for turnings. The shaded area will be cut off.

2. Hold the corner in place by working straight stitches into both sides of the diagonal fold.

Cords

When making up a cushion or other small item, it is often necessary to neaten the edges and for this purpose a hand-made cord is useful and decorative. Cords may also be used for bag handles and as a means of suspending a hanging. They are not difficult to make and can link up with the decoration. Use thread either the same colour as the background material or a contrasting colour taken from the embroidery. Alternatively, you can make an attractive multi-coloured cord. The thickness of the cord will be determined by the thickness of the thread or the number of threads used.

Simple twisted cord

Use two threads, each three times the length of thread required for the finished cord: for example, for a cord 60 cm (2 feet) long, take two threads each 180 cm (6 feet) in length. Knot the threads together at each end. Fasten one end over a hook. Insert a pencil at the opposite end, holding it in place close to the knot. Stretch the cord tightly and revolve the pencil clockwise over the threads. Continue twisting until the two threads are tightly twisted along the whole length. Keep the cord firmly stretched throughout. Place your finger in the centre point of the twist and, keeping the thread taut, fold one knot over the other. Release the folded end, ensuring that the cord forms its own natural tight twist. Tie the knotted ends together. Practice will show you the thickness of thread needed to produce the size of cord you require.

A simple twisted cord: position of cord and dowel (or pencil) ready for twisting.

Tied cord

When learning, use only four strands, ideally two strands of two colours. Take two strands of one colour in each hand. Allow three times the length of the finished cord when calculating the length needed for each thread. Tie a knot at one end and hang it over a hook, so that you can get a good tension. Each group of two threads is looped over the other group alternately.

A tied cord.

Tassels

A simple tassel can be produced by making an overhand knot at the end of a cord, then fringe out the ends and trim them evenly.

Tiny tassels of fine linen thread or large ones of thick wool may be made with the following method. Wind thread round some thin cardboard, the depth of the required tassel. The number of turns will depend on the thickness of tassel you need. Chubby ones tend to look more attractive than slender ones. If making several for a set, remember to count the number of turns to keep them to the same size.

Take a blunt needle and a long thread. Back stitch along the top of the threads, making sure that all are enclosed. Slip the threads off the cardboard and wrap them round an overhand knot at the end of a cord already made. Stitch through the top of the threads and through the knot to hold the tassel securely. Finish by wrapping the stitching thread round the tassel threads below the knot. Take the needle back up the centre to come out close to the cord at the top. Fasten off securely. Trim off the bottom of the tassel.

To make a more elaborate tassel the area above the bound threads can be covered in. Start by making a circle of thread round the cord and secure it. Work about twelve blanket stitches over this thread, around the top of the tassel. Continue working blanket stitch into the loops of the previous row, round and round until you just reach the bound threads. Work the last line of blanket stitch into these and finish off by taking the thread up the centre and down again. Trim off the bottom of the tassel.

Wind thread round cardboard and work back stitch along the top. Secure the tassel round overhand knot by stitching. Wrap stitching thread round tassel below the knot. Work buttonhole stitch round the top of the tassel

Freehand embroidery

Freehand stitches

The freedom and adaptability of these stitches make them practical for almost any project and they are the basis of the stitches for many other techniques. When worked freely it is not necessary to either count the threads or follow the grain of the material. A great many freehand stitches have been used over the centuries; some stitches are characteristic of certain countries and often one can identify an embroidery from the stitches or threads used. The method of working the stitches has scarcely changed but nowadays they are worked with modern threads and materials.

Freehand stitches can be worked on the outlines of a design, as fillings if worked closely, or with regular spacing. Practise the stitches and get used to working them on different materials and in different threads. Keep all your experiments so that you can refer to them in the future, and make a note of the thread and colour you have used. Some stitches are worked through the material; others, such as couching, lie on the surface and are held down with a second thread. Most of the stitches for other embroidery techniques follow the basic formation of one or other of the freehand stitches. Freehand stitches can be combined with appliqué and some outline stitches are worked in with blackwork fillings. Although the formation of stitches may be the same, when working counted thread methods, it is necessary to work in a controlled way and a certain number of warp or weft threads will need to be counted for each stitch. Similarly when doing canvas work, a stitch worked may closely resemble or be the same as one of the freehand stitches but, because of the nature of the background material, the stitch will have to follow the threads of canvas and will always be angular.

It is important to choose stitches in relation to the design. For a narrow smooth line, stem stitch or couching are the most effective. Stitches such as back and running may be whipped to produce a hard line. Whipped chain stitch gives a hard corded effect. If a broad stitch is required, you may use Cretan or Roumanian stitch but if you need a stitch with a texture you may choose raised chain band or French knots.

Experiments with stitches will often give unexpected results. Blocks of stitches worked in different directions can produce an interesting play of light. Colour, too, forms an important factor and a stitch worked in one colour may look quite different in another colour even on the same ground. Similarly, the colour of stitches in the same thread will appear to vary when worked on different coloured backgrounds.

Most materials can be used for freehand stitches. Consider whether you need a fine cotton material or a coarse one such as hessian/burlap. Furnishing and some dress materials are good, as are more conventional linens and cottons. A loosely woven material will need to be mounted on a backing material, and the stitching should be worked through both materials.

Choose a thread which is smooth enough to go through the material easily. When learning stitches it is easier to use a single thread such as soft embroidery cotton, or a coton perlé, rather than a stranded thread which may be difficult to handle. A single thread will produce well-defined stitches. Yarns with texture are unsuitable for most freehand stitches and will need to be couched down. The thickness of thread needs to be considered in relation to the material and stitch, just as the size of the stitch needs to be adjusted to the thickness of thread.

Most freehand stitches will be worked with a crewel needle or, if the thread and material are coarse, with a chenille needle. When whipping a stitch, as in whipped chain, use a blunt tapestry needle for the second stage of the stitch to avoid splitting the first line of stitchery.

A slate/scroll frame or a ring frame will help to give a good even tension when working freehand stitches and will stop the work from puckering between the stitchery. A backing fabric will also help to avoid puckering, especially where areas of stitchery are dense.

For successful work, start and fasten off a thread securely, keeping the threads as flat as possible on the wrong side. Avoid using a knot when starting a stitch. Work which is to be mounted on completion may fail to lie flat if there are knots on the back. Ironing embroidery on garments or table linen may be difficult if knots have been used and if knots are used on the back of loosely woven material, they may eventually work through to the right side. Either work small running stitches along the line or within the area to be stitched, towards the point where your freehand stitch is to be started (this method is suitable for fine threads), or leave an end of about 7·5 cm (3 inches) on the wrong side at the start of the stitching. When some stitches have been worked, thread up the end and darn it into the back of them. To fasten off, darn back into the stitches worked on the wrong side. If very thick threads are used, or if you are using textured threads in couching, use some fine thread for stitching over them on the wrong side. Cut off the thick thread at least 1 cm ($\frac{1}{2}$ inch) away from where it has been taken through the material.

To join a thread, fasten off and re-start, bringing up the new thread in a position to continue stitching without a visible break.

If the thread needs to be taken across the back of the work always darn threads into stitches on the wrong side. If there are no stitches into which to darn the threads, fasten off and re-start, as shadows may be seen through the material. If working on transparent fabric, thread should not be visible on the right side between areas of stitching.

Right above *Box decorated with freehand stitchery, appliquéd PVC/vinyl, beads and sequins. Stem stitch is used for the semi-circular motifs and the gold cord is couched in position.*
Right *Two pockets decorated with freehand stitchery. Stitches include straight (single and in clusters), French knots, and woven wheels. For the pocket on the right, hand-made twisted cords are stitched down to form a linear design.*

Running stitch

Work from right to left (left to right). Bring the needle up at the beginning of the line to be worked. Insert the needle down and up, with the space between the stitches either the same or varied according to your design. Uneven lengths of stitches and spaces can produce an attractive simple decoration. Never work stitches so long that they will catch in use. Running stitch may be used as a lightweight filling for shapes, particularly if a smooth rhythm is created with the direction of stitches. If a design has been transferred to the material by the prick and pounce method, do not use this stitch, as part of the painted outline would be left exposed. It may be used to soften the outline of appliquéd material, or as a method for attaching material to a background.

Straight stitch

Each straight stitch is worked independently, whether spaced or worked closely. Bring the needle up in the required position for the first stitch. Take it down before coming up in the position for the next stitch. If working straight stitches with a stranded thread, untwist the thread as you work, to ensure that the stitches lie flat. The length of the stitches will depend on whether they are on embroidery for practical use or on a mounted panel. In the latter instance, they may be any length, providing the work is stretched out firmly and well mounted, so that the stitches lie really flat on the material. It is best to work on a frame.

When straight stitches of even lengths radiate from a central point, they form *star stitch*. This can be used as a stitch on its own, or as part of a group of combined stitches. Worked as an all-over pattern, the changing direction of the stitches will give an interesting play of light.

Back stitch

This is a useful stitch for outlining, especially when a fine smooth line is required. It looks like a continuous running stitch, with no spaces. Work from right to left (left to right). Bring the needle up one stitch length in from the beginning of the line to be worked. Take the needle back to the start of the line and up one stitch length forward from the first stitch. Take the needle down into the same hole as the end of the first stitch. Repeat this movement to the end of the line.

Variations of this stitch include *whipped back stitch* where a needle holding a second thread is taken beneath each stitch, always from the same side. In *threaded back stitch*, the second thread is taken under each stitch from top to bottom and bottom to top alternately. The thread used for both these variations does not go through the material, except at the beginning and end of the row of back stitch. The second thread used in each instance may be of a matching or a contrasting colour. The type of thread used may also be varied.

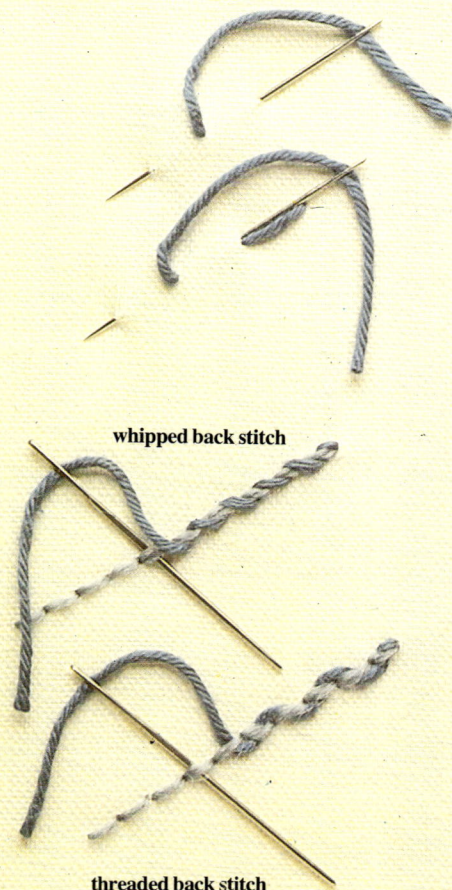

star stitch

whipped back stitch

threaded back stitch

Fern stitch

This simple arrangement of straight stitches may be useful for leaf veins, grasses, for border lines or for breaking up the surface of the background, using a fine thread. It is worked from top to bottom. Groups of three straight stitches are worked in succession, one of which lies down the centre on the working line with the other two radiating from it. Bring the needle up for an outer stitch and take it down on the centre line. Next bring the needle up on the centre line, down into the same place as the end of the first stitch, up on the opposite side and down in the same place again. The stitches adjacent to the centre should be diagonal. Repeat these three stitches along a continuous line.

Stem stitch

Stem stitch is worked in lines and is good for outlining. The lines may be either close or spaced, and the stitch can also act as an interesting filling. Work it from the bottom of a line towards the top, away from you. Bring the needle up at the beginning of the line. Take it down a short distance forward and up half-way back, but close to the first stitch. Go forward again so that the second stitch will be the same length as the first, take the needle down and back to the end of the previous stitch. Repeat this movement to the end of the line, keeping the stitching on the same side of the needle each time the needle is inserted. Stem stitch may be whipped as for back stitch if a corded effect is required.

When working this stitch as a filling, continue to keep the stitching on the same side of the needle each time, and always stitch in the same direction. Do not turn the work for a return journey, always start from the bottom of a line and work towards the top.

Chain stitch

This is a versatile and useful stitch which may be worked as a line stitch or as a filling.

Work chain stitch from the top of a line, down towards you. Bring the needle up at the top of the line. Insert the needle down in the same position and take it out a short distance below. Place the thread under the point of the needle from left to right (right to left) and pull the needle through. Arrange the thread so that the chain lies flat and is a good rounded shape. Too long a stitch will give a spidery effect. For the second stitch, insert the needle into the first chain stitch, alongside the thread. To fasten off, take the needle down outside the last chain stitch to make a holding stitch. To join a thread, fasten off in this way with a tiny holding stitch. Bring up the new thread into the last chain and continue working.

Chain stitch may also be whipped to create a corded effect.

whipped stem stitch

Detached chain stitch

Each stitch consists of one chain stitch complete in itself before starting on the next. After working one chain, fasten it off with a holding stitch, the length of which may vary. The stitches may form part of a regular pattern or can be worked in varied sizes and in different thicknesses of thread.

Magic chain

As in ordinary chain stitch, this is worked from the top of a line towards you. It consists of a continuous line of chain stitch but by threading the needle with two threads of different colours, each alternate stitch is in the second colour. To learn the stitch, use one dark and one light colour in the needle. Start working as for chain stitch but when the needle is about to be pulled through over the two threads, remove the dark one from beneath the point of the needle and let it lie over the needle. Pull the needle through over the light stitch. You will have made a simple chain stitch in the light colour. Repeat the second stitch, this time lifting the light thread from underneath the point of the needle, and you will obtain a dark stitch. It is necessary to give the thread which is not in use an extra pull to remove it from the surface of the material. Continue to the end of the line when you will hold the final chain in place with its matching thread. The second colour may be taken through on the inside of the last chain. As a variation, instead of alternating the stitches, work a few chain stitches of one colour and then some of the next.

Twisted chain

This is one of the variations of chain stitch, and is worked as a line stitch. It should be worked down towards you. Bring your needle up at the top of the line. Hold the working thread down with the left (right) thumb. Insert the needle slightly lower, in a slanting direction, into the material on the left (right) of the thread. Bring it out to the right (left) with the thread lying under the point of the needle.

Zig-zag chain

This makes an attractive border stitch. It is worked in a similar way to simple chain stitch, but instead of placing the needle in straight, it is inserted in a slanting position, with the direction of each chain alternating. To keep the stitches lying flat, it is necessary to take the needle down through the thread at the end of each loop.

Broad chain

This produces a narrow braid-like stitch, also known as heavy chain. Work from the top of a line towards you. Bring the needle out at the top of the line. Make a short running stitch, bringing the needle out slightly lower down the line. Pass the needle under the running stitch and take it down where it was brought up. Bring it up again a little further down the line ready for the second stitch. The running stitch is only used for the start. For the second and successive stitches, pass the needle under the previous chain, not through the material. For the best results, do not pull the thread too tightly.

Open chain

This is a wider stitch than those already described. It gives a ladder-like effect.

It can be learned either by marking out two rows of tacking/basting stitches 5 mm ($\frac{1}{4}$ inch) apart or by working on a striped material with stripes of this width. Bring the needle up on the left (right) side. Hold the thread down with the left thumb (right thumb). Insert the needle exactly opposite on the right (left) and bring it out below the first position on the left (right) in a slanting position. The thread should lie under the point of the needle. The loop should be slack so that when working the second stitch, the needle is inserted just inside the loop on the right (left) hand side.

Open chain may be varied by reducing and increasing the slant of the needle. The less the slant, the closer will be the stitches. If working on a curve, insert the needle so that the horizontal threads are at right angles to the curve.

Rosette chain

To learn this more difficult stitch, work it between two lines of tacking/ basting stitches 5 mm ($\frac{1}{4}$ inch) apart or on a striped material. Work from right to left (left to right). Bring the needle up on the right (left) of the top line. Hold the thread to the left (right) with the left (right) thumb. Insert the needle in an upright position, with the working thread looped under the point of the needle from left to right (right to left). Pull it through. Slip the needle under the thread and continue with the next stitch.

The success of this stitch depends on choosing a suitable scale for the thread in use; too fine a thread will be disappointing. The stitch may be worked in lines and on curves. If it is worked in a circle, the spacing will need to be carefully planned, with the rosettes facing outwards.

Fly stitch

To learn this, work on either side of a vertical line of tacking/basting. Bring the needle up on the left (right) side. Hold the thread down with the left (right) thumb. Insert the needle in a slanting position on the right (left) equidistant to the tacking line, and up on the line, with the thread beneath the point of the needle. Pull up the thread until it lies flat on the material. Hold it down by taking the needle down just below the stitch. Bring the needle up in the position required for the next stitch.

Feather stitch

This is best worked from the top of a line downwards. Looped stitches are worked alternately from the left and right. To learn the stitch, work lines of tacking/basting 5 mm ($\frac{1}{4}$ inch) to each side of the centre line. Bring the needle up at the top of the centre line. Take the needle down on the left side slightly lower and slant it so that you can bring it out on the centre line, with the thread under the point of the needle. Repeat this movement, slanting the needle from the right side to the centre. If worked with two stitches to the left and two stitches to the right, the stitch becomes *double feather stitch*.

double feather stitch

Buttonhole stitch

Work from left to right (right to left). Bring the needle out on the line and insert the needle to the side and above it. Bring it out directly below, on the line, making a straight upright stitch on the wrong side. The thread must be placed under the point of the needle for each movement which is repeated along the line.

There are many variations of this stitch: the spacing may be varied, the length of the straight part of the stitch may be even or uneven or grouped. Rows of the stitch may be placed back to back, or fitted into each other and circles may also be worked. This stitch is also called *blanket stitch*.

Herringbone stitch

Work from left to right (right to left). Each movement is worked by inserting the needle horizontally, pointing the needle towards the left (right) at the top and bottom of the line of stitching alternately. Thus, a series of overlapping diagonal straight stitches is created. By varying the amount of material picked up on the needle, and the space between, different effects can be obtained.

Herringbone stitch may be worked in with other freehand stitches when building up borders or motifs. It is also used sometimes for appliqué and it is the stitch used in shadow work known as shadow stitch.

Coral stitch

Work from right to left (left to right). Bring the thread up at the beginning of the line. Hold the working thread along the line to be worked with the left (right) thumb. Pick up a small amount of material on either side of the line to be worked, with the needle at right angles to the line, and pass the working thread under the point of the needle. Varied effects will be obtained depending on the thickness of thread, the depth of each stitch and the closeness of the stitches. If worked closely and with a small amount picked up on the needle, you will get a bead-like effect which is often useful for an edging. A more dotted effect will result from greater space between stitches.

Scroll stitch

This creates a simple decorative line and may be built up into a filling. Work from left to right (right to left). Bring the needle up at the left (right) end of the line. Insert the needle towards you, on the line, picking up a small amount of material. Pass the working thread behind the eye of the needle from left to right (right to left) and under the point from right to left (left to right). Pull the needle through to complete the stitch. This is best worked with a firm thread. Experiments will show how close you wish to place the scrolls.

Cretan stitch

This is particularly attractive yet comparatively simple to work. It can be worked in lines or can be worked closely as a filling stitch. It is worked from top to bottom, towards you. To learn the stitch it will help to make two vertical lines of tacking/basting stitches, placed about 1·5 cm ($\frac{5}{8}$ inch) apart. Bring the needle up at the top, a short way in from the left hand line. Insert the needle from right to left, slightly lower, picking up one-third of the distance between the running stitches and with the working thread under the point of the needle. Repeat this stitch in reverse, by inserting the needle from left to right and slightly lower than the previous stitch.

Variations on this can be made by altering the amount picked up on the needle, and by varying both the width of the stitch and the distance between stitches. Experiments will show that varied thicknesses of thread can be used, and the overlapping of Cretan stitch worked in different directions can give an interesting all-over effect.

Fishbone stitch

This can be worked in lines, or as a filling stitch, particularly for small shapes such as leaves. Work from the top of a line, towards you. To practise, it may help to work two vertical lines of tacking/basting 1·5 cm ($\frac{5}{8}$ inch) apart. Bring the needle out at the top of the right hand line. Take it down half-way between the two lines, so as to get a diagonal stitch; bring it up at the top of the left hand side. Repeat this stitch in reverse by inserting the needle just below the first stitch in the centre, and out on the right hand line. Repeat these two movements to the end of the line. If working a leaf shape the stitches at the tip will be shorter, with the centre line indicating the leaf vein.

Roumanian stitch

This is another broad line stitch which may also be used as a filling stitch. It is worked from top to bottom towards you. It consists of a series of straight parallel stitches, each of which is held down with a short diagonal stitch in the centre. To practise the stitch, work two vertical lines of tacking/basting, 1·5 cm ($\frac{5}{8}$ inch) apart. Bring the needle up at the top of the left hand line of stitches. Take the needle down at the top of the right hand side, and with the thread under the point of the needle, bring it up just above the stitch made, to the right of the centre. Take the needle over the straight stitch, insert it to the left of the centre, bring it out just below the first horizontal stitch on the left line, ready to repeat the two movements. Try to keep the small central holding stitches directly beneath each other to get the most attractive results. If working on a curve, space the stitches slightly on the outer curve, keeping the horizontal stitches at right angles to the line being worked.

Seeding

These stitches are useful as filling stitches and are worked in a haphazard way. It is a useful way of breaking up an area of background where some texture is required. Bring the needle up and take it down as though working a tiny running stitch. Bring it up in the same place as at first, in order to make a double stitch in the same position, taking the needle down to complete this. Bring the needle up ready for your second seeding stitch. The length of stitch will depend on the thickness of thread. As a guide, make your stitch about the same length as the thickness of thread so that you obtain a seed-like effect. The most successful seeding is that where the stitches are not too long.

French knot

This knotted stitch is not as easy to work as some of the previous stitches, so it is best to practise it with different thicknesses of thread to become accustomed to it. Once you have mastered it, it is quite simple. Bring the needle up in the required position. Hold the working thread loosely between the thumb and forefinger of the left (right) hand. Push the thread away from you with the needle but do not take it through the material. Make a movement with the needle towards the right (left) passing the point of the needle over the thread. Then pass the needle down into the fabric close beside the thread, through the loop formed. Before pulling the needle through, pull the thread up close to the needle. This last movement will give you a well-defined French knot. To get knots of a different size, use a finer or thicker thread and a smaller or larger needle. Do not wind the thread round the needle more than once. French knots may be worked singly, or closely to fill up an area. Spaced out irregularly, they may be used to break up a background.

Woven wheel

This is a useful stitch which forms a small motif complete in itself. It may be used singly or several may be worked together, either as an all-over pattern or spaced. Different effects will be obtained from varying the thickness of thread, but it is necessary to consider the scale when planning the size of stitch. Start by working a star stitch. Then bring the needle up in the centre. Pass the needle under two threads. Continue round the star by taking the needle back over one thread and forward under two, wrapping thread round each spoke. These stitches do not go through the material. Work round the star in this way until the wheel is filled at the end of the spokes. Take the needle through to the wrong side before starting another woven wheel.

Raised chain stitch

This stitch is also known as cable chain stitch. It consists of looped stitches worked on a foundation of spaced horizontal straight stitches, which are made first. Work from top to bottom towards you. To learn the stitch work two lines of vertical tacking stitches about 5 mm ($\frac{1}{4}$ inch) apart. With embroidery thread, work straight stitches between the lines of tacking stitches. Next bring the needle up at the top of the line, above the first horizontal stitch. Pass the needle under the horizontal stitch but not through the material, pointing the needle upwards, and with the working thread to the right (left). Take the needle under the horizontal thread, pointing it downwards and with the working thread under the point of the needle from left to right (right to left). Gently pull up the thread to form a looped stitch. Repeat these two movements until the last horizontal stitch has been used. Take the needle down through the fabric after the last stitch.

Variations include different lengths of horizontal stitch on which several lines of looped stitches are worked closely or spaced. This stitch provides a textured surface.

Bullion knot

As with French knots, this stitch needs practice. Once you know how to do it, you will find it an attractive and useful stitch which will give texture. Bring the needle up at the left (right) end of the required position of the stitch. Insert the needle at the right (left) end of the required length of the stitch bringing it out at the left (right) end. Do not pull the needle through; twist the working thread round and round the needle, close to the emerging point. Place the left (right) thumb on the twists to hold them in place and carefully pull the needle and working thread through the material and twists. Then pull the needle and thread back in the opposite direction. This movement makes the coiled thread lie flat, in the required position for the stitch. Tighten by pulling the working thread, and take the needle through to the wrong side at the left end of the stitch ready to come up again for the next stitch. If you have not done enough twists, they will not fill the space; too many twists will cause congestion.

Cloud filling

As indicated by its name, this is a filling stitch and it is simple and quick to work. Start by working a foundation of small straight stitches spaced as shown. Then with either a contrasting colour or the same, these foundation stitches are threaded through by picking up a stitch in the top row, then one in the lower row, gradually working towards the opposite side. The lacing does not go through the material until the end of a line. The second and alternate lines are worked so that the loops meet under the same stitch. Variations can be obtained by changing the spacing of the foundation threads which may be close or far apart. This may be useful to combine with other freehand stitches, in appliqué and in crewel work.

Couching

This may be treated as an outline stitch as it incorporates a smooth flowing line of thread and it is used extensively when doing embroidery with metal threads. The basic stitch is made by laying a thread on the surface of the material in the required position. This laid thread is then held in place with a finer thread, the couching thread, with small stitches which lie at right angles to the main thread. Bring the needle up on one side of the thread and take it down on the opposite side, making a tiny stitch. Repeat the next stitch at a reasonable distance away, about 5 mm to 1 cm ($\frac{1}{4}$ to $\frac{1}{2}$ inch). The laid thread is taken through to the wrong side only at the beginning and end of the line being couched. At the end of a line, fasten off by taking the thick thread through to the wrong side and cut off within 1·5 cm ($\frac{5}{8}$ inch). Stitch over the end with straight stitches in the fine thread. Because of this, the couched thread may be as thick or as fine as you wish. On a decorative hanging to be seen from a distance, heavy thread such as 6-ply rug wool, hand-made cord or string can be couched effectively. A textured thread such as bouclé or weaving yarn may be used. The tying-down stitches may be in a fine thread of the same colour which scarcely shows, or in a heavier thread in a contrasting colour.

Couching is best worked on a closely woven material. If a loosely woven one is to be used, it should be backed with a fine backing material before working the stitchery.

Once you can work the basic stitch, variations may be tried. Experiment by varying the distances between the couching stitches, by varying their lengths and by using a variety of stitches such as buttonhole, herringbone, cross, open chain or fly stitch for holding down the laid thread.

As a variation from the smooth line the couching of a group of stranded threads may be a means of creating thickness. Instead of keeping the threads lying flat on the surface, a bunched effect can be achieved by allowing the stranded threads to be slack and working a tying stitch tightly at intervals.

Mounting finished embroidery

Work a line of tacking/basting stitches around the edge of the finished piece of work, making sure that there is at least 2·5 cm (1 inch) around the edge for turning and glueing the embroidery onto the backing.

Cut a piece of strong cardboard the size of the finished piece and stretch the embroidery over it, making sure that the warp and weft threads are kept parallel and that the tacking/basting likes on the edge of the cardboard. The piece of work is then glued into place and the corners mitred. Finally, the embroidery can be backed or glued onto a piece of hardboard/particleboard or very stiff cardboard and framed. It's preferable to frame embroidery without glass, to display its texture.

Circular sampler

Once you have become used to working with needle and thread and practised the stitches shown in the previous pages, you'll want to start using these stitches in a finished piece of embroidery. A sampler is a good project to start with, and a circular sampler, such as the one shown here, is more impressive than a rectangle or square.

The embroidered area of the sampler measures about 10 cm (4 inches) in diameter and includes a variety of stitches, including raised chain stitch, open chain stitch, French knots, fern stitch, threaded back stitch, feather stitch and woven wheels. Soft/matte embroidery cotton, stranded embroidery cotton/ floss and knitting yarn have been used for textural contrast, but you can experiment with raffia, tapestry yarn or even metallic threads. A thick yarn, such as rug wool, can be included by couching it down with a silky thread, and beads can be added to the design, either singly or on lengths of thread. Many interesting effects can be achieved with these techniques.

Mounting a sampler

When the sampler is completed, mount it onto a piece of stiff cardboard. First work a line of tacking/basting round the edge of the work, making sure that there is at least 2·5 cm (1 inch) round the for the body, two pieces of green and two pieces of blue for the wings and slipstitch them in place.

Work the lines of yellow coral stitch in six strands of stranded cotton. Then work the lines of back stitch in yellow, blue and red coton perlé and the French knots in navy blue coton perlé and six strands of white stranded cotton.

Making up the accessories

To make up the pincushion, place one plain square on one embroidered square, wrong sides facing, and machine stitch them together round three sides, 1·2 cm ($\frac{1}{2}$ inch) from the edge. Use red thread to match the fabric. Stuff the pincushion firmly with polyester stuffing. Stitch the last side together by hand. Withdraw threads from the edges to the stitching to make a fringe.

To make up the needlecase, machine stitch one plain and one embroidered square together along the left-hand side, 1·2 cm ($\frac{1}{2}$ inch) from the edge. Then machine stitch the two pieces of canvas to the inside of the plain piece of fabric, 1·2 cm $\frac{1}{2}$ inch) from the machine-stitched outer edge. Fringe fabric edges.

Key to butterfly diagram
A French knots in navy blue
B French knots in white stranded cotton
C coral stitch in lemon stranded cotton
D back stitch in lemon coton perlé
E chain stitch in white stranded cotton
F back stitch in white stranded cotton
G back stitch in red
H back stitch in blue
I back stitch in lemon coton perlé

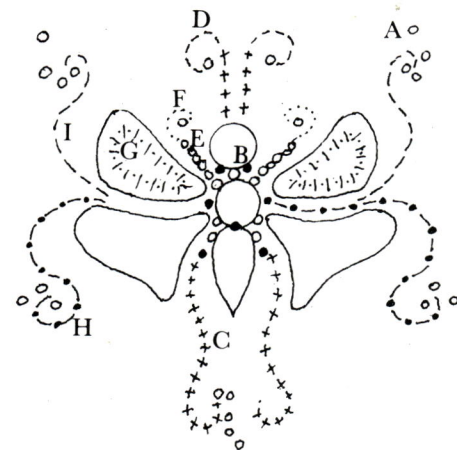

edge for turning under. Cut a piece of strong cardboard the size of the area inside the tacking/basting and stretch the embroidery over it, making sure that the warp and weft threads are kept parallel. The tacking/basting should lie along the edge of the cardboard. Glue the work in place, mitring the corners (see page 22) and remove the tacking/basting. Finally, the sampler can be glued onto a piece of mounting board/matboard and framed, with or without glass.

Butterfly Sewing Accessories

Make this pretty needle case and pincushion for your sewing basket or as a gift.

Materials required
Red or natural canvas, 2 pieces 10 cm (4 inches) square
Red linen, 40 × 10 cm (16 × 4 inches)
Scraps of black, blue and green felt
Stranded cotton/floss, 1 skein each of lemon on yellow and white
Coton perlé/pearl cotton, no. 5, 1 ball each blue, red, lemon yellow and navy blue
Small amount of polyester stuffing

Working the embroidery
Cut four pieces of red fabric, 10 cm (4 inches) square. Trace off the actual size design and transfer it onto the right side of the fabric on two of the squares using the transfer paper method. Using the tracing as a pattern, cut three pieces of black felt

Aquarium panel

This panel is a challenging project, because although only a few embroidery stitches are used, subtle effects are achieved with the use of brilliant colours and the contrasting textures of three different kinds of thread. The finished panel measures 40 × 23 cm (16 × 9 inches) before framing.

Materials required

Blue linen, 45 × 28 cm (18 × 11 inches)
Strong cardboard, 40 × 23 cm (16 × 9 inches)

Threads:

stranded cotton/floss, 1 skein each dark pink, mid-rose, pale pink, old gold, mid-orange, gold, dark emerald green, pale leaf green and apple green coton perlé/pearl cotton no. 5, 1 skein each brown, yellow, red, pink, orange and black tapestry wool, 1 skein each dark green, mid-green and mustard brown

4 silver plastic domes or sequins for the fish's eye and air bubbles

Working the embroidery

Have the design enlarged photographically so that the grid fills an area 40 × 23 cm (16 × 9 inches). (If you do not have access to a photographic enlarging service, use the grid lines to enlarge the design by hand.) Trace off the enlargement and transfer the main outlines to the fabric using the transfer paper method.

Mount the fabric in a slate/scroll or ring frame and work the stitches following the key. Stitch the domes in place as shown in the photograph.

Making up the panel

Stretch the completed work. When it is dry, place it on the cardboard, fold the turnings to the underside and glue them in place with fabric glue, mitring the corners.

Key to diagram

stranded embroidery cotton/floss
1 satin stitch in dark pink
2 satin stitch in mid-rose
3 satin stitch in pale pink
4 satin stitch in mid-orange
5 satin stitch in old gold
6 satin stitch in gold
7 French knots and back stitch in dark emerald green
8 fly stitch and back stitch, also feather stitch in apple green
9 fly stitch and back stitch in pale leaf green
10 satin stitch in apple green

Coton perlé

——— brown backstitch
○○○ brown knot stitch
——— yellow backstitch
●●● yellow coral stitch
–·–·– red backstitch
+·–·+ red coral stitch
– – – black backstitch
● black satin stitch
· black French knots
●●● red satin stitch

Tapestry wool

I back stitch and fly stitch in mid-green
II coral stitch in mid-green
III back stitch in dark green
IV French knots in mustard brown

Belt in freehand stitches

Here is a simple design which is planned so that you can use it for many purposes. Apart from the belt, you may like to use the motif on the yoke or pocket of a dress, on the pocket of jeans or a skirt.

For the belt, five motifs are spaced so that the belt can be adapted for any size, whether larger or smaller. The pattern is for a 65 cm (26 inch) waist, the finished belt being 70 × 5 cm (28 × 2 inches).

Materials required

Donkey brown smooth flannel or similar background material, 80 × 10 cm (32 × 4 inches)

Calico/unbleached muslin, 90 × 20 cm (36 × 8 inches) or wider if necessary for your frame

Interlining for belt backing, 70 × 5 cm (28 × 2 inches)

Buckle, interlocking type, size 5 cm (2 inches)

Sateen lining, 65 × 7·5 cm (26 × 3 inches)

Crewel wool, 1 skein mid-grey (A) and 1 skein sienna (B)

Stranded cotton/floss, 1 skein biscuit (C) and 1 skein pale grey (D)

Working the embroidery

Use a slate/scroll frame if you have one of a suitable size, or use a ring frame. Mount the background ma-terial onto the calico and mark out the outline of the belt with tacking/basting. Mark out also the centre front and back of the belt, and the position where the material will be turned back for the buckle.

The centres of the motifs are positioned as follows:

F – centre back

G, H – 11 cm (4½ inches) on either side of F

J, K – 11 cm (4½ inches) on either side of the centre front

Work tacking/basting to mark these positions, and transfer the designs.

Work chain, stem and fly stitches using three strands of stranded cotton and one strand of crewel wool, and French knots using three strands of crewel wool. Work the embroidery as follows, referring the numbers to the areas on the diagram and the letters to the threads in the materials list.

1 and 2 outline in stem stitch (D).

2 fill with chain stitch (A).

3 left hand side – outline in stem stitch (C), right hand side – outline in stem stitch (C) and continue to the top of the belt along the right hand side of 4.

3 and 4 fill with chain stitch (B).

5 outline in stem stitch (D).

6 fill with French knots (A).

7 fill with chain stitch (A).

8 outline in stem stitch along the right hand side and work two lines from the base (D).

9 outline in stem stitch (C), and fill with fly stitch worked alternately in (C) and (D).

10 outline in stem stitch on the right hand side (B).

Making up the belt

When the embroidery is complete, trim the calico to the tacking/basting indicating the width of the belt. Lap the top edge of the flannel with the right side uppermost over one edge of the belt backing, so that the tacking/basting lies directly over the edge of the belt backing all the way along. Machine or hand stitch through these two layers, half-way between the two edges.

Fold the belt backing under the belt. Turn under the lower edge of the belt, so it covers the raw edge of the backing and lace the two edges of the background material together all the way along.

Position the two halves of the buckle at each end of the belt. Turn each end through the buckle and stitch it in place. Fold under the edges of the lining and hem it in position to neaten the back of the belt, making sure that it is not visible from the right side.

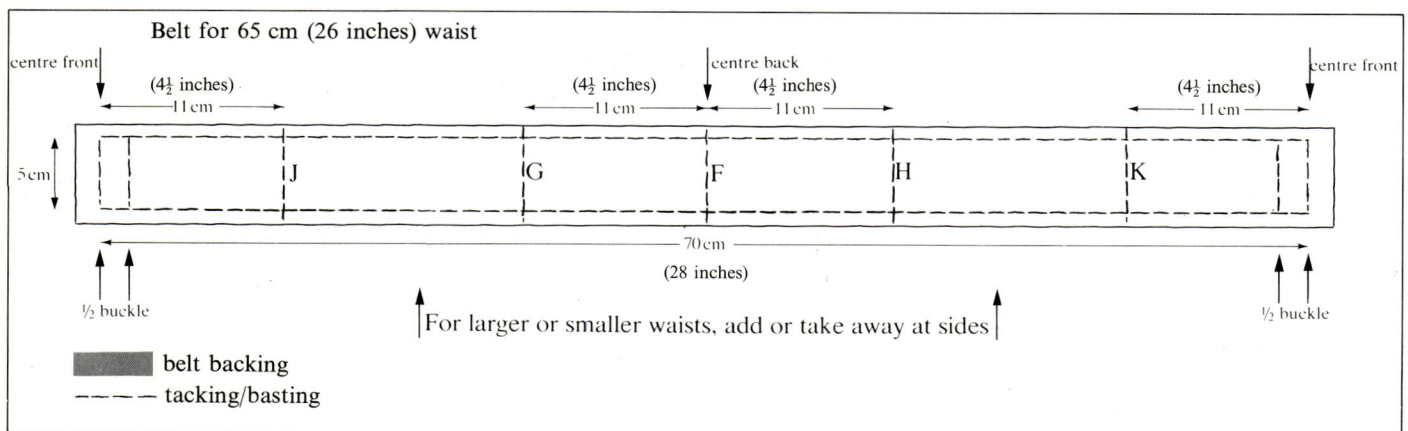

Belt for 65 cm (26 inches) waist

centre front · (4½ inches) 11 cm · J · G · centre back · (4½ inches) 11 cm · (4½ inches) 11 cm · F · H · K · (4½ inches) 11 cm · centre front

5 cm · 70 cm · (28 inches) · ½ buckle · ½ buckle

For larger or smaller waists, add or take away at sides

belt backing
tacking/basting

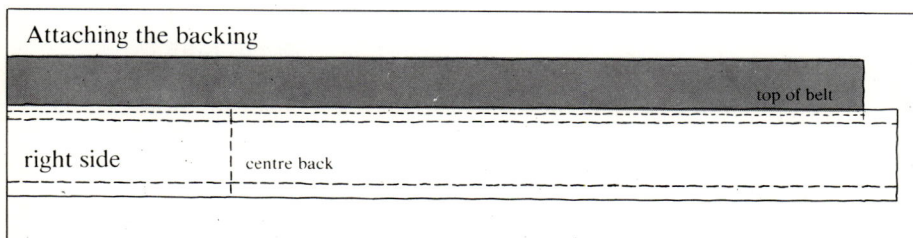

Attaching the backing

top of belt
right side · centre back

Lacing the backing

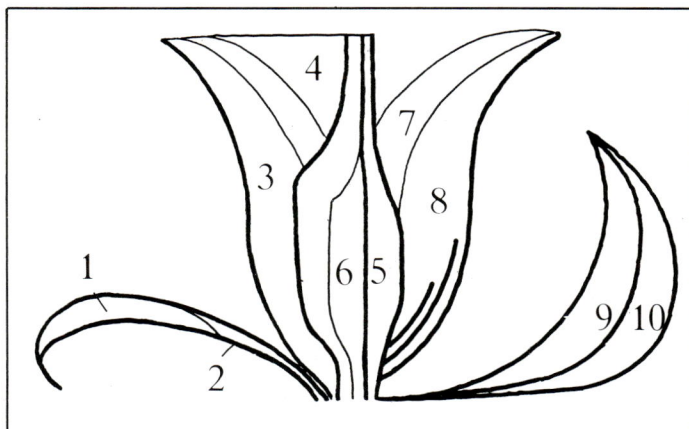

1 and 2 outline is stem stitch (D).
2 fill with chain stitch (A).
3 outline in stem stitch (C) and continue to the top of the belt along the right hand side of 4.
3 and 4 fill with chain stitch (B).
5 outline in stem stitch (D).
6 fill with French knots (A).
7 fill with chain stitch (A).
8 stem stitch along the right hand side and two lines (D).
9 outline in stem stitch (C), and fill with fly stitch worked alternately in (C) and (D).
10 stem stitch on the right side (B).

Rose bedspread

A beautiful embroidered bedspread and pillow cover such as these might well become family heirlooms. The wild rose design goes round all four sides of the bedspread, and three motifs are used on the pillow cover. In addition to stitches already introduced, the embroidery includes two new ones – satin stitch and long and short stitch.

Materials required

Linen, calico/unbleached muslin or other closely woven cotton to cover bed, including allowances for overhang, seams and hems.

A ready-made pillowcase, or fabric to cover pillow.

Stranded embroidery cotton/floss in pale olive green, mid-olive green, olive green, bright green, brown, buttercup yellow, pale pink, mid-pink and pink (finish 1 skein of each colour, then estimate the amount required of each to complete the embroidery).

Note: Make sure the background fabric is pre-shrunk before starting the embroidery.

Working the embroidery

Enlarge Fig. 3 photographically or by hand, using Fig. 1 (actual size) as a guide. Trace off enough motifs to go round the bedspread on all four sides. The motifs are positioned approximately 12 cm (5 inches) from the edge.

Work the embroidery using three strands of cotton throughout. Work the flower petals in long and short stitch using three shades of pink and following Fig. 1 for placement of colours. Work the leaves also in long and short using three shades of green.

Work the flower centres in satin stitch using two strands of pale olive and one of mid-olive green.

Work the stamens in French knots, using buttercup yellow.

Work all the stems (except the

Key for leaf stems
1. Pale olive green
2. Medium olive green
3. Olive green
4. Bright green
5. Brown

ones marked with colours 1 and 4 on Fig. 3) with two rows of stem stitch, one in brown (underneath) and one in mid-olive green.

Work the thinner stems in stem stitch using two strands of bright green and one of pale olive.

For the pillow cover use three main motifs and a linking border (Fig. 2).

Press the completed embroidery on the wrong side under a damp cloth.

Fig. 1

Fig. 2

Fig. 3

Key
1 Orange red
2 Mid-blue
3 Dark blue
4 Bright orange
5 Pale canary
6 Lilac
7 Mauve
8 Chestnut brown
9 Dark gorse yellow
10 Maroon
11 Old rose
12 Pale blue
13 Olive green
14 Yellow green
15 Mid-olive green
16 Pale olive green

Flower garland

Embroider a garland of summer flowers on a white shirt and it instantly becomes luxurious and fashionable. The garland is a life size motif which can be traced from the page and it is a simple matter to pick out one or two flower motifs to decorate the collar or cuffs. Bright, summer garden colours are used for the shirt illustrated but the design could be worked in shades of one colour, if you preferred or in an all-white scheme on a coloured shirt.

Materials required

Stranded cotton/floss orange red, mid-blue, dark blue, bright orange, pale canary, lilac, mauve, chestnut brown, dark gorse yellow, maroon, old rose, pale blue, olive green, yellow green, mid-olive green, pale olive green.

To work the embroidery

Trace the design and transfer to the right hand side of the shirt. Reverse the design for the left hand side. Work the embroidery following the colour key. Use two strands of cotton throughout. All the flowers and leaves are used in satin stitch. Stems are worked in stem stitch.

Press embroidery on the wrong side under a damp cloth when completed.

47

Crewel work

The thread traditionally used for this work is known as crewel wool. Today crewel wool is still used and the work is based on the traditional stitches used on the wall and bed hangings and large curtains which were in fashion in the seventeenth and early eighteenth centuries. At that time the designs were large and usually took the form of a central tree shape rising from uneven mounds on which various animals were often resting. Large curving foliated branches radiated from the central trunk, sometimes with flowers and birds filling the spaces. Other types of designs include patterns built up of motifs depicting plants, trees, animals and birds. Flower designs gradually became lighter and by the nineteenth century, crewel work consisted of long and short stitches in designs of the period. It is worth studying the fascinating stitches and colours.

Nowadays crewel work can still be used for large wall hangings and bedspreads but it is also worked in finer detail for dress inserts and decorative accessories.

Material for crewel work needs to be firm to bear the weight of the closely embroidered wool. Loosely woven fabric such as tweed should be mounted on a backing material before starting the stitchery.

Crewel wool is available in a large range of colours and tones. Most crewel wool is mothproofed and colour-fast, making it suitable for decoration on furnishings. Usually one or two strands of crewel wool are used, unless the work is on a very large scale and needs more strands. Persian wool, available in almost as many colours as crewel wool, is also an attractive thread to use for this method.

It is best to use a crewel needle for the stitching, and to work on a frame. If using a ring frame, find one that is large enough to mount the complete section to be worked to avoid disturbing any solid areas already stitched.

The beauty of crewel work really lies in the many fine stitches which lie flat on the surface of the material. Once you are familiar with these, they can be added to the freehand stitches described in the previous chapter and worked on a smaller scale in a thread other than wool.

Right and facing page *Details from an early eighteenth-century crewel work hanging.*
Below *A sampler of crewel work.*

Split stitch

This is a useful outline stitch as it creates a smooth line and is quick to work. Work in any direction. Bring the needle up at the beginning of the line. Take it down a short distance away. Go back about half-way along this stitch and bring the needle up again through the centre of the stitch, splitting it in two. Then go forward and down again. The stitches should be small on curves in order to get a smooth line. Split stitch may be built up into a filling stitch.

Satin stitch

This consists of straight stitches worked closely together to form a smooth band or block of stitchery. To practise, work two horizontal parallel lines of split stitch about 5 mm (¼ inch) apart. Bring the needle up close above the top line of the split stitch, at one end. Take the needle down below the bottom line of split stitch. Repeat this stitch continuously by bringing the needle up close to the stitch at the top, so that your second and successive stitches lie alongside and touching the previous stitch.

When working satin stitch, you should always have a long stitch across the wrong side of the work between stitches, to ensure a good tension.

To work shapes in satin stitch, your stitches will not all be the same length. If a change of direction is needed, the occasional short stitch may be included.

Satin stitch is best worked with a single thread. Although it will take longer to work, the result will be worth the extra time spent.

Long and short stitch

This is a method of filling shapes with an arrangement of straight stitches, which are blended to create a smooth surface. The direction of the stitches needs careful planning and it is essential to practise the stitches until you are satisfied with the result.

Start by working long and short in straight horizontal lines before attempting to fill a shape. Select three tones of a colour, dark, medium and light. Use one strand of crewel wool in the light tone and work a line of split stitch across the top. This acts as a guide for a smooth line and it slightly raises the edge of the work. Now bring the needle up about 1 cm (½ inch) below the line of split stitch. Take it down on the outside of the split stitch, with the needle in an upright position. Then bring it up about 5 mm (¼ inch) below, close to the first stitch and work across the line with long and short stitches alternately. Thread up the medium tone of wool. The second line of

stitches is worked by bringing the needle up into the end of each stitch in the first line, and down into the material. Work another row in the medium tone before working the final row in the dark tone. Note that the stitches in the second and successive lines are all the same length until you reach the last row when the stitches will again be long and short alternately.

A line of split stitch on the base line will give a straight and smooth ending to the practice piece.

Next try working long and short stitches within a shape; mark in pencil the direction in which you will work your stitches. Split stitch may be worked in lines to divide up a shape and you will find that these stitches blend in with the long and short.

There is a general tendency when working long and short to make the stitches too short. Unless they are long enough the work will become congested with short stitches.

split stitch

satin stitch

Block shading

This consists of rows of satin stitch worked in graduating colours or tones of a colour.

Work a line of split stitch on the outline then bring the needle up into the material and down on the outline. The second and successive lines are worked by bringing the needle up into the material, and down into the extreme end of the previous row. This method is best worked in a single thread of crewel or Persian wool on a closely woven material.

Laid fillings

Patterns of stitches worked on a basic grid of straight stitches were used as fillings for large leaf shapes on the heavily embroidered curtains and bedcovers of the seventeenth and eighteenth centuries. Adapted for present-day use, they form a useful means of decoration in any weight of wool, cotton or metal thread. These fillings are unsuitable for small shapes unless worked on a very small scale.

Laid fillings should be worked on a frame as it is essential that the threads lie flat on the surface of the material. Start working at the widest part of the design, or in the centre. Bring the needle up on one edge of the outline. It is usual and helpful to follow the grain of the material. Take the needle down on the opposite side. Bring the needle up on the same side of the shape, a short way from the first stitch (about 5 mm

[¼ inch] if working in one strand of crewel wool. Cover the whole area with a series of spaced parallel stitches, then bring the needle up on an adjacent side and work on a second set of straight stitches over the first set and at right angles to them. Then hold down the intersections of the crossed threads with a small diagonal straight stitch. This mesh may be used as a basis on which patterns can be worked in straight, satin, cross and woven stitches.

The scale of the square mesh will depend on the thickness of thread used. A variety of threads and colours may be used, and beads and sequins can be added. The patterns do not need to fill the mesh entirely, and as you become accustomed to the method, you can vary the size of the mesh and thickness of thread.

Below *Assorted filling stitches.*

51

Evening bolero

Graceful curves of chain stitch decorate this bolero, made from a paper pattern of your choice.

Materials required

Pattern for a bolero
Medium weight fabric as required
Lining fabric (optional)
Bias binding to match fabric
Fine synthetic gold yarn
Crewel or Persian wool, 1 skein each moss green, peacock blue, purple

Working the embroidery

Pin the pattern pieces to the fabric and cut them out. Enlarge the design as indicated on the diagram and transfer it to the bolero front, placing it as indicated. Work the motif in the gold yarn using chain stitch. Work the border, starting 1 cm ($\frac{3}{8}$ inch) inside the finished edge with a row of chain in purple and one in moss green, a row of herringbone stitch in gold yarn and a row of chain stitch in peacock blue.

Make up the bolero using standard dressmaking principles, adding a lining of desired. Bind the edges.

Fig 1
1 square = 10mm

Place mats

Bright bands of colour decorate the linen place mats shown on page 54.

Materials required

Gold-coloured linen, 1 m ($1\frac{1}{8}$ yards)
Fine synthetic gold yarn
Crewel or Persian wool, 1 skein each dark brown, peacock blue, vermilion, sage green, mink brown

Working the embroidery

Cut six mats, each 30×38 cm (12×15 inches). Machine stitch 1·2 cm ($\frac{1}{2}$ inch) from each edge. Fringe up to the stitching.

Starting at the outer short edge, work the embroidery in the following order:
1 work chain stitch in dark brown, then work over this in herring bone stitch in peacock blue
2 work chain stitch in gold yarn
3 work chain stitch in vermilion
4 work chain stitch in sage green
5 work chain stitch in mink brown, then work over this in herringbone stitch in gold yarn

Shoulder bag

Modern Greek peasant embroidery inspired this colourful shoulder bag.

Materials required

Hessian/burlap or coarse linen, 40 × 62 cm (16 × 24½ inches)
Linen fabric
Double knitting yarn/knitting worsted, 10 strands, each 90 cm (36 inches) long, of dark green, pale yellow, yellow brown
Fine synthetic gold yarn
Crewel or Persian wool in pale yellow, chestnut brown, pale turquoise, maroon, dark beige, dark green, light brown, light green, mid-blue, mid-turquoise, dark turquoise, vermilion, dark pink-beige, light pink-beige, yellow, yellow-green, cream

Working the embroidery

Cut fabric into two pieces, each 40 × 35 cm (16 × 12¼ inches). Oversew the edges.

Enlarge the design to measure 34 × 29 cm (13¼ × 11¼ inches) and transfer it to one or both fabric pieces, positioning it 3·5 cm (1¼ inches) below the top edge.

Using two strands of crewel wool or one strand of Persian, work the embroidery as follows:

A buttonhole ring in pale yellow, outlined in chain stitch in chestnut brown
B buttonhole ring in pale turquoise outlined in chain stitch in maroon
C chain stitch in dark beige
D chain stitch in dark green
E chain stitch in dark green (two rows), pale turquoise, light brown, light green and dark green
F buttonhole stitch in pale turquoise
G chain stitch in maroon, over-worked in herringbone in gold yarn
H chain stitch in yellow-green and mid-blue
I chain stitch in pale turquoise outlined in mid-turquoise, with mid-turquoise crosses
J chain stitch in yellow and maroon outlined in vermilion
K buttonhole stitch in dark pink-beige, light brown, light pink-beige and cream
L buttonhole rings in gold yarn.

Making up the bag

Place the two bag pieces together with right sides facing. Machine stitch along side and lower edges just outside the embroidery. Fold under the top edges; tack/baste, and press edges. Cut and stitch a lining, if desired, in the same way.

Braid the knitting yarn strands to form the handle and tie a knot in each end. Stitch the knots to the upper corners.

Slip the lining into the bag, wrong

sides facing, and slipstitch the folded edges together. If there is no lining, hem the upper edges in place.

Musical Angel Cushion

This charming cushion cover (shown on page 52) is reminiscent of Indian embroideries.

Materials required

Linen, 40 cm (16 inches) square
Velvet/velveteen the same size
Crewel or Persian wool in the following colours: black, navy blue, pink, pink-beige, salmon pink, deep pink-beige, emerald green, vermilion, old gold, light beige, dark beige, light brown, mid-blue, turquoise, lilac-blue, coral pink, dark brown, white, light green, mid-green, dark green, cyclamen, deep cyclamen, maroon
Fine synthetic gold yarn
Decorative braid, 1·6 m (1⅝ yards)
Cushion pad/pillow form 38 cm (15 inch) square

Working the embroidery

Enlarge the design to measure 36 cm (15 inches) square and transfer it to the linen.

Work the embroidery as follows, using one strand of thread and referring to the diagram on this page.

Wings

A buttonhole stitch in gold yarn
B buttonhole stitch in pale pink
C buttonhole stitch with chain stitch between in pink-beige
D buttonhole stitch in salmon
E buttonhole stitch in deep pink-beige
F chain stitch in emerald green, outlined in gold yarn
Crown
G buttonhole stitch in vermilion
H chain stitch and French knots in gold yarn; satin stitch in old gold
Face and hands
I face tones – stem stitch shading in light and dark beige, outlined in light brown; mouth – stem stitch in coral pink; eyes – stem stitch in dark brown and white
Clothing
J satin stitch in old gold with French knots in gold yarn
K chain stitch in dark and light green
L buttonhole stitch in vermilion

and cyclamen, outlined in chain stitch in deep cyclamen

M chain stitch in maroon, outlined in stem stitch in old gold

N chain stitch in vermilion, cyclamen, maroon and gold yarn, outlined in maroon

O chain and satin stitch in cyclamen and vermilion, outlined in maroon

P French knots in gold yarn

Q chain stitch in mid- and dark green; French knots in light green

R chain stitch in old gold and light brown; French knots in gold yarn
Background

S buttonhole rings in black with stars over-worked in gold yarn.

Work the background in chain stitch in navy blue, mid-blue, turquoise and lilac blue.

Making up the cushion

Press the embroidery. Place the embroidery and the velvet backing together with right sides facing. Stitch round three sides, taking 2 cm (1 inch) seams. Turn the cover right side out, insert cushion pad and slipstitch the opening edges together. Stitch braid round the edges.

Griffon and birds

This richly coloured wall hanging is worked on brown linen and finished with a knotted fringe.

Materials required

Brown linen, 82 × 50 cm (32 × 20 inches).

Crewel or Persian wool, 1 skein each of the following colours: pale yellow, pale orange, bright orange, amber, deep amber, rust, mustard, pale blue, mid-blue, silver blue, pale silver blue, baby blue, sky blue, deep olive green, purple, gold, pale olive green, cinnamon.

Working the embroidery

Enlarge the design so that it measures 28 cm (11 inches) in width. Mark the centre of the fabric with two rows of tacking/basting, and mark the centre with a pencil. Transfer the design to the fabric.

Work the embroidery following the stitch and colour keys.

Work bands of stitches in various colours below the design.

Making up the wall hanging

Press the embroidery. Stitch down both sides 1·2 cm (½ inch) from the edge and fringe back to the stitching.

At the top edge turn under 7 cm (3 inches); stitch. Hem the lower edge. Cut 18 cm (7 inches) lengths of cinnamon, rust and deep amber wool. Using 10 threads at a time, knot a fringe through the hem, using a crochet hook.

Stitch key

�	buttonhole (stitches close together)
	buttonhole filling
⊗	buttonhole ring
	detached buttonhole
ΛΛΛ	chain stitch
++++++	couching
○─○	broad chain
	Cretan stitch
○ ○ ○	French knots
XXXXX	herringbone stitch
++++	oriental stitch
	long and short stitch
	rosette chain
	Roumanian stitch
//////	satin stitch
□□□	open chain

Colour key

1 pale yellow
2 pale orange
3 bright orange
4 amber
5 deep amber
6 rust
7 mustard
8 pale blue
9 mid-blue
10 silver blue
11 pale silver blue
12 baby blue
13 sky blue
14 deep olive green
15 purple
16 gold
17 pale olive green
18 cinnamon

Motifs

Here are some traditional crewel embroidery motifs which can be used on a variety of furnishings. Use them singly or in groups. Crewel or Persian wool can be used, but the designs look just as effective worked in cotton embroidery threads. Some suitable stitches are shown on pages 28–37 and 50–51.

Laid work

The technique of laid work was created originally to produce a speedy and economical way of covering large areas of material with stitchery. Laid work is so called because it consists of straight stitches which are laid on the surface of the right side of the material, little of the thread being visible on the wrong side. Because of the effect caused by the length of the stitches, it was a means of displaying the beauty and sheen of an untwisted floss silk thread in large patterns. In museums and churches, lavish silk hangings and ecclesiastical vestments show this work, much of it from Italy.

Today, this type of work may be useful for covering large areas of design with threads in an economical way because the method uses a minimum amount of thread. It is particularly good for decorative panels, curtains or bedcovers as well as for decoration on dress or accessories.

The material for laid work should be closely woven and any design for its use should ideally include bold shapes. It can be combined with freehand stitchery. A smooth effect will be obtained by using a thread which is stranded, such as two strands of crewel wool or three strands of stranded cotton, as these will be flat and will blend together. Rounded threads can be used but these will not cover the material so well as they are not easy to hold in place. Always work with the material mounted on a frame.

Start by bringing the needle up on the outline at the widest part of the shape. Lay the thread flat down, away from the edge and take the needle down on the outline opposite. Bring the needle up on the same side close to the first stitch and take it back to the starting line, and down close to the point of entry. Fill in the whole of the shape in this way, working from alternate sides each time. The stitches on the right side will be long, while those on the wrong side will be tiny straight stitches which follow the outline. Do not pull the stitches too tightly or they will be distorted when holding stitches are worked.

The direction of the stitches may also be changed by occasionally not taking a stitch to the extreme edge of the shape. Then bring the needle up at the edge, as you would normally, for the return journey. This will give a slight slant to the next stitch, which will enable a gradual change of direction to be made.

Colouring or tones may be changed within an area of laid work. Plan any changes so that three or four stitches are alternated with the same number of the next colour to be used. Alternatively a change of tone may be done smoothly by mixing the strands of thread in the needle (for example, one strand of the tone already worked and one strand of the next tone to be worked) before completely changing to the successive tone.

Once the threads have been laid, they must be held in position with some form of stitchery. This may be in lines following the shape of the outline or at right angles to the laid threads. Stitches suitable for this include split, stem, chain and couching. Any design for the stitching will need to be done visually as you will have covered the pattern lines.

Laid fillings may be worked over a background of laid work; the best effects will be obtained by working the square grid diagonally across the laid threads.

For a bold effect any of the outline stitches may be used to outline the work. If you are using a stranded thread, untwist the threads from the needle as you work, so that the strands lie alongside each other. It will also help to take the needle down between the strands.

Surface needleweaving

Traditional needleweaving is included in the section on drawn thread work. Surface needleweaving is a development of the traditional method. Instead of weaving over threads of material which have been exposed by the withdrawal of others, independent straight threads are laid on the surface of the material and it is over these that the weaving is done.

Surface needleweaving is most attractive if worked freely, with varying lengths of laid threads. It is only used on work for decorative purposes as the loose stitching would catch if in practical use. Use a closely woven fabric and work on a frame.

Learn the simple method by working five long straight stitches which lie closely at one end and which splay out slightly towards the other end. Then, using a blunt needle, weave in and out of the laid threads for as many lines as you wish, keeping a good tension. It is usual to leave part of the laid threads exposed.

As a variation, to give dimension, bring the needle up through a round wooden bead and lay the threads so that they radiate from the centre hole. The threads being woven will be worked on threads slanting from the top of the bead to the surface of the material.

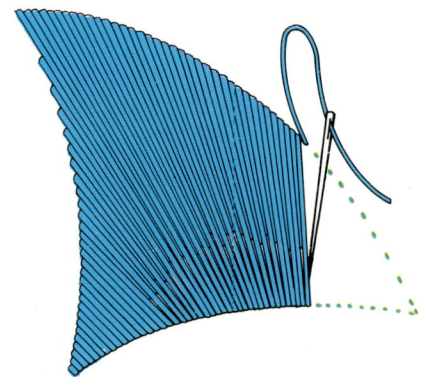

Top *Laying threads.*
Above *Gradually changing the direction when laying threads.*

60

Above *Laid threads held in place with additional stitchery: three forms of couching and fly stitch.*
Right above *A panel with foliage and flowers in laid work. The bird is worked in long and short stitch.*

Above *Surface needleweaving.*

Appliqué

Appliqué consists of building up a design by applying shapes of one material to another and is an embroidery method which has been used for many centuries in several countries. Visits to museums will show the variety of this kind of work and the most simple examples will be contrasted with others in velvets and silk damasks. Traditionally, some appliqué is pictorial while other designs are of regular repeating patterns, such as scrolling, usually outlined boldly with cords. The finish of the work indicates its period and country of origin: some examples show the applied material held in place with hemming stitches while pieces worked at the beginning of the twentieth century in England were held in place with close buttonhole stitching. Today, the approach is flexible and the way in which we apply the material is an integral part of the design.

Appliqué may be used for decoration on small items such as boxes, small pictures and garments, as well as on large-scale hangings, church vestments and altar frontals or on other items which will be viewed from a distance. It is a means of creating a design in a relatively quick way, and it can be embellished with additional stitchery if required.

When collecting interesting pieces of material some people will turn to the disciplined technique of patchwork where the mixing of different types of fabric is not advisable. In appliqué, however, almost any fabrics can be combined, whether transparent or opaque, textured or smooth, although when learning, you should use materials of a similar weight on one piece of work as it is quite difficult to apply a heavy material alongside a lightweight one.

When selecting a background material, choose one which is firm and of medium weight. Dress materials, furnishing fabrics, hessian/burlap and felt may all be used. Avoid using a fabric which will stretch. Sometimes your design will entirely cover the background and in this instance a firm backing of calico/unbleached muslin is all that is necessary, without an additional background material.

One of the problems which you may encounter is the puckering of both the applied material and the background material surrounding it. The use of a frame will help to keep the fabrics flat, and it is also a help to mount your background fabric onto a backing material of linen, calico/muslin or sheeting/broadcloth. Collect remnants for this purpose.

It is best to use only materials which are non-fraying such as cottons or woven woollens. Generally, fabrics of man-made fibres are more difficult to handle than those of natural fibres. Materials which fray badly should not be used for appliqué unless they are backed with dressmaker's iron-on interfacing of an appropriate weight. Transparent materials must not be backed. Avoid using delicate fabrics on items which need to be strong enough for hard wear. As a general rule, most appliqué should be dry cleaned.

The scope for designs which can be interpreted in appliqué is almost unlimited. You can use ideas from cut paper shapes and ink blots. Simple drawings and photographs may also be used. Avoid sharp angles until you can handle materials without difficulty. Simplify as much as you can and do not try to produce naturalistic effects.

A certain piece of tweed may spark off the desire to create a design of tree bark, or a piece of horizontal-striped furnishing fabric may evoke the feeling of sea and sky. A small piece of left-over red material could have a multitude of uses, for example, a soldier's uniform, a flower head or a car. A bag of fabric scraps is very useful for appliqué.

Transparent materials, sometimes difficult to apply, can change the colour of the background material. Experiment by placing one layer of coloured organza onto your background, then a second colour and watch how it changes. Try also the effect of using net. The background will change each time you add a layer.

Right *Detail from panel 30 of the Overlord Embroidery (see page 8).*

Framing up

Wash a piece of backing material in hot water to pre-shrink it. It should be 7·5 cm (3 inches) longer and wider than your background material. Mark the centre of the width and length with tacking/basting. Mount the piece on a slate scroll frame with the warp threads running from top to bottom (see page 14); leave the material slack so that when the frame is placed flat on a table, the centre of the material just touches it.

Press the background material; snip or remove the selvedges and mark the centre of the width and length with tacking/basting. If possible, use the material so that the warp threads run from top to bottom. Place the wrong side of this material over the framed backing material, matching the centres of each.

Still keeping the frame slack, pin the two materials together, working outwards from the centre of each side and smoothing the material as you pin. Work tailor tacking/diagonal basting stitches all over to hold the two materials together.

Use a sewing thread to work straight stitches all round the raw edges of the background material. Starting with a knot at the end of the thread, bring the needle up at the centre of one side into the backing material and straight down into the background material so that the stitches are at right angles to the raw edges. Work to the end of the first side. The stitches should be about 5 mm ($\frac{1}{4}$ inch) long and 5 mm ($\frac{1}{4}$ inch) apart. Return to the centre and work to the opposite end before repeating this process on the two adjacent and opposite sides.

If you are not using a backing material, the background material should be framed up in the usual way.

Small pieces can be worked in a ring frame and if you decide to use a backing material, it should be the same size as the background, once shrunk. Blend the two together with tailor tacking/diagonal basting all over, matching the fabric grains.

For a small motif, at the hem of a skirt, for example, tack/baste backing material to its wrong side, just large enough to work the motif. When the work is finished, trim the backing close to the stitched motif.

The design may be put onto the fabric before or after framing up.

Tighten up the frame if putting a design onto framed-up material.

Applying materials

The frame should be slack when applying small areas of material, just as it was when the background material was applied.

When cutting out material for applying, consider what method will be used to attach the material to the background. You may need to allow turnings in order to avoid raw edges, particularly if the appliqué is to be on hard wearing clothing such as jeans. Allow turnings of 3 to 6 mm ($\frac{1}{8}$ to $\frac{1}{4}$ inch) all round a shape, depending on the fabric. If two applied pieces will touch, extend the under piece by 1·5 cm ($\frac{5}{8}$ inch) so that the upper piece will overlap it, and do not turn under any fabric on the under piece.

For decorative work, where wearing properties do not have to be considered, the raw edges need not necessarily be neatened or covered with stitching. If this is the case, only small holding stitches are necessary.

Use one of the conventional methods of transferring the shapes onto the appropriate pieces of material which will be applied. Alternatively, make a tracing of the design and cut it up into pieces to use as paper patterns which can then be pinned onto the fabric to be applied and cut round. Always try to match the grain of the material to be applied to that of the background. It will help to mark your pattern pieces with an arrow so that you can match it to the warp of the material. Once the method of applying is mastered, however, you will find it possible to turn some fabrics from the true grain.

Backing the fabric with dressmaker's iron-on interfacing may be done either by cutting the backing to the required shape before ironing onto the wrong side of the material or by painting the design onto the non-adhesive side of the backing which is ironed on before being cut out. When putting an outline onto iron-on interfacing remember to reverse the design so that when it is cut out, the shape will be correct for the right side.

Turn any turning allowances to the wrong side and tack/baste them down all round, keeping the knots on the right side for easy removal. Snip 'V'-shapes on any curved edges

to enable the material to lie flat.

With the frame slack, place the wrong side of the prepared pieces to the right side of the background material, the underneath parts first. For example, if working a landscape, the sky would be applied first followed by the fields or hills and then the trees; similarly, apply the material for a building before its roof or door. Pin and tack/baste the material in place, using tailor tacking/diagonal basting on large areas. Tighten the frame a little so that it is still slightly slack. Hem pieces with turnings. Fine fabrics can be held in place with very tiny running stitches which will be almost invisible.

To apply material without turnings, the same principle is used until the final hemming. If a decorative panel is being worked, where no consideration needs to be made regarding practicability, freehand or running stitches may be used without worrying about the raw edges of material. Useful decorative stitches include coral, Cretan and straight stitches. These stitches will help soften the outline as well as hold the material in place. The best stitches for garments, when no turnings are used, are herringbone or buttonhole stitch as these will also neaten the edges. Additional emphasis can be given to certain areas by increasing the thickness of thread or the denseness of stitches. Pieces of net may be used to hold down some materials in decorative work, with the net extending beyond the edge of the applied piece in some places.

If a hard outline is needed, as in heraldry, the shapes can be outlined with couching. If you are working couching over the edge of an applied shape, you may find it a help to hold the piece down first by working tiny straight stitches, taking the needle up into the background and down into the applied material. Use a matching sewing thread so that the stitches, which will be about 3 mm ($\frac{1}{8}$ inch) apart, are not visible after couching.

When applying soft leather, suede or vinyl, use this method with tiny straight stitches at right angles to the edge. As pins or tacking/basting cannot be used to hold down any of these non-woven types of material (or the holes will show), work long stitches across the shape at the widest points, bringing the needle up into the background material at one side and down on the opposite side. Repeat these holding-down stitches at intervals in both directions and over any points. Remove these stitches when the tiny straight stitches have held the leather in place. Invisible thread may be used for stitching down leather and vinyl if you do not wish the stitches to show.

If you want to raise the surface of the applied material from the background material, make a felt padding (see page 86) before applying the material. Small areas which need to be raised, possibly on clothing, can be padded from the wrong side, using the trapunto quilting method (page 184). If no backing material is being used, it will be necessary to stitch some muslin as a backing over the required area.

Once the applied material is held in place the frame should be fully tightened before working freehand stitches. Backgrounds often need breaking up and straight stitches, French knots and clusters of beads may be useful for this.

If the work will be viewed from a distance, stand your frame in an upright position and stand well away from it. Usually one finds that certain areas need emphasizing, others may appear to be too prominent. It is surprising how different the work will look from a distance compared to the effect when you are actually working on it.

Finally remove any remaining tacking/basting stitches, and take the finished work off the frame. Only stretch appliqué if it is really necessary. It is usual to cut away the backing material carefully from the wrong side in any areas where material has not been applied on the right side but it can be left if needed for strength.

Above *Tailor tacking/diagonal basting*
Above right *Mount the background material onto the backing with straight stitches*
Right *Match the grain of the applied material with that of the background.*

Right *'Hedgerow' design in appliqué. The background is a furnishing fabric and the applied shapes are of various materials including nets and printed cottons. Decorative stitches include running, detached chain, straight, couching and French knots.*

Landscape in felt

This delightful felt picture has an attractive simplicity. The picture illustrated is 38 cm (15 inches) wide, but plan the background and road to fit the size of your frame.

Materials required

Blue felt for the background in the required size plus 10 cm (4 inches) for turnings
Scraps of felt in green, yellow, sand, red, blue and orange
Scraps of white cotton fabric
Stranded embroidery cotton/floss to match the fabrics
Brown and black knitting yarn
All purpose adhesive/glue
Thin cardboard
Hardboard/particleboard or stiff cardboard to fit the frame

Making the picture

Trace the outlines of the houses and other features from the photograph. Enlarge the drawings to the required size. Draw the outlines on thin cardboard and cut out each shape. Using these templates, cut out the grass, the yellow path and the sand-coloured road. Using slipstitch sew the grass to the background, then the path and finally the road.

Cut out houses in felt and white cotton. Glue a white house to the wrong side of each felt house. Cut out the trees. Pin trees and houses in position and stitch them to the background. Embroider tree trunks in stem stitch using brown yarn. Embroider roof details in stem stitch with black yarn.

Cut out the vehicles and stitch them in place. Work details in stem stitch or couching using embroidery cotton. Work wheels in couching.

Mounting the picture

Cut the board a little smaller than the size of the frame to allow clearance for the turnings. Place the picture face down and put the board on top. Glue the felt turnings to the board, mitring the corners.

66

Quick appliqué techniques

Appliqué can be very elaborate or very simple, formal or whimsical, like the felt picture shown here. You can get attractive results using time-saving techniques such as fusible web and machine stitching.

Fusible web is of two basic types: one consists of a single, fine layer which is fused simultaneously to the backing fabric and the motif, and the other has a peel-off backing and is applied in two stages.

To use the single type, cut it a little smaller than the motif and position it on the background fabric. Then lay the motif on top and press it in place as shown in Fig. 1. You may find it easier to secure the motif and the web to the background fabric with two or three pins in the centre, then press the edges in place and finally remove the pins and press the entire motif.

Web with backing is applied first to the wrong side of the motif fabric, with the backing layer upwards. The shape is then cut out, the backing layer peeled off and the motif pressed in place on the background fabric.

Very small motifs can be applied with fabric glue.

With any of these methods it is advisable to practise first with scraps of spare fabric.

Once applied, the motif should usually be edged with stitching of some kind. Ordinary machine zig-zag (Fig. 2) is suitable for casual clothes and accessories; a close zig-zag produces satin stitch, which is preferable on garments that will receive hard wear. Some machines do decorative stitches. If yours is equipped in this way, see what different and interesting effects you can create.

You may prefer to embellish the work with hand-stitching, such as the buttonhole stitch shown in Fig. 3, herringbone, coral, or another decorative stitch.

Appliqué perse

This technique (whose name means 'Persian appliqué') consists simply of cutting motifs from a printed fabric and applying them to a plain background. It is a good – and economical – way of giving a coordinated look to a decorating scheme, as you can use scraps of fabric left over from curtains or loose covers/slipcovers, cutting motifs to apply to cushions. The technique can also be used effectively on clothing and personal accessories.

Cut the motif carefully, first stiffening it with interfacing (or use fusible web as described above), and tack/baste or fuse it to the background fabric. Finish the edges with machine or hand stitching.

Shadow appliqué

This appliqué is used on sheer fabrics to make beautiful table linens, blouses, lingerie and other delicate items.

First mark the motif on the main fabric (organdy is a good choice for this), using tailor's chalk or pencil. Cut a piece of fabric for the motif (which may be the same as the main fabric or a little heavier), cutting it a little larger than the motif. Tack/baste it to the wrong side of the main fabric. Using matching embroidery thread, work back stitch along the lines of the motif. Then very carefully cut away the excess fabric round the motif. If you prefer, you can apply the motif with ordinary sewing thread, then work over the lines with a decorative stitch using embroidery thread.

Fascinating effects can be achieved with shadow appliqué by using different thicknesses of fabric for the motifs. The addition of some surface appliqué further enriches the work.

Kitchen Wall Tidy

This cheery wall tidy to hang in the kitchen is made from scraps of printed fabrics. The tidy could also be made for a work corner, to contain sewing or writing materials, or for a teenager's room, to hold brush, comb, ribbons, hair bands and other accessories. The tidy illustrated makes clever use of printed fabrics for the strawberry and little girl motifs. The fabrics you have on hand may suggest other kinds of motifs; use your imagination and you could come up with something really original.

Materials required

Coarse, cream-coloured linen, 95 × 60 cm (37½ × 23½ inches)
Blue bias binding, 7·5 m (8¼ yards)
Assorted fabrics for pockets
Iron-on interfacing for motifs and pockets
2 plastic curtain rings 2·5 cm (1 inch) in diameter
Dowel 55 cm (21½ inches) long

Making the tidy

Unravel all four edges of the linen fabric for about six threads to make a fringed edge. Turn side and bottom edges to the right side to a depth of 2·5 cm (1 inch) including fringe. Press and tack/baste. Pin and machine stitch the bias binding to the turned hems so that the fringed edge shows, mitring the corners. Turn down the top edge 4·5 cm (1¾ inches) and tack/baste. Stitch binding across as before, so that there is sufficient space above the top row of stitching to make a casing for the dowel.

For the pockets, enlarge the diagram as indicated. Darken the outlines of the pockets and motifs with a felt-tip pen, then trace the outlines onto iron-on interfacing, placing the interfacing shiny side up. Cut out the pieces and iron them to the wrong side of the appropriate fabrics.

Cut out the motifs and position them on the pockets, tack/baste them in place and apply them, using either machine zig-zag stitch or close buttonhole stitch.

Cut out the stiffened pockets and bind their edges with bias binding. Topstitch them in place on the tidy in the positions shown, using thread matching the binding.

Stitch the remaining length of binding to enclose the edges. Cut

2·5 cm (1 inch)

two short lengths to tie in bows around the curtain rings and stitch these in place on the tidy.

Cut the long piece in two, stitch both lengths to the wrong side of the tidy and tie the ends in a bow for hanging.

Bath set

Circles of crochet are appliquéd to terrycloth towelling to make this pretty bathroom set.

Materials required
Terrycloth towelling, 1 m (1⅛ yards)
Crochet cotton in four colours
Medium-sized crochet hook

Making the towel and mitt
For the towel, cut a piece of terrycloth 80 × 53 cm (31½ × 21 inches) and hem all four sides.

For the mitt, first make a pattern. Place your hand on a sheet of paper, fingers together and thumb pointing upwards. Draw round the hand, then smooth the outline as necessary. Add 3 cm (1¼ inches) turnings to the outer edges. Pin the pattern to a double layer of terrycloth and cut it out. Mark the stitching lines between the thumb and the rest of the hand.

Turn up a 3 cm (1¼ inch) hem on both wrist edges. Place the pieces together, right sides facing, and stitch along the seamlines. Trim the turnings and neaten them together.

Turn the mitt right side out.

Making the motifs
Crochet a strip 9 cm (3½ inches) deep and the width of the towel using contrasting cotton and double/single crochet. hand-stitch the strip in place on the towel.

Using several colours as shown and double/single crochet, work four circles, 9 cm (3½ inches) in diameter. Stitch them to the strip.

Similarly, make a strip 5 cm (2 inches) deep for the entire wrist edge of the mitt and six circles, 5 cm (2 inches) in diameter. Stitch them in place as shown.

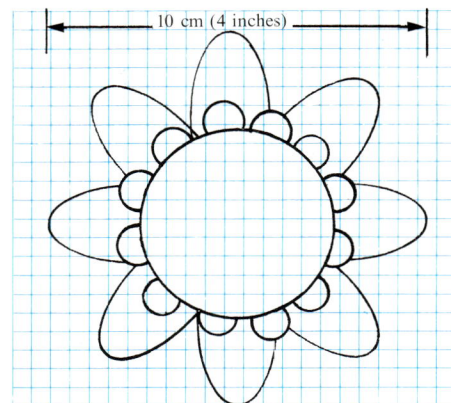

Sunflower cloth

Here is an idea for quick appliqué. Work sunflower motifs in crochet to match the colours of a tablecloth.

Materials required
Fabric 137 cm (54 inches) wide, 1.4 m (1½ yards)
Ric-rac braid, 5½ m (6 yards)
Crochet cotton in several colours
Medium-sized crochet hook

Making the cloth
Trim the selvedges and ends of the fabric to make a square. Turn under 5 mm (¼ inch), press, then turn a 2·5 cm (1 inch) hem, mitring the corners. Hand-stitch the hem in place.

Following the flower shape on the diagram, work the desired number of motifs in double/single crochet, working the centres first and then the petals. Arrange the motifs on the cloth and hand-stitch them in place.

Stitch ric-rac braid to the edges of the tablecloth, or work a crochet edging.

10 cm (4 inches)

Name belt

Here is a novel idea for an appliqué – work initials, or your complete name, onto a belt. Choose a variety of textures for the best effect: thin cotton, coarse linen, chintz, velvet, corduroy and tweed are some possibilities.

Materials required

A variety of fabrics in different textures and colours

Backing fabric, such as curtain/drapery lining, to waist measurement plus 10 cm (4 inches) $\times \frac{1}{2}$ m ($\frac{1}{2}$ yard)

Iron-on interfacing, the same amount as backing fabric

Lining for belt, ·2 m ($\frac{1}{4}$ yard)

Fabric adhesive/glue

Leather thonging or cord, 1·7 m ($1\frac{7}{8}$ yards)

Making the design

If the name is short, simply repeat it for the required length. Or reverse it, and place the two versions back to back as shown.

For a long name that is likely to

fill the belt shape, repeat the first or last letter at the opposite end, as shown with 'Dorothy', so that the name is complete when the belt is fastened.

Making the patterns

Measure the waist, add 5 cm (2 inches) for the underlap and mark this measurement on a sheet of paper. Mark it again, 6·5 cm ($2\frac{1}{2}$ inches) above the first line and join the lines to make a rectangle. Curve

Fig 7

Braid mats

Simple place mats made of linen or similar fabric can be easily decorated with strips of braid or ribbon to make striking table settings.

Materials required for six mats

Fabric 46×93 cm ($17 \times 36\frac{1}{2}$ inches)

Braid or ribbon, 2·8 m (3 yards)

Making the mats

Cut the fabric into six pieces, each 23×31 cm ($8\frac{1}{2} \times 18\frac{1}{4}$ inches), following the threads. Draw three or four threads about 1·5 cm ($\frac{5}{8}$ inch) from

the edge on all four sides. Zig-zag stitch or hem stitch (see page 134) the inner edge of the fabric, then pull away the remaining threads to make a fringe.

Cut the ribbon or braid to fit the mat, allowing 1·2 cm ($\frac{1}{2}$ inch) for turning under. Tack/baste each strip in place, then slipstitch or topstitch all round.

the rectangle as shown, by marking points A and B, 2·5 cm (1 inch) above each corner and joining these points to the centre (C) in a gentle curve. Trace off the shape and put the tracing aside.

Trace off the required letters from

the alphabet given and enlarge them to a height of 6·5 cm (2½ inches). Arrange the letters on the original belt pattern, putting the extra letter, if any, on the underlap on the left side. Don't worry about spacing the letters evenly; uneven spacing can look very attractive. Glue the letters in place and then cut them out. Keep the space patterns separate from the letters.

Working the appliqué
Pin the letter shapes to the fabrics, draw round them with a pen and cut them out, leaving extra fabric all round. Apply iron-on interfacing to

the wrong side, then cut along the marked outlines.

Cut the space shapes in fabrics, adding 1·2 cm (½ inch) margin all round (don't mark outlines).

Using the tracing of the belt pattern, mark the shape on the backing

fabric, then cut it out, adding 5 cm (2 inches) turning allowance on all edges.

Tack/baste the space pieces to the backing fabric, checking the positions with the letters and remembering that the letters will overlap the spaces by about 1·2 cm (½ inch).

Now tack/baste the letters in place. Set the machine to a fairly wide satin stitch and zig-zag over the edges of the letters.

Making up the belt
Trim the backing fabric to within 1·2 cm (½ inch) of the appliqué. Clip the curves and cut across the corners.

Press the turnings to the wrong side. Stiffen the belt with interfacing.

Trim the traced belt pattern by 3 mm (⅛ inch) all round and use it to cut the lining, adding 1 cm (⅜ inch) turnings on woven fabric.

If you are using non-fraying fabric such as imitation suede, simply glue the lining to the wrong side of the belt. If you are using woven fabric, first clip the turning allowance then turn it to the wrong side. Pin and tack/baste the lining to the wrong side of the belt; stitch it in place.

Cut the thonging or cord into four equal lengths. Fold each length in the centre and stitch it to the belt.

Appliqué panel 'Cyclamen'

The design for this panel is based on a drawing of one cyclamen flower. The appliquéd material is padded by the trapunto method (page 184) and added interest is created by echoing the flower shape with a padded mount.

Materials required

Background material: 60 cm (24 inches) of 90 cm (36 inch) deep beige soft cotton
Backing material: white cotton 65 × 45 cm (26 × 18 inches)
Thick polyester wadding/batting 45 cm (18 inches) square
Hardboard/particle board 50 × 30 cm (20 × 12 inches)
Cardboard 45 × 30 cm (18 × 12 inches)
Material for appliqué:
  pink cotton, 13 × 18 cm (5 × 7 inches) (petals 1, 6, 8)
  light cream Viyella® or cotton, 24 × 12 cm (9½ × 4½ inches) (petal 10) beige Viyella® or cotton 8 × 23 cm (3 × 9 inches) (petals 2, 4, 5, 7) khaki-coloured Viyella® or cotton, 18 × 4 cm (7 × 1½ inches) (stem 9) printed cotton, 10 × 7·5 cm (4 × 3 inches) (petal 3)
  brown suede or felt, 7·5 × 5 cm (3 × 2 inches) (flower centre 11)
1 skein of stranded cotton/floss to match each piece of material
Yarn, a small amount for padding suede
3 thicknesses of dark brown thread for couching
Fabric adhesive/glue
Felt, 50 × 30 cm (20 × 12 inches) for finishing off the back of the panel
2 2·5 cm (1 inch) curtain rings
Picture wire

Working the appliqué

Frame up the backing material on a slate/scroll frame. Cut out a piece of background material 60 × 40 cm (24 × 16 inches), and with the frame slack, mount it on the backing material.

Enlarge the design to full size (page 18) and transfer it to the background material using the running stitch method (page 18).

Make a tracing of each piece of the design to be appliquéd, extending the design by 1 cm (½ inch) where one fabric will lie under another. Use these tracings as patterns when cutting out the appropriate pieces of fabric.

Pin and tack/baste these in place on the design, in order from 1 to 10.

Using one strand of stranded cotton, work straight stitches in a zig-zag way over the raw edges of all the pieces except 7 and 9. Over the edges of these two, work close herringbone stitches.

Stitch round the outer edge of the suede, and poke in some yarn padding before stitching the inner edge in place. Fill the centre with close chain stitch in 6 strands of stranded cotton. Work back stitch over the chain stitch, to fill the area.

Work the lines of couching surrounding the top left petal and the right hand side of the flower, using three different thicknesses of dark brown thread.

Turn the work to the wrong side, pad each petal and the stem in turn, using the trapunto quilting method (see page 184).

Mounting the work

Remove the material from the frame and mount it on the hardboard, following the method for the gold-work panel on page 88.

Cut out the cardboard mounts which surround the flower shape.

Cover each piece with polyester wadding, gluing it in position.

Cut out the background material to cover the mounts allowing turnings of 2 cm (¾ inch) all round. Stretch the fabric over the wadding, pin it at the edges of the cardboard, and glue the fabric edges to the back of the cardboard, snipping the turnings on curved edges and cutting away any surplus material at the corners. Allow it to dry before removing the pins.

Glue the mounted areas in position on the edges of the mounted panel.

Stitch the felt to the back of the panel to neaten it. Stitch a curtain ring to each side of the panel 15 cm (6 inches) from the top and attach a length of picture wire.

1 square = 2·5 cm (1 inch)

≡ couching lines

▓ mount

30 cm (12 inches)

(20 inches)

Collage

There are two basic differences between appliqué and collage. First, in collage, materials are glued in place, rather than sewn. Second, all sorts of materials can be used in addition to, or instead of, fabric. Paper is a popular medium, but you can also use seeds, grasses, buttons, bits of string and braid or parts of an old watch – anything that can be stuck down onto a background.

The projects in the following pages illustrate the versatility of collage, using materials as diverse as delicate lace, terrycloth towelling and even pasta.

The essential equipment for collage is a suitable adhesive/glue, scissors – a large pair for cutting up fabrics and a small pair for cutting details, a backing of some kind and, finally, the collage materials themselves.

Most professional collage designers use a fabric adhesive because it is clean and convenient to use, but any all-purpose clear-drying adhesive can be used. It should be used sparingly, spread either with a matchstick or with a toothpick. Use the fingertips if you prefer. Adhesive is always applied to the back of each collage piece, which is then glued in place, rather than onto the background.

Backgrounds

When you have chosen your background fabric, mount it onto board or cardboard. First stiffen it, if you like, with iron-on interfacing. Allow 5–7.5 cm (2–3 inches) extra on all sides for turning under. Either glue the turnings to the back of the board or lace them together across the back, using strong thread.

Fabrics for fabric collage

Begin by making a collection of fabric scraps in as many colours and textures as possible. No matter how small it is, a remnant will be useful for some kind of effect. Generally it is uneconomical to buy fabric from the bolt, except for backgrounds. Dressmaking friends are usually delighted to contribute remnants of fabric to a ragbag. Remnant sales can be a source of collage pieces, and sample books of furnishing fabrics are useful because they sometimes contain several pieces of one type of fabric in different shades. Household sales can also provide beautiful old fabrics.

Collect all sorts of material for different effects in collage work. Sheer curtain fabrics, for example, are useful because they can be used to suggest smoke, sea, clouds or shadows. Silk and cotton sheer fabrics are soft and can be pleated and bunched. Nylon net is stiff and will lie flat on the background. Chiffon is particularly good for sky effects. Fur fabrics are obviously ideal for animal collages. Wide-wale corduroy is excellent for ploughed fields. Silks provide rich, lustrous textures that lend excitement to a collage.

Lion wall hanging

This bright, amusing collage, suitable for a child's room, is simple and fun to make.

Materials required

Olive green hessian/burlap 40 × 30 cm (16 × 12 inches)
Iron-on interfacing
Gold terrycloth towelling
Scraps of felt in gold, pink, deep pink, cream, black, white, brown, green, red, yellow, blue and orange

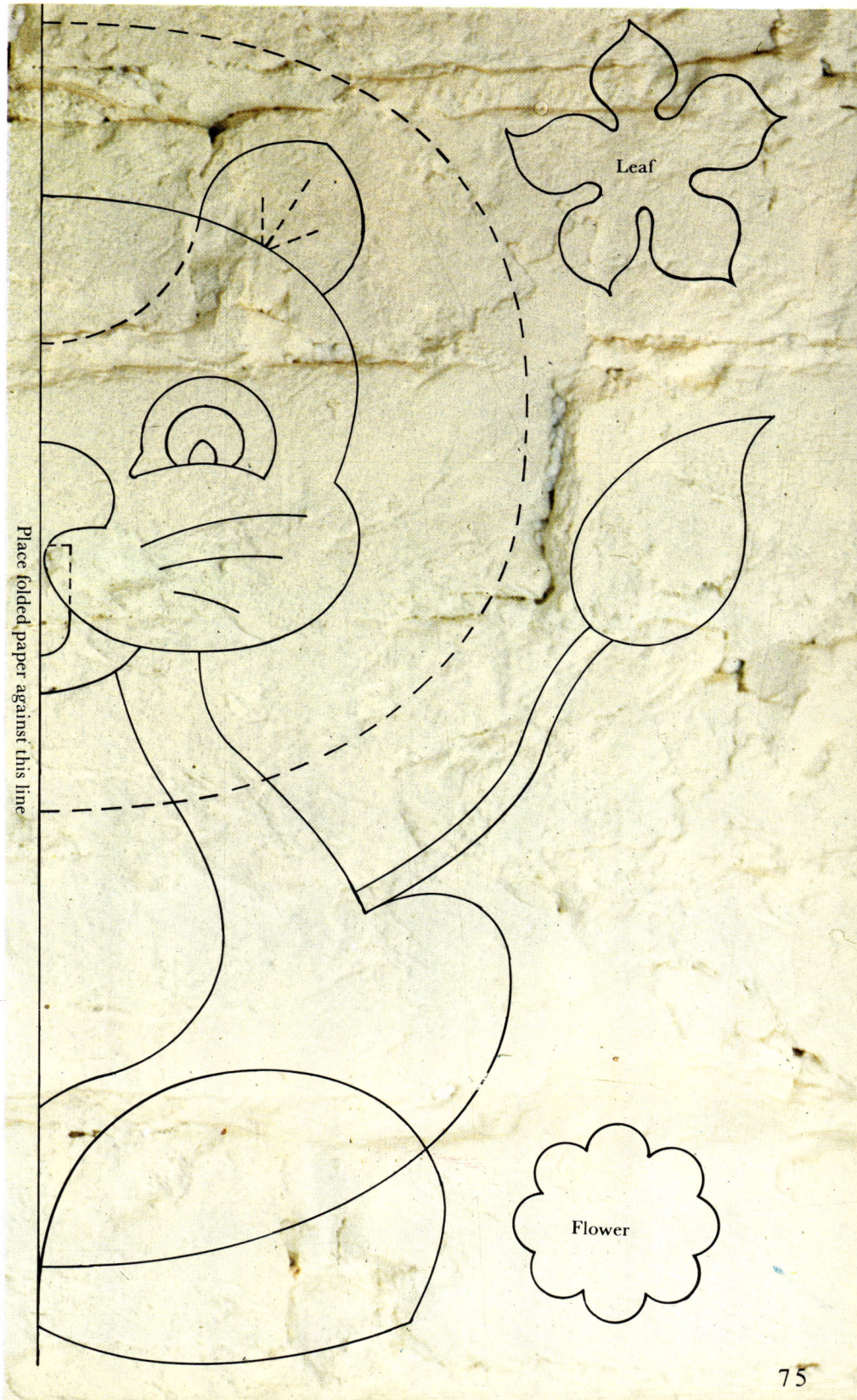

Place folded paper against this line

Leaf

Flower

Scraps of thin wadding/batting
Scraps of brown, dark brown, gold and black braid
Chunky/bulky knitting yarn in gold
Black guipure lace daisies
Light green·raffia
Thick black embroidery thread
Narrow dowel or bamboo, 2 pieces 40 cm (16 inches) long
Fabric adhesive/glue
String

Making the collage

Trace off the design onto a folded sheet of tracing paper, then trace it off again for the complete shape.

Trace the lion's body onto the shiny side of the interfacing, omitting the tail, paws and all broken lines except the forelock. On the matt side re-trace the eyes, nose, whiskers and forelock. Trace the paws onto separate pieces of interfacing.

From the interfacing body cut away the chin (including the tongue), the head and the ears.

Cover the head and paws with towelling, the body with gold felt, the chin with cream felt and the ears with pink felt.

Glue bits of yarn to the ears as indicated by the broken lines. Place the head right side down and tape the ears in place. Glue narrow dark brown braid round the edges of the ears. Trace a pattern for the tongue and cut it out in deep pink felt. Glue the tongue to the wrong side of the head at the upper corners. Place the head right side down and tape the chin in place.

Trace and cut interfacing patterns for the nose, eyes, irises and pupils and cover them with black, white, brown and black felt respectively. Glue narrow black braid round the back of each eye as shown. Glue the nose and eyes in place, using the traced features underneath as guides, then add irises and pupils. Mark the positions of the whiskers with pins. Using a needle, bring the black embroidery thread through at the inner corners and glue it in a curve as shown.

For the forelock glue short lengths of yarn closely together at the top of the head, overlapping it slightly. Turn the ends to the wrong side and glue them in place. Glue 4 cm ($\frac{1}{2}$ inch) lengths of yarn all round the underside of the head to form the mane.

Trace off the tuft of the tail on to interfacing and glue lengths of yarn all over it, starting at the edges and working inwards.

Make a paper tracing of the bib and cut it out in wadding. Glue it lightly to the body. Glue the paws in place and trim them with braid.

Place the head right side down and tape the body in place.

Make the flowers and leaves of interfacing and cover them with felt. Glue a daisy to the centre of each flower.

On the long edges of the hessian turn under and stitch 6 mm ($\frac{1}{4}$ inch) hems. Make 2·5 cm (1 inch) casings at top and bottom.

Spread glue on the back of the lion (excluding the mane) and glue it to the background, about 10 cm (4 inches) from the lower edge. Glue the leaves in place, then glue strips of raffia at each side. Glue gold braid in place for the tail and add the tuft. Glue the flowers in place.

Insert the dowels in the casings. Tie on lengths of string for hanging.

Regency house

This charming English country house and the elegant lady and gentleman evoke the world of Jane Austen. You can copy it in your own choice of materials, or you could make a collage 'portrait' of your own house.

Constructing the picture

First make a drawing of your house, or take a photograph. It's best to show the house 'head on', rather than from an angle, to avoid tricky problems of perspective. Make a tracing of the picture and cut this up to make patterns.

Cut the background 'sky' fabric the size of the finished picture and mount it on iron-on interfacing. Apply the trees behind the house and then the house itself, doors, windows and other architectural features. Then apply paths, shrubs and other foreground features, working towards the foreground of the picture.

Ideas for effects

Skies look especially pretty if shaded chiffon is used over cotton. Net or chiffon scraps make realistic clouds. *Trees, bushes and shrubs* Use a variety of different fabrics and fray the edges. Muted shades of green

look better than bright ones, but yellow-greens can be used for sunlit areas. Lace, dyed or painted green and placed over bits of untwisted brown braid, suggests leaves over branches.

Flowers Ribbons and bits of braid massed together suggest flower borders, which look more convincing than individual blooms. Avoid using too many bright colours.

Stones and brickwork Textured fabrics can represent different kinds of building materials, though bricks are best painted on with watercolours. Shadows can be represented with a layer of black net over the fabric.

Roofs Corduroy can look like slate or tiles, and rough-textured tweed also looks effective. Fur fabric can suggest thatch.

Paths and paving Cut these from matt finish fabric or felt. Paving stones can be cut separately and applied to a darker background.

Windows These should be black unless the curtains are a special feature. Single strands of braid can be used for window frames. The outer frames should be carefully cut and mitred at the corners.

Doors Glazed or satinized fabrics make effective doors, and panels can be detailed with a single strand of braid. For door hardware use metallic thread or beads.

Dating the collage

Your house 'portrait' may become a family heirloom, so it is a nice idea to give it a date. For the lettering and numbers use a single strand of braid.

Edwardian lady

The emphasis in this collage is on the fabric, especially the lace, and the clever blending of colours.

Materials required

Cream moiré ribbon 9 cm (3½ inches) wide, 23 cm (9 inches)
Cream and dark brown lace 6 cm (2½ inches) wide, 8 cm (3 inches) of each
Coffee and dark brown lace 1·2 cm (½ inch) wide, 25 and 45 cm (10 and 18 inches) respectively
Scrap of black lace 1·2 cm (½ inch) wide
Scraps of coffee, dark brown and cream ribbon 5 mm (¼ inch) wide
Stiff cardboard 17·5 × 30 cm (7 × 12 inches)
Green felt 5 cm (2 inches) larger than the cardboard all round
Iron-on interfacing
Fabric adhesive/glue
2 toothpicks

Making the design

Mount the felt on the cardboard, turning the edges to the wrong side and gluing them in place.

Enlarge the figure as indicated and trace it off twice onto iron-on interfacing, placing the shiny side up. Using one interfacing figure, cut out the main pieces: hat, torso, arms, train and skirt (together) and parasol.

Cover the left arm piece with moiré ribbon, leaving a small margin where it meets the body. Glue a bit of cream lace on top and glue the piece to the complete interfacing figure.

Cover the torso in moiré ribbon and glue it in place, overlapping the left arm.

Similarly cover and glue down the right arm; cover it with cream lace and add coffee lace to the wrist and neck. Cut a hand from the coffee ribbon and glue it down.

Cut the frill section off the skirt. Cut the frill pieces apart and cover each with a strip of coffee, dark brown or black lace (see photograph), folding under and gluing the lace ends at the right-hand side, and leaving a bit of excess lace at the left-hand side. Glue the frills in place.

Mask the cut edge of the train (broken line) with wide cream lace, then glue slightly gathered dark brown lace along the lower edge. Glue the train and upper skirt in

1 square = 2·5 cm (1 inch)

Diagram to draw flower centre
(to trace)

Leaf (to trace)

Diagram to draw bud
(to trace)

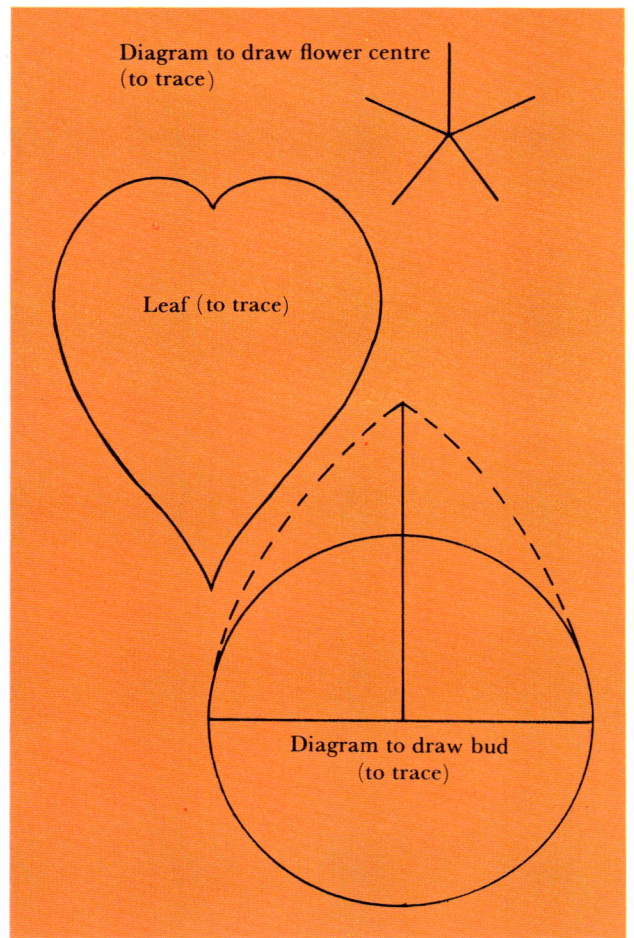

place, overlapping the frills.

Cut separate pieces of interfacing for the sash, the ends of the bow and the bow itself, and cover them with dark brown ribbon. Glue them in place.

Cut wide dark brown lace into suitable shapes to cover the hat and glue them in place, finishing with a motif in the centre to hide the cut ends. Glue bits of narrow cream lace round the brim.

Glue the figure in place on the background.

Cover the parasol piece with scraps of moiré ribbon and cream lace and edge the top with coffee and dark brown lace. Glue toothpicks in place for the handle and ferrule and tie a bow at the base with cream ribbon. Glue the parasol to the background.

Seed picture

Pastas, dried beans and seeds are a more unusual kind of material for collage design, but they are colourful and great fun to work with.

Materials required

An assortment of beans, seeds and pasta; those used here include pearl barley, split peas, rice and macaroni
Thin piping cord, about 1 m (1 yard)
Decorative braid, 1·2 cm ($\frac{1}{2}$ inch) wide. ·7 m ($\frac{3}{4}$ yard)
Narrow braid, ·5 m ($\frac{1}{2}$ yard)
Scraps of hessian/burlap
Scraps of knitting yarn
Stiff cardboard 45 × 36 cm (18 × 14 inches)
Coarsely woven background fabric 5 cm (2 inches) larger all round than cardboard
Clear-drying adhesive/glue

Making the collage

Mount the fabric on the cardboard, gluing the turnings in place on the underside.

For the flowers, draw circles the required size on tracing paper. (The largest flower shown is 13 cm [5 inches] in diameter.) Trace the centre lines from the diagram and extend them to the edges. Trace the required number of leaves and buds from the diagram. Arrange the tracings on the background and mark them on the fabric using dressmaker's carbon.

Now decide on the arrangement of items for each flower, bud and leaf. Two of the flower centres shown are made of coiled piping cord, but you might prefer to make all the centres of beans or pasta. The leaves are cut from hessian and edged with yarn.

Apply a thin layer of adhesive to one petal or bud at a time. Small fillings such as rice and pearl barley can be sprinkled liberally over the area, then gently pressed in place and the excess shaken off. Split peas and larger beans should be individually placed. Apply the braids for the stems before applying the leaves.

Metal threads and beads

Metal thread work

Metal thread work is completely different from any other needlecraft technique because the threads which are used have a unique richness and sheen. Much of the work's success is dependent upon careful manipulation of the threads and this is not a process which can be hurried.

The splendid embroideries known in style as Opus Anglicanum, made in England during the twelfth and thirteenth centuries, started a wonderful tradition of metal thread embroidery. Since then, work of such magnificence has not been repeated but metal thread work has, nevertheless, been used with great skill heraldically, on military uniforms, for domestic embroidery as well as for the church. Other countries also produce lavish and simple examples of metal thread work often combined with silk threads. Museums which exhibit textiles will usually include some pieces of metal thread work. These will give inspiration and the opportunity to study how different effects are achieved by changing the direction of the couched threads and how padding is used. Examples of present-day metal thread work, usually in the form of small panels, can often also be found at exhibitions.

The cost of metal threads today prohibits them being used as lavishly as in the past, but there are good inexpensive synthetics which can be used on their own or they can be combined with the metal threads which contain a small percentage of gold or silver. When buying the latter, it pays to get the best quality as these will not tarnish so much as those of a less good quality.

Some metal threads may only be laid on the surface of the material and be couched into position, as they are unsuitable for threading in the needle. A few metal threads may be used for direct stitching, these being ones which can also be combined with blackwork or drawn fabric work. The coiled varieties of metal threads are cut into small pieces and threaded as though using a bead. As well as the conventional metal threads, knitting and crochet yarns which include metallic or Lurex®

strands may also be used as a contrast.

This type of needlecraft needs to be worked on a closely woven material, chosen carefully as a foil for the lushness of the metal threads. For small pieces such as a jewel box or a pendant, pieces of raw silk or Thai silk would be suitable. For larger items, furnishing fabrics and some dress materials are good. Usually the background fabric should be mounted on a backing material (see page 64), as the weight of the metal threads and the closeness of stitchery would tend to pucker a background without a backing. Always work on a frame, using a ring frame only for pieces where the design can be contained within the ring area. To move a ring frame over part of the embroidery would damage the metal threads.

Designs for metal thread work need to be simple and planned according to the way the threads will be used so that their beauty can be exploited to the full. Start with bold shapes and avoid sharp points at first. For detailed or heraldic designs, it is best to use the prick and pounce method for transferring a design onto material.

To make a sampler of stitches, draw overlapping circles or lines on a piece of material not larger than about 15 cm (6 inches) across. In each of the areas experiment with different methods of couching, using different threads or thicknesses of thread to become accustomed to their manipulation.

Metal thread work can be combined with appliqué, and with stitches in threads of silk, cotton, wool or synthetic yarn. Gold or silver kid leather or vinyl may be added in small quantities as a contrast to threads.

Equipment
The following pieces of equipment are necessary for metal thread work:

Slate/scroll or ring frame
Crewel needles in different sizes, including size 10 for use with purls.
Chenille needle size 18 for taking ends of couched threads through to the wrong side.

Nail scissors (straight) for cutting metal threads.
Stiletto for making holes and for manipulation of threads (if available).
Beeswax to strengthen the couching thread and help it cling to the metal thread.
Tweezers to avoid handling certain threads.
Maltese silk is available in two tones of gold and in grey; used for couching down threads and for threading purls.
A cardboard box lid roughly 10 cm (4 inches) square, the inside covered with felt, for holding purls when cutting.
Pure sewing silk in place of Maltese silk, in any colours required.
String in yellow or white for padding gold or silver threads.
Felt in yellow or grey for padding gold or silver threads.
Invisible nylon thread is useful in cases where the stitches should not show.

Threads
There is a wide range of metal threads available, and only the most readily available kinds are mentioned here. Some are couched into place, others are threaded. The real Japanese gold and silver threads, used for centuries for church embroidery because of their non-tarnishing properties, are no longer made.

Substitute Japanese gold is synthetic and non-tarnishable; it is easy to handle for couching and is very bright in appearance. It comes in different thicknesses and is also made in silver.

Imitation Japanese gold comes in a slightly dull warm gold, with a dull finish. It makes a good contrast to the other brighter threads and is inexpensive and not difficult to use for couching. It comes in four different thicknesses of gold and is available in silver.

Passing thread was traditionally used as a couched thread on ceremonial embroidery. Purchase the best quality available as, having a metal content, it is likely to tarnish. The finer passing thread may be threaded in the needle and be used for laid fillings, blackwork and drawn fabric work.

Plate is a narrow flat thread mainly used in ceremonial work.

Twists come in different weights, the heavier ones resembling cords. Most are synthetic today although some real ones are available at a price. Instead of taking the couching thread over the twist, the needle is taken down into the twist, thus producing an invisible holding stitch.

Pearl purl consists of a coiled wire, each coil looking like a tiny bead. To use it, slightly stretch the coil, holding each end of the length of thread required between thumb and first finger of each hand. Stretch it only sufficiently to allow a fine thread such as Maltese silk to lie between the 'beads' of the coil in couching. It is not necessary to couch between each 'bead'. Curve the pearl purl in the hand to obtain the shape required. To turn a corner, use the flat side of a stiletto. The ends of pearl purl are not taken through to the wrong side.

Lurex® threads are high quality synthetic threads, made as couching threads and twists, and come in a variety of colours as well as in silver and gold. Lurex passing threads and cords are also available, and are made in silver and gold colours.

Purls, unlike the above metal threads (including pearl purl), which are couched in place, are threaded like a bead. They consist of very fine wire closely coiled into a tiny spring-like length.

Rough purl has a dull surface.

Smooth purl is brighter and more shiny than rough purl.

Check purl has a bright chequered finish.

Attractive effects can be obtained by using purls of each finish. Using the box lid to avoid handling the purls, snip off the length required with nail scissors. Bring a no. 10 crewel needle threaded with Maltese silk through to the right side of the material at the point where the purl is to be laid. Pass the purl through this as you would a bead and let it fall to the material. Take the needle down at the opposite end of the length of purl and bring the needle up ready for the next piece of purl. Restrict the lengths of purl to short pieces, never longer than 1 cm ($\frac{3}{8}$ inch). Tiny pieces will look like tiny beads.

Below 'Baby Bird' design in a variety of stitches and threads. Note the tones and spacing of the couching threads and the use of strips of kid for basket stitch. Pearl purl is used for the feet.

Couching

Select a tying thread, either Maltese silk or pure sewing silk. Use a short length of about 30 cm (12 inches), to prevent it from wearing thin in use. Before threading the needle, run the silk thread through a piece of beeswax two or three times. The wax strengthens the thread and prevents it from knotting as you work. It also helps the thread to cling to the metal and keep it in place.

It is a good plan to do some experiments with fine string, before starting on the actual metal threads, to practise changing the direction of the couching. It is possible to practise corners and turnings in this way, without wasting metal threads. String can be purchased in different colours and in different tones of off-white, so interesting effects can be achieved.

Metal threads are usually couched in pairs as the material is covered more satisfactorily in this way. Fold a length of imitation or substitute Japanese gold thread and lay the pair of threads on the surface of the material. Start with a knot in the silk thread, on the wrong side of the material. Then work two back stitches which will be covered with couching. Bring the needle up on one side of the fold and down on the opposite side. Continue to couch down the pair of threads, bringing the needle straight up on one side and taking it straight down on the opposite side. Repeat this stitch at intervals of about 5 mm ($\frac{1}{4}$ inch). Each tying stitch should always be at right angles to the metal thread,
except at corners.

After working a few stitches, try a right-angled turn. There are two ways of doing this, depending on the distance of the last tying stitch from the corner. If close, work one diagonal stitch on the outer thread, then continue with normal couching. If the last tying stitch is further from the corner, work a separate diagonal stitch over each thread before proceeding with the normal couching. In all couching, the tying stitches should be regularly spaced.

If working a slightly more acute angle, the same principle is used except that the inner thread is not taken right into the corner. Make a good turn with the outer thread, taking it just beyond the point, and hold it down with a tiny stitch at the point, and the next stitch will be across both sides of the folded outer thread; the next will hold down the turn of the inner thread.

On points which are sharper it will be necessary to cut the inner thread at the point, leaving 2·5 cm (1 inch) to take through. Leave another 2·5 cm (1 inch) before starting the couching again.

For a very sharp point it will be necessary to cut off both the outer and inner thread at the point, leaving 2·5 cm (1 inch) of each to take through to the wrong side. The point will be created by taking one thread down slightly beyond the other.

Take metal threads through to the wrong side either by threading each end in turn into the eye of a chenille needle or by threading a folded piece
of strong thread, about 12 cm (5 inches) long, through the eye of a chenille needle so each metal thread end can be slipped into the loop and then be gently taken through to the wrong side. Fold the thread ends back, on the wrong side, and work oversewing stitches into the back of the couching stitches to hold them in place. It is best not to take the threads through every time you finish a thread, but to wait until there are several after completing an area. This will save the threads from getting caught up on the underside of the material during working.

When couching more than one line, the tying stitches should be bricked (positioned like brickwork). In order to get the pairs of thread lying closely, bring the needle up on the outside of the second or successive pair, and take the needle down close to the previous pair. When turning threads at the end of a straight line of couching work a small stitch over both threads at right angles to the other couching stitches. If working curves as on a circle, the tying stitches need careful planning; those in the centre will be closer than those on the outer edge.

As a variation from the usual bricking, tying down threads may be arranged in other patterns and contrasting colours can be used instead of the usual matching thread. For example, red and orange will add warmth to gold threads whereas blue and green will cool it. Silver and aluminium threads can be varied by couching down with white, blue or mauve.

Left Car panel in metal thread work including couching, beads and padded PVC/vinyl. The wheels are check purl radiating from the centre.

1. A right-angled corner: work a diagonal stitch on the outer thread.

2. A right-angled corner: work a separate diagonal stitch over each thread.

3. An acute angled corner.

4. A very sharp corner: cut both threads.

5. Taking a metal thread through in the eye of a needle.

6. Taking a metal thread through by means of a loop.

7. Bricking.

8. Bricking: take the needle down close to the previous pairs of threads.

9. Bricking: for a circle the centre tying stitches are closer than the outer tying stitches.

Or nué

A traditional way of working metal threads consists of couching pairs of metal threads horizontally and continuously. The design is produced by the colour of the stitches. If, for example, you are working a heraldic shield, the background could be worked in gold threads couched down in gold coloured silk. As you reach the device, change the tying threads to the colour required. Work close tying stitches until the end of the shape is reached, leave the coloured thread and continue in the background colour. Turn the pair of threads at the end of the line, continue couching until you reach the coloured thread, continue with this to the end of the device. Then use the background colour. Simple or elaborate designs may be worked in this way. Paint the outlines of the design onto the material before starting. Work with as many coloured threads as are needed, leaving each threaded in a needle, ready to pick up as the appropriate point is reached.

Padding with string

String padding may be used for raising couched threads from the surface, with the string well spaced unless working basket stitch. Use yellow string for gold threads, dyeing it, if necessary.

Wax the string to stop it from unravelling. Lay it on the surface of the material at right angles to the couching and, using a waxed sewing thread, stitch into the centre of the string from each side alternately. At the beginning and end, work two stitches over the string, close to the ends.

String is also used as a means of padding purls. After the string is held in place, work satin stitch with lengths of smooth, rough or check purl. These may be stitched on as a straight stitch or as one which slants.

Basket stitch

Stitch down lengths of string in parallel lines with the distance between each not less than the width of the string. Couch down two metal threads at right angles to the string and with a double stitch on the outside of the first string. Pass the metal threads over two strings and hold them down firmly in between the second and third string, then in between the fourth and fifth string.

Continue in this way until the end when a double holding stitch should be worked. Cut off the ends leaving 2·5 cm (1 inch). Start again at the beginning of the line with two metal threads, this time passing over only one string at the start, then hold the metal threads down between the third and fourth string. Continue in this way, bricking the stitches as you work. The third line of metal threads will be couched down as in the first line.

Many variations of this theme may be made by working the tying stitches with uneven spacing. Also, different threads can be used such as fine twists, silk threads, and strips of kid leather or suede.

Padding with felt

Felt padding is used under couched threads, pieces of purl, gold and silver kid, or other applied materials. A small amount of padding produces changes of light, additional to that created by the couching of threads in different directions. One or more layers of felt may be used, depending on the height required. For an average padding on an area of about 2·5 cm (1 inch) square cut out three pieces of felt; one should be the size of the area to be padded, the next slightly smaller and the third smaller still. Tack/baste this one into the centre of the shape to be padded, followed by the next size, gradually building up until you reach the largest piece. This should be held firmly in place with small straight stitches. Done in this way, to any thickness, the padding is smooth and gradual. It may be necessary to increase the size of the top piece of felt to accommodate the quantity of padding.

Sewing down twists

These are used as single lines, or for outlining. Bring the needle up on the inside of the cord which should be held down in the direction to be worked. Take the needle back and down into the next twist, so that the thread lies within the twist. To turn a corner, make stitches into both sides of the cord, pressing it into a point. If the corner is very pointed, it will be necessary to cut the cord leaving 2·5 cm (1 inch), and start again slightly lower, taking both ends through to the wrong side. By gently making a hole in the background material with a stiletto, it is possible to take a cord through by means of a loop of thread in a chenille needle as described for couching.

Heraldic and ecclesiastical work

Heraldic work needs to be disciplined, as the correct drawing and tinctures of a coat of arms or crest should be strictly adhered to. The more conventional metal threads are used, such as pearl purl for outlining, and the purls for devices. Couching will also be used. The threads are often combined with appliqué.

If you wish to do some work for the church, start by making something small such as a stole or a burse on which you can use your skills. It is advisable to have the co-operation of the church when planning a piece of work as the design is important and should be done by a professional, preferably someone who understands the medium of embroidery. Consider the making up at the time of designing as this is vital and the quality of the hang of vestments may depend on an interlining or on the choice of a suitable fabric.

Padding with string.

Basket stitch.

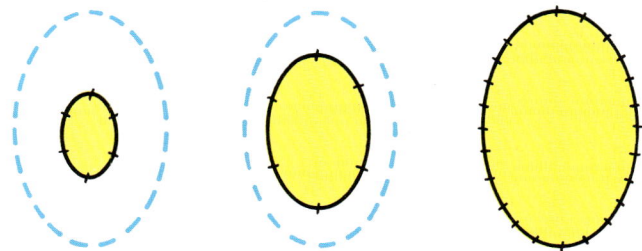

Padding with felt.

Above *Fleur-de-lis in basket stitch with uneven spacing. The string is laid horizontally.*
Left *Shield worked in or nué.*
Top right *Crown emblem. Note the use of lines of rough and check purl over a string padding on either side of the jewelled band. Chips of purl create the rough texture, and long and short stitch fills in the base.*

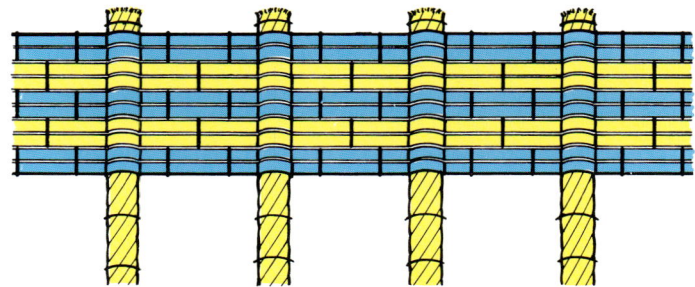

Goldwork panel 'Cyclamen'

This small decorative panel is worked from the same design as the appliqué panel on page 73.

Materials required

Closely woven cream-coloured material, 30 × 25 cm (12 × 10 inches)
Fine white cotton material for backing, 35 × 30 cm (14 × 12 inches)
1 skein coffee-coloured stranded cotton/floss
1 skein dark brown stranded cotton
4 metres (4¼ yards) medium weight imitation Japanese gold
30 cm (12 inches) dull gold twist
10 cm (4 inches) fine pearl purl
5 cm (2 inches) rough gold purl
1 reel light gold Maltese silk or 1 spool gold-coloured sewing silk, for couching
Yarn for padding
Strong cardboard 19 × 14 cm (7½ × 5½ inches)
Strong thread for lacing

Working the embroidery

Mount the background material on the backing, using either a ring frame or a small slate/scroll frame.

Enlarge the design to full size (page 18) and transfer it to the background material using the running stitch method (page 18).

Work the embroidery in the following order:

1 work the back stitching using one strand of stranded cotton
2 couch the imitation Jap gold in pairs following the outline (the close couching on one petal should be worked from the outer edge towards the centre)
3 stitch two lines of twist on either side of the couched imitation Jap gold on the top left petal
4 stitch the pearl purl in place
5 work the French knots using two strands of stranded cotton
6 position a few very small pieces of rough purl amongst the French knots, to add sparkle.

Loosen the frame and turn the work to the wrong side. Using the trapunto method (page 184) carefully pad the areas marked P making sure that the surface is smooth on the right side.

When complete, remove the work from the frame and cut away the excess backing material.

Mounting the work

Place the material, right side up, on the cardboard. Pin the material to the centre of each side of the cardboard, ensuring that it is straight.

Turn the mounted work over to the wrong side and lace the edges of material together working from the centre of each side outwards towards the edges. At the corners cut away any surplus material to avoid bulk, before hemming in place.

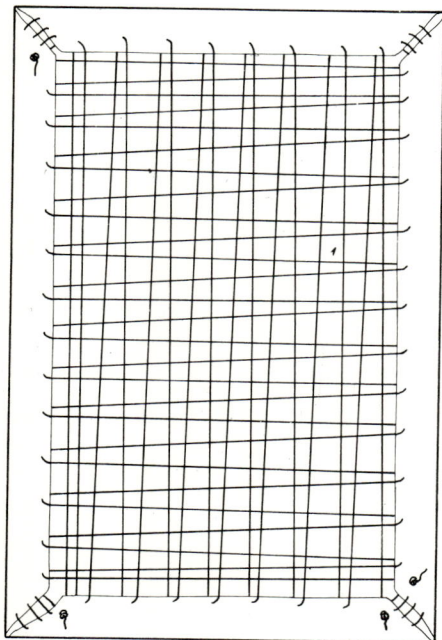

Mounting work: lace the edges of the material on the wrong side.

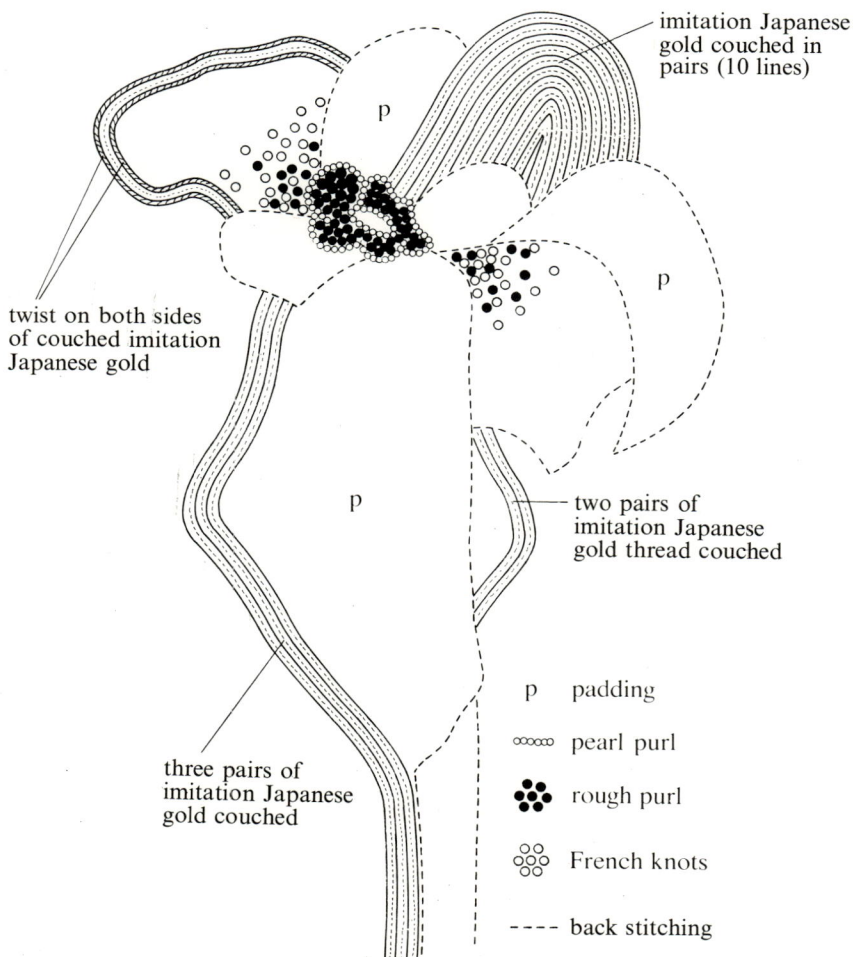

imitation Japanese gold couched in pairs (10 lines)

twist on both sides of couched imitation Japanese gold

two pairs of imitation Japanese gold thread couched

three pairs of imitation Japanese gold couched

p   padding

∞∞∞   pearl purl

⬤⬤⬤   rough purl

°°°   French knots

- - - -   back stitching

Bead work

Beads have always been a form of decoration; originally natural materials such as dried seeds or shells were treasured by hanging round the neck. There are many uses for beads in needlecraft and even just one beautiful bead may be the focal point of an embroidered pendant, or a box top. In fact, beads should always be used sparingly in embroidery to avoid over-decoration.

Although some people make their own beads, it is the commercially manufactured glass and china beads which are most often used in embroidery. Lovely glass beads are made in a variety of shapes, sizes, colours and cuts. They may be used as a restrained embellishment to free embroidery, possibly mixed with clusters of French knots and they may be added to metal thread work. More lavish work can be achieved by treating beads as the sole form of decoration on clothing for a special occasion or on accessories, evening bags being the most popular items to make in bead work.

Bead work should be worked on a frame. A slate frame is best unless you are doing only a small piece which can be contained within the area of a ring frame.

A fine thread such as mercerized sewing cotton or nylon is used and it should be strengthened by passing it several times through a piece of beeswax. The thread should match the bead when possible, and the thickness will depend on the beads being used. A beading needle is fine, long and flexible.

Bring the thread up on the right side of the material in the position for the first bead. Thread the needle through the bead, and allow it to drop onto the material. Settle it in position and take the needle through the material on the opposite side of the bead to hold it in place. Continue in this way with the next bead. The tension of the thread should not be too tight or it will break, and not too loose or the beads will move.

For quicker work, and to get a continuous line of beads, bring the needle up at the beginning of the line. Thread the required number of beads, take the needle down at the end of the line. Then hold the beads in place by couching between each bead or between every second or third bead.

As a variation when each bead is to lie on its side, a bead may be attached to material with its hole facing upwards. For this, hold the bead in place by bringing the needle up through the centre hole and down on the outside of the bead. Work two or three stitches in this way to hold each bead.

Another variation which will give added dimensions, will be obtained by stitching one bead on top of another. Bring the needle up and thread a round bead, then take the needle through the hole of a second, slightly smaller, bead. Then take it back down through the hole of the first bead.

To raise the beads from the surface of the material, couch some string or piping cord in place. Then thread a length of beads just long enough to cover the cord when the thread containing the beads is brought up on one side and is taken down on the opposite side.

Strong fastening off in bead work is vital. Turn the work to the wrong side and work back stitches into the material behind the beads.

Sequins

Although sequins are not strictly beads, the method of using them is included here as they are sometimes used with beads. Sequins come in many colours and in a variety of sizes and shapes. To sew on a round sequin, bring the needle up in the centre hole and take it down at the outside edge. Repeat this either once or twice, with equal spacing between stitches.

A sequin may also be attractively attached by means of a tiny bead. Bring the needle up through the centre hole, thread it through the small bead and back down through the hole of the sequin. Invisible thread may be used for stitching.

Right *Two early twentieth-century bags decorated with beads.*

Sewing down a single bead.

A continuous line of beads.

Couching between beads in a continuous line.

Attaching a bead with its hole facing upwards.

Stitching one bead on top of another.

Counted thread work

Blackwork

Blackwork is a technique best known historically for the patterns worked in double running in Elizabethan times. Portraits of that period show the delightful fine blackwork stitchery on collars and sleeves.

Blackwork consists of small straight stitches arranged in patterns on an evenly woven material. Traditionally worked in black thread on white material, today we use a range of tones to give some variation. For decorative purposes, fine gold or silver metallic thread can be added, but this would not be practical on articles needing constant laundering. Providing the thread used is of a suitable scale, blackwork can be worked on either a fine or a coarse fabric.

Blackwork can be used on household linen, furnishings, on clothing and accessories. A conventional evenweave material is good to learn on as the loosely woven material is easy to work and the patterns will be even and regular. By using a less even fabric such as linen, the stitch patterns will not turn out to be quite so even. It is not necessary for the complete item to be made up in the evenweave material required for the blackwork as a band or border can be set into a garment. A box top decorated with blackwork can be made up with the sides and base in a strong, coloured fabric. Blackwork patterns worked on a hessian-type fabric could be used for appliqué on a bold decorative panel.

It is important to choose a thread which is suitable and experiments will help you decide which you prefer. Generally the thread should be about the same thickness as the woven thread of the material, although the thickness of thread may be varied within one piece of work since some stitch patterns will look good in a fine thread, and others look better in a thicker one.

The actual threads which can be used are fairly limited. Suitable ones include coton perlé/pearl cotton and, for finer work, one strand of stranded cotton/floss or pure sewing silk. Crewel or Persian wool or a knitting yarn are practical for coarser work. On hessian/burlap, soft/matte embroidery cotton is successful. If you wish to include some metal thread, choose one which can be threaded and which will not deteriorate if drawn through the material.

As in all counted thread methods, use a blunt tapestry needle which will not split the threads of material as you work. Blackwork does not necessarily require the use of a frame but it can be helpful to have the material stretched out.

Blackwork patterns may be used as borders or motifs and can be planned on graph paper. If the patterns are to be included in a free design, use shapes which are simple. The scale of design will depend on the fineness of the material you are using. Suitable subjects include simplified plant forms, buildings, figures or birds. Choose filling patterns which give the feeling of the area to be worked; this is an interesting stage as one pattern may suggest bricks whereas another will suit a leaf filling.

Some of the little patterns are dense when worked and will be even denser if worked in a heavier thread. Other patterns are lighter in appearance, and one can create different tones by the choice of filling patterns. The planning of balance of tones can be achieved by cutting out pieces of newspaper, selecting pieces with varying closeness of print, and dark areas from illustrations. Move them around until you feel the arrangement is well balanced. Glue the newspaper down, for reference, and select your blackwork patterns to coincide with dark, medium or light tones.

Do not think that because of its name this technique can only be worked in black. Traditionally worked in black and white, the method has been adapted to present-day requirements. There is nothing to stop us from working in colour or on colour, or both. The most successful blackwork is that in which the stitch patterns, because of their delicacy, form a contrast to the background. On a light background, this can be achieved by using a thread in dark brown, bottle green, maroon or navy blue as an alternative to black. Equally well, a thread of white, cream or another pale colour is effective if worked on a dark ground. As a variation, in addition to the use of patterns of different density, up to about three tones of a colour may also be used, but avoid using a tone too close to that of the material as the patterns would fade into the background.

Each of the stitch patterns is made up of a series of small straight stitches, some horizontal, some vertical and some diagonal, each worked by counting threads. It is done either in back stitch, or in double running if the work needs to be reversible as on a stand-up collar. Sometimes cross stitch is included. Pattern darning works in well with blackwork.

The scale of stitch will vary from two to three or four threads of material, depending on the material. To keep the attraction of the work, do not use long stitches. Replace one long stitch with two or more short stitches. Some patterns need to be worked over an even number of threads as it is not possible to work a stitch adjacent to the centre of a stitch worked over three threads.

Right *One panel in a series of the same design embroidered by different methods (see contents page 6 and page 105). This panel and the details taken from it show a variety of blackwork fillings.*

Back stitch

Start by leaving an end on the right side, which can be darned in on the wrong side, when some stitches have been worked. Back stitch is worked as described for freehand stitches (page 28) with the needle picking up twice the length of the required stitch, then back to the end of the first stitch and forward under twice the number of threads as the length of each stitch. If each stitch is to cover four threads, the needle will pass under eight before being brought through the surface again. When working a square corner, the needle will pass under the material in a diagonal direction to maintain the rhythm of the stitches. Fasten off by running into the stitches on the wrong side for about 2·5 cm (1 inch). Do not make a bump with several back stitches in one place.

If the material in use is loosely woven, take care not to take dark threads across the back between patterns as this will leave a dark shadow. It is better to fasten off between motifs.

Double running

If working a continuous scrolling pattern or if the work needs to be reversible, double running is used. It consists of carefully planned running stitches with the spaces being the same number of threads as the stitches; a return journey is made with running stitches filling in the gaps. When working the return journey in double running, take the needle in at the top of a stitch, and bring it out at the lower edge of the same stitch. This will prevent a stepped effect and should produce a smooth continuous line. To start and fasten off, pick up on the needle alternate threads of material working for about 2 cm ($\frac{3}{4}$ inch) towards the beginning of the line. Fasten off in the same way, back from the end of the line. By picking up only one thread on the needle, these tiny stitches will sink into the fabric under the running stitches.

Building up patterns

It is useful to have a small spare piece of material on which to experiment with patterns. There are many traditional patterns which can be adapted, be built up into motifs or borders, or have the spacing changed. Variations can also be made by omitting or adding stitches, and by using different weights of thread. If working a pattern within a given shape, start working in the centre in order to obtain a focal point. Work up to the design outline but do not go over the edge. It is easy to fill in a missing stitch at the end but it is not easy to remove one which is too long. Outlining may enhance a design, and can be worked on a whole design or sometimes just on part of a shape to give interest. Smooth outlining can be obtained with couching, back stitch or chain stitch. A knotted outline can be produced by working coral or scroll stitch. If a metal thread is included use it sparingly for whipping back stitch or chain stitch. Laid fillings (see page 51) can be included in blackwork, with the laid squares or patterns worked on them in metal thread.

Back stitch.

Double running.

Far right *Fuchsia and butterfly design showing the use of filling patterns of varied density to provide different tones. Some gold thread has been included.*
Right *One blackwork pattern worked in different thicknesses of thread for an all-over effect.*

Cross stitch and Assisi work

This type of work, as indicated by its name, consists of various forms of cross stitch worked into designs on an evenweave or some other loosely woven material. Cross stitch has been used for many centuries, and will be found on old samplers, peasant costume and household articles in many countries.

Working this simple stitch is repetitive and therefore to many people it is a form of relaxation. Simple or elaborate designs may be worked using self colour, monochrome or polychrome twisted or stranded threads. A variation of thread within one piece of work can give added interest. The thread should be about the same thickness as the threads of the material and a blunt needle should be used.

Pattern books of designs are available from needlework suppliers, but it is not difficult to plan one's own patterns, using graph paper. One square on the graph paper will represent one cross stitch on the material.

To adapt a drawing for cross stitch, start with a simple shape and draw it onto graph paper in pencil.

Then, using a pen or ball-point pen, work round the shape using the grid line nearest to the freehand outline, so that you have used only horizontal or vertical lines. Each square on the graph paper will be interpreted on the material with one cross stitch.

The method of starting and finishing off a thread is done as in the other counted thread methods. Leave an end on the right side and darn this in after some stitches are worked. Fasten off by running the thread through worked stitches for about 2·5 cm (1 inch); do not sew over and over in one place as this will leave a lump.

Assisi work

The main characteristic of Assisi work is that, although cross stitch and double running stitch are used throughout, it is the background and not the design which is filled with the stitches. This technique comes from the village of Assisi in Italy. Traditional designs often consisted of curiously shaped animals and birds and the colours used were threads of blue or scarlet on an ivory ground.

Use the same materials and threads as for ordinary cross stitch, and avoid using other than an evenly woven material or the shapes may be spoilt by distortion. The design should be well planned on graph paper, with one square equal to one cross stitch and this will be worked over two, three or four threads, depending on the fineness of the material.

Start by outlining the design with double running or back stitch. All the outline stitches must lie either horizontally or vertically to enable the cross stitch to fill the entire background between the pattern shapes. Once the design has been outlined, fill in the background with cross stitch worked in horizontal lines, working half the stitch first and completing the stitch on the return journey.

To soften the edges of a heavily embroidered area of Assisi work, work bands of double running.

Below left *Motif in Assisi work with detail (below).*
Right *Cushion in cross stitch with detail (bottom).*

Cross stitch

This is a simple diagonal cross worked over a square of two, three or four threads of material. It is usual to use the same size stitch throughout one piece of work. On the wrong side the top stitch of the cross should lie in the same direction throughout. A right-handed worker will find it easiest to work from right to left and will produce a cross stitch with the top thread (the second diagonal) lying from bottom left to top right, whereas a left-handed worker will probably work from left to right and will have the top stitch of the cross lying from bottom right to top left. It is best not to turn the work sideways as the stitches can easily become confused.

There are two ways of working cross stitch: by completing each stitch before starting the next or by working half of each stitch in a row before completing the second part of each stitch on the return journey. Cross stitch may also be worked diagonally.

Italian cross stitch

This consists of a cross stitch surrounded by a square of straight stitches. To obtain a clearly defined stitch use a thinner thread than for ordinary cross stitch.

Work each stitch over three or four threads of material. Bring the needle up at the left of the line to be worked (A). Make a straight stitch by putting the needle in to the right and bringing it back out at the starting point A. Make a diagonal stitch to the top right, bringing the needle back out at A. Make a vertical straight stitch from A bringing the needle out at the end of the first horizontal straight stitch. Repeat these three movements to the end of the line. The third movement of the second stitch will act as the upright stitch on the right of the first cross. At the end of the line, work back to the beginning by inserting the needle in an upright position towards you and thus completing the crosses. The second line of stitching, worked over the first, will complete the square of the first line.

Long-legged cross stitch

Although this is a stitch usually worked on canvas, it can be worked on an evenweave material in attractive patterns, leaving the background plain. It is also useful as a single line stitch.

Long-legged cross stitch can be worked horizontally and vertically, turning the work sideways for the latter. It may be worked from left to right or from right to left. As a variation, work in rows alternately from left to right and right to left. This creates an attractive plaited effect. It is important not to lose the sequence of alternate lines or the effect will be spoilt.

Start with a single cross stitch over a square of two (or three) threads. Each stitch is formed by inserting the needle in a vertical position pointing towards you and under two or three horizontal threads of background material. The second and successive stitches are worked in two movements, the needle being inserted in and out two (or three) vertical threads forward from the previous stitch, thus forming the long leg of the stitch. Complete the stitch by inserting the needle in and out through the same holes as the end of the previous stitch. The first and last stitches of each row are simple cross stitches. As for Italian cross stitch, avoid using too thick a thread for this stitch.

Other variations of cross stitch are given in the section on canvas work. Rice stitch, oblong cross and Smyrna stitch may well be worked into patterns on an evenweave material.

Handkerchief sachet in cross stitch.

Pattern darning and geometric satin stitch

Pattern darning

Pattern darning is another of the counted thread methods and it may be worked in very simple or really elaborate patterns. When worked, it resembles weaving as it consists of horizontal or vertical running stitches which follow the warp or weft threads of the background material. The running or darning stitches are worked over and under a different number of threads of material and it is the relationship between the stitch and space which creates the pattern. Accurate counting of threads is necessary, so it is worked on an evenweave or a loosely woven material such as hessian/burlap, tweed or linen. It has many uses and may be worked on clothing, either on the garment itself or as an inset on a yoke, collar, cuffs, pocket or belt. Pattern darning may be worked on net/marquisette as a curtain or room divider, and a simple border can be built into an all-over pattern on a cushion or bag. It combines well with blackwork patterns.

The pattern on the wrong side of the work will be the reverse of that shown on the front. To avoid thread on the wrong side from showing through to the right side, fasten off the thread rather than take it for more than 2·5 cm (1 inch) across material which is not being covered with stitchery.

The choice of thread will depend on whether you wish the pattern darning to cover the material or whether you wish to add only a slight decoration with the background showing through the stitches. In the latter instance use a single rounded thread such as coton à broder, coton perlé or tapestry wool, depending on the thickness of material. If you do not want the material to show through the pattern, use a stranded thread such as crewel wool or stranded cotton/yarn, the fine strands will lie side by side, giving a smooth surface. Knitting or Persian wool can be used on hessian or a heavy tweed.

Designs for this work can be planned on graph paper. The smaller the spaces between the stitches, the denser the decoration will be. Ravellings from a material may be used to give a slight texture to the surface of the same material.

Any colour schemes may be used, but the effect of material showing between the stitches will tend to reduce the strength of colours and it may be necessary to work in a darker tone to achieve the required effect.

Pattern darning can be worked in the hand for small areas, but for a complex pattern on a large area it is easier to work on a slate/scroll frame. Work from right to left (left to right) and turn the work at the end of a line if working in the hand. Otherwise, work each line from right to left (left to right), fastening off at the end of each line.

Start by leaving an end on the right side, which can be taken through to the wrong side and darned into a few stitches, taking care not to alter the tension of the stitches on the right side. Extra care is needed if working on sheer fabric.

If working an elaborate pattern, make a line of tacking/basting down the length of the area to be worked. Start working in the centre of a line so that you have the pattern darning centred. The first line of stitches is the most difficult as this needs careful counting. Once this is correct, you will have these stitches to act as a guide. If a successive row starts immediately below the one above, work a back stitch instead of a running stitch as the first stitch, in order to keep a good tension. Loose stitches will spoil the effect, and the stitches on the right side should not be so long that they will catch in use.

Geometric satin stitch

The design on the wrong side of pattern darning appears in reverse of that on the right side, but in geometric or counted satin stitch there is a stitch across the back of each stitch on the right side.

Geometric satin stitch should be worked on a material whose threads can be counted easily. An evenweave material will give the most satisfactory results. Use a frame for all geometric satin stitch.

Borders and motifs as well as all-over patterns can be done in this stitch. Self colour, monochrome and polychrome are all effective and an interesting result can be obtained by the play of light if the direction of the stitches in one colour is changed.

Satin stitch is common to many needlecraft techniques. In geometric satin stitch the stitches must all lie with the warp or weft threads of the material. Using a blunt tapestry needle, leave an end of thread on the right side which can be darned in on the wrong side when some stitches are worked. Take the needle down at the end of the appropriate number of threads. Bring the needle up alongside the beginning of the first stitch, thus having a long stitch across the back of the work. Repeat this stitch throughout. Avoid using long stitches as these will catch in use.

To help the stitches lie side by side when working satin stitch with a stranded thread, untwist the thread from the needle and take the needle down through the strands for each stitch.

As a variation from the more usual patterns, it is interesting to work at random, creating irregular patterns using the same stitch.

Left *Detail of the tablecloth on pages 92–3, showing areas of geometric satin stitch, eyelets, pattern darning and pulled work.*
Right *Detail of a bag in pattern darning showing a variety of patterns.*

Drawn fabric work

Early examples of this work were done in Greece and Turkey in one colour on a contrasting ground. However, it is the drawn fabric work in self colour which is best known, as found in examples of coverlets and gentlemen's waistcoats of the eighteenth century. At that time, drawn fabric work was sometimes combined with quilting for warmth.

Drawn fabric work is often called pulled work to avoid confusing it with drawn thread work. Whereas threads are actually withdrawn from the fabric in the latter type of work, in pulled work the threads of the background material are only pulled out of place. Thus it is the open patterns created by the formation of the stitches which characterize this type of work rather than the stitches themselves.

Drawn fabric work can be worked as a border, or it can be built up into geometrical patterns or used as fillings in a free design. It can be used for household linen and furnishings, for accessories or as insets for clothing. Outlining is optional as in blackwork. Stitches which may be used for outlining include whipped chain, coral or scroll.

To get the full beauty of the patterns, use a loosely woven material and select a thread which is finer than the woven threads of material. The thread needs to be strong because of the pull on each stitch. Linen thread is good, as are fine coton perlé/pearl cotton and crochet cotton. Stranded cotton/floss should be used in short lengths to keep fraying to a minimum. A contrast can be made by using varying thicknesses of thread, but patterns where more than one stitch is made into one hole cannot usually be adapted in this way.

Use a fine blunt tapestry needle, size 24, for most work. Starting and fastening off will require a finer, pointed needle because the blunt needle is too large to run under tiny stitches.

There are many stitches which may be done in pulled work and the most useful of these are detailed below. Some are variations of stitches already mentioned, others are exclusive to this type of work. It is necessary to keep a good tension and to prevent the threads of fabric, in spite of being pulled, from going off the straight. As it is almost impossible to correct this fault later, some people find it easier to work on a frame, but the material must not be stretched tightly.

Stitches for this work vary in density, some being fairly closely worked, others being more sparsely placed giving a lighter effect. Select a suitable stitch and, if using stitch patterns within a design, a variety will give added interest. Most stitches should be worked over two or three threads of material, unless otherwise indicated.

A simple edging for pulled work is done by drawing out the fourth thread from the edge, all round. Work a line of double back stitch four threads in from the withdrawn thread over four threads all round using a thread about the thickness of the threads of the background material. Fold the material to the wrong side so that the back stitch rests at the top of the fold. Now work a satin or straight stitch, over the fold, to hold it in place, between each back stitch. When you have worked all round the hem, work in the opposite direction, making a satin stitch over each previous one, forming a cross on the wrong side. By pulling the stitches firmly, the hem will be held in place securely enough for the surplus material to be carefully cut away on the wrong side.

Far left *Small mat in fine drawn fabric work. Stitches include eyelets, satin, ringed back, diagonal pulled.*
Left *A house design in drawn fabric work. This is one panel in a series of the same design embroidered by different methods (see contents page 6).*

Satin stitch

In drawn fabric work this stitch is also called *whip stitch*. It is the simplest stitch and is worked in the same way as the crewel work version, with a thread passing across the back of the work between each stitch. Pull the thread tightly after each stitch.

Satin stitch is versatile and is the basis for many variations. It may be spaced, turned, stepped, used as a single line or built up into arrangements of all-over patterns.

Square stitch

Also known as *four-sided stitch*, this attractive stitch may be used for single lines, particularly at hems. Work from right to left (left to right). More than one row may be worked to give added weight. Three positions of the needle are needed to form one stitch. The first stitch of each successive stitch after the first, forms the last side of the square of the previous stitch.

Three-sided stitch

When worked, this produces a row of triangles with points facing up and down alternately. Work from right to left (left to right) over an even number of threads, usually four, repeating each movement twice as double stitches are necessary to form the patterns. There will be two threads on the surface of the right side of the material on each side of every stitch.

Bring the needle up at the top of the line to be worked. Take it down four threads below and two to the right (left). Bring the needle out four threads to the left (right). Take the needle back into the first hole at the top and out into the left (right) hand hole at the bottom. To start the second triangle, take the needle into the same top hole and out four threads to the left (right). Continue in this way along the line.

Successive rows may be worked by leaving one or two threads of material before the next row.

Ringed back stitch

A series of back stitches are combined to make small octagons which form rings when the stitches are pulled tightly. Each ring is made up of two lines of stitching.

Pick up two threads of material for each stitch whether horizontal, diagonal or vertical. As in the three-sided stitch above, two stitches appear on the right side in the same position each time. There will be long stitches on the wrong side as with all back stitch.

satin stitch

square stitch

Diagonal pulled stitch

This may be worked as a single line but it is most effective if worked into an all-over filling. It consists of a series of straight stitches with the needle either vertically or horizontally under three or four threads of material. Each stitch is worked twice. Turn the work at the end of each row and fit the successive rows into the same holes as the previous row.

Window filling

This forms a lightweight filling if worked with a fine thread. It is worked as a series of double diagonal stitches, and worked across a square of three threads. When passing from one diagonal to another, the needle should pass under seven threads, leaving one thread between each V, and each line of diagonals.

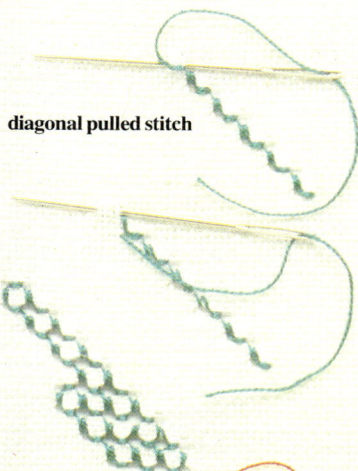

Eyelet holes

There are different forms of these. The most simple version is the eight stitch eyelet, known as an *Algerian eyelet*. Work over a square of six or eight threads of material. The eight straight stitches radiate from a centre hole with the needle taken down into the centre hole and up at the centre of each side and at each corner alternately.

A *detached eyelet* is worked in a similar way but the stitches are taken between every thread along each side of the square. The needle is still inserted into the centre hole between each stitch. As so many stitches are taken into the centre hole, the thread should be fine enough to lie side by side round the hole and by working with an even tension, a clear hole should be visible. Detached eyelets may be worked as a single stitch, or as a filling with the stitches of adjacent eyelets worked into the same holes.

As a variation, eyelets may be varied in size, partly worked only, or worked in different threads. Eyelets may be worked as the centre of a motif built up of satin stitch, turned at the corners in the same way as in an eyelet.

A *lozenge-shaped eyelet* is worked in the same way as a simple eyelet, but with diagonal stitches radiating from a central hole between two vertical and two horizontal stitches.

Chevron cross stitch

A series of cross stitches, each worked with a double stitch, is effective if worked tightly in a fine thread as a pulled stitch. Repeat each movement twice. Work the first half of the stitch by inserting the needle diagonally and then vertically. On the return journey, complete the cross stitches in the same manner, inserting the needle diagonally and vertically alternately. This can be worked as a line stitch or as an all-over filling, the second and successive rows being worked into the same holes as the previous row.

diagonal pulled stitch

window filling

Algerian eyelet

detached eyelet

lozenge-shaped eyelet

chevron cross stitch

Drawn fabric evening bag

This charming drawstring bag in drawn fabric work is simple to make. The loosely woven material is decorated with stitches in self colour and a little synthetic gold thread. The basic pattern for the drawstring bag can be used for other embroidery methods such as blackwork, pattern darning or geometric satin stitch on an evenweave material, or for freehand stitches on a dress or furnishing fabric. The loose weave used for drawn fabric work permits the colour of the lining to show through.

Materials required

Evenweave linen with 12 threads to each 2·5 cm (1 inch), 68 × 23 cm (27 × 9 inches)

Lightweight silk or cotton material in a contrasting colour for the lining, 75 × 15 cm (30 × 6 inches)

2 circles of cardboard, each 11 cm (4½ inches) diameter

Threads:

5 skeins coton perlé/pearl cotton no. 3

2 balls coton perlé/pearl cotton no. 5

Working the stitches

Cut out a piece of linen 50 × 23 cm (20 × 9 inches) and work a line of tacking/basting down the centre of the fabric, dividing it in half widthwise.

Work 24 Smyrna stitches down the tacking/basting. To emphasize them, work each movement of each stitch twice. On either side of the Smyrna stitches work the lines of stitchery shown on the chart.

The woven bars are worked by laying four threads of coton perlé no. 5 closely on the surface of the material; then weave under and over each pair of threads to form a loop through which the cords are threaded.

Join up the side seam with back stitch, right sides together and matching the stitches. Turn the work to the right side and cover the seam with Smyrna stitches which will match up with the first 24 worked on the opposite side. Trim the fabric to 1·5 cm (⅝ inch) from the base of the decorative stitching, turn under and tack/baste in position.

Making up the bag

Cut the lining material into three pieces, one 41 × 15 cm (16 × 6 inches), and two circles each 15 cm (6 inches) in diameter. Place the round cards in the centre of each circle of lining material. Lace the edges together from side to side across the back.

Join the strip of lining down the short side. With the wrong side outside, turn 1 cm (½ inch) at the lower edge to the wrong side. Oversew this to the edge of one card, with the covered side of the card to the right side of the base of the lining.

Cut out a circle of linen 15 cm (6 inches) in diameter. Place it wrong side down over the covered side of the second circle of card and lace into position.

Place the side of the bag in position on the base (covered side downwards). Pin it into place, easing where necessary, and oversew.

Fold over the top of the bag between the fourth and fifth eyelet, and stitch into the back of the gold square stitch. Trim the unworked fabric to 1·5 cm (⅝ inch) below this. Drop the lining into the bag with its wrong side facing the wrong side of the bag. Turn in the raw edge at the top of the lining and hem into place at the base of the eyelets.

Make two cords each 40 cm (16 inches) long, using coton perlé no. 3. Make two tassels 5 cm (2 inches) long. Work buttonhole stitching on the tassel in metallic thread.

Thread each cord through the woven bars from either side. Join the ends of the cords and attach the tassel at each side.

Smyrna stitches down centre then work bands of stitches as chart on either side of centre

50 cm (20 inches) · 23 cm (9 inches)

fold over · base of bag · centre

eyelets
square stitch (gold)
woven bars
square stitch (gold)
Smyrna stitch
ringed back stitch with cross stitch in gold metallic thread
satin stitch coton perlé no. 3
square stitch
ringed back stitch with cross stitch in gold metallic thread
satin stitch
square stitch
diagonal satin stitch coton perlé no. 3

Use coton perlé no. 5 except where indicated
1 line of graph paper represents one thread of material

Canvas work

Many people are introduced to canvas embroidery by working a painted canvas. This is sometimes incorrectly referred to as tapestry work as many of the designs are based on seventeenth and eighteenth century tapestries which were, in fact, woven on a loom. Copies of these beautiful designs are worked by entirely covering a canvas background with stitches.

There are a few early examples of canvas work dating from the Middle Ages, and there was a great deal worked in Elizabethan times at the end of the sixteenth century, particularly cushions, coverlets, bags and book covers.

Since that time canvas work has been done in different styles, either with the original tent stitch or with a variety of stitches. The colourings, too, have changed through the centuries. The strong but pleasing colouring of canvas-embroidered chair covers of the eighteenth century, depicting classical scenes or stylized floral designs, is contrasted by the harsh colouring and popular designs of dogs, flowers and parrots of the Berlin wool work which was in such favour in the nineteenth century.

Today we still use the great variety of stitches which has evolved over many years, but by using designs and threads of our own time, we can avoid direct copying and produce a lively form of canvas work unique to the twentieth century.

Canvas work differs from other embroidery techniques in that the stitchery covers the entire background. A strong fabric is produced which can be used not only for decorative purposes, but also where strength and hard wear are required. Because all the background is worked, canvas work is not quick to do, and it requires accuracy, particularly if working a repeating pattern. Although it is not included in the section on counted thread work, canvas work is in fact dependent on the counting of threads.

Tiny decorative items such as pendants or paperweights can be made, as well as items made for hard wear such as chair seats, stool tops, church kneelers, small rugs, cush-ions and handbags. An insertion of canvas work may be set into clothing or used as an accessory such as a belt or button. Canvas should be dry cleaned, not washed.

Canvas

The quality of canvas varies considerably. Buy the best that is available if making something which is intended to last; the cheaper varieties are suitable for decorative work. The mesh of the canvas which is indicated when you buy it, refers to the number of warp threads to 2·5 cm (1 inch). Some canvas will not have an equal number of warp and weft threads in a square. This will not matter unless you are working from a chart where the finished size of the embroidery is critical.

There are two sorts of canvas which may be used, double mesh and single mesh. Double mesh is suitable for cross stitch and its variations such as long-legged cross stitch, rice stitch and oblong cross. Double mesh canvas is used for most painted canvas when a half-cross stitch or tent stitch is worked. This canvas is made in sizes from 7 to 12 holes to 2·5 cm (1 inch), the most popular one having 10 holes to 2·5 cm (1 inch). This generally comes in widths of 65 cm (26 inches) or 90 cm (36 inches).

The single mesh canvas is easier to work on and it comes in a wider range of meshes. It has the advantage that any of the stitches, including the cross stitch family, may be worked on it. Single mesh canvas is generally made in meshes varying from 10 threads to 2·5 cm (1 inch) to a fine mesh with 24 threads to 2·5 cm (1 inch). For cushions, kneelers and chair seats, a canvas with 16 or 14 threads to 2·5 cm (1 inch) is suitable to work on, and will produce hard-wearing results. For small objects, use a canvas with 18 threads to 2·5 cm (1 inch); for bold experimental work using thick threads, a canvas with 10 threads to 2·5 cm (1 inch) is appropriate. These canvases are generally available in widths of 65 cm (26 inches) or 100 cm (40 inches).

Right *A cushion worked in a variety of canvas work stitches.*

Canvas work should be done on a slate/scroll frame to prevent it becoming warped. Do not use a ring frame for canvas work as this will push the threads of canvas out of place. If you want to be able to carry it around easily or take it with you when travelling, it can be worked without a frame. Certain stitches such as tent stitch will tend to pull the canvas out of shape more than others. Diagonal working of tent stitch and cross stitch helps to avoid too much distortion. However, the stretching of the canvas when the stitching is finished will generally rectify any faults. Always test the threads to make sure they are colour-fast. For stretching allow 5 cm (2 inches) of canvas outside the area for stitchery on all four sides.

Threads

Certain threads are specially prepared for canvas work. This means that they will be hard wearing, colour-fast and with a good colour range. Interesting variations can be made by using more than one of these wools on a piece of work. As the stitches should entirely cover the canvas, experiment to see how many strands of any one thread are needed to do this without a congestion of threads.

Tapestry wool is mainly used for painted and trammed canvases on 10's double canvas.

Crewel wool is available in a vast range of colours and tones, is hard wearing, colour-fast and usually mothproofed. It is a fine thread and therefore is suitable for almost any canvas as several strands may be used in the needle at once, enabling the number to be varied according to the stitch being worked.

Persian wool is an attractive thread to use on canvas. It is skeined with three strands together; these are easily divisible and the number of strands used will depend on the mesh size of the canvas. The colour range is comparable to that of tapestry and crewel wools.

Two-ply rug wool, sometimes known as thrums, is strong and hard wearing but the colours are limited. This wool is useful on coarse canvases and for hard wear.

For more decorative and less functional canvas work, almost any thread can be used, providing it will pass through the canvas comfortably.

Soft embroidery cotton with a matt finish will produce clearly defined stitches.

Knitting, crochet and weaving yarns, which are made in fashion colourings, have attractive textures which give a contrast to the usual threads. For highlights, coton perlé no. 3 has a good sheen and the finer no. 5 can either be worked with more than one strand, or can be added to a needle threaded with wool, before stitching. Alternatively a single thickness can be added to stitches already worked.

Synthetic raffia may also be used for highlights.

There is no quick and easy way to calculate quantities of thread for canvas work. Every instance is different, with varying canvas, different threads and changing stitches. As a guide, a hank of crewel wool weighing 25 grams (1 ounce) will complete about 15 cm (6 inches) square if working tent stitch on 16's single canvas. A small skein of tapestry wool 8 metres (26 feet) in length will cover an area 10 × 7·5 cm (4 × 3 inches) if working tent stitch on 10's double canvas. See also page 13 for hints on thread calculation.

Tapestry needles should be used to avoid piercing the canvas. Size 20 is a good all-purpose needle, size 18 is for thick threads and size 22 is for fine threads.

Designs

Designs for canvas work may be geometrical, all-over repeating patterns or free. However, because of the mesh on which the stitches are worked, it is not possible to obtain smooth or flowing curved or diagonal lines, although vertical and horizontal stitches will produce straight lines. To adapt a line drawing for canvas work, refer to the method for cross stitch on page 70 where graph paper is used.

All designs can be plotted on graph paper to form a chart. The choice of graph paper will depend on the mesh of canvas. For example, if working on 16's single canvas, you can use 16 or 8 squares to 2·5 cm (1 inch) graph paper. In this way, the stitchery will work out the same size as the chart, providing the stitches are either over one thread of canvas for 16 squares or over two threads of canvas for 8 squares. However, if you cannot get a graph paper to scale with the canvas, it is necessary

to count the threads in each direction which will be used for stitchery and use the same number of squares on the graph paper. When plotting a chart, consider working some stitches over one thread, and some over two, three or four. If you intend to work over an odd number of threads, you will need to be careful not to mix these with stitches over an even number of threads.

When working from a chart, it is often helpful to mark out the canvas with tacking/basting to produce squares of 2·5 cm (1 inch). On 16's canvas tacking/basting stitches will appear after every sixteenth thread.

All-over patterns can be built up directly with stitches on the canvas. Mark the centre of the canvas horizontally and vertically and work outwards from the central point.

Free designs can be marked on white paper in black ink and placed under the canvas. Then the design can be painted on the canvas with artist's oil colour mixed with a little pure turpentine. Never use a felt pen or ball-point pen which is not waterproof.

Stitches

Canvas stitches consist of those composed of cross stitches and those made up of straight stitches. When planning stitches for a design, count the threads not the holes. When working canvas stitches, the threads of the canvas should not be moved out of place, except when working eyelet holes. If you have difficulty in getting the thread through a hole previously used for another stitch, a finer thread should be used.

Make a knot at the end of a thread. Take the needle through to the wrong side, leaving the knot on the right side, about 3 cm (1¼ inches) away from the first stitch, to the left or right, above or below, depending on the direction of the first stitches. Once the first few stitches have been worked over the thread on the wrong side, the knot can be cut off. When some stitches have been worked, start and finish off by running through the stitches on the wrong side for about 2·5 cm (1 inch).

Right *A sampler of canvas stitches.*

Cross stitch

This can be worked as an outline stitch with a different stitch as a filling, as a filling stitch or as a single stitch to break up a large area of tent stitch. The top stitch should lie in the same direction throughout a piece of work. Cross stitch can be worked over two or more threads of single canvas or over one intersection of double mesh canvas. As for cross stitch on evenweave, cross stitch on canvas may be worked in two ways. One method is to work each complete stitch in turn, working from right to left (left to right). It is best to work backgrounds and large areas in this way, preferably working diagonally to reduce the likelihood of the canvas being pulled out of shape. To give added texture to a single stitch, slip in a second under stitch before pulling the top stitch tightly. The second method is to work half of each stitch along a line and to complete the cross stitch on the return journey.

Rice stitch

This stitch is sometimes called *crossed corners*. It can be used in borders, motifs, backgrounds or as single stitches. It has a lovely texture and is usually worked over a square of four single threads or over a square of two double threads. It is a very strong hard-wearing stitch. It consists of a large square cross stitch, over which each corner is crossed diagonally. The stitches on the wrong side are either horizontal or vertical. Work in lines from right to left (left to right).

As a variation, the corner stitches may be worked in a contrasting colour to the large cross, in which case the crosses are worked first before working the corner stitches. These could be worked in a different thread to the cross stitches, such as coton perlé worked over wool, but the corner stitches should not be too fine. If a thick thread is used for the corner stitches, only a tiny amount of the centre stitch will show, giving a bead-like effect. Rice stitch mixes well with other stitches. If worked over a square of four threads, other stitches worked over two threads, or tent stitch worked over one thread make a good contrast to rice stitch. It can also be worked as a single stitch to break up a tent stitch background.

Oblong cross stitch

This variation of cross stitch makes a good filling stitch and is effective if worked as a background. It is worked in the same way as cross stitch but the height of the stitch is twice its width. If worked over two vertical threads of canvas, its height will be over four horizontal threads. As in cross stitch, it may be worked by completing each stitch before working the next, or it may be worked with one line of diagonal stitches which are crossed on the return journey. If you have difficulty in covering the canvas with the stitches, work a line of back stitch across the centre of each stitch. As a variation, *alternating oblong cross stitch* makes a delightful background or filling stitch. Work a line of oblong cross stitch, omitting each alternate stitch. The second line is worked in the spaces, with the top of each two threads above the bottom of the stitches in the first line. The stitches in the third line will lie immediately below the first line, working into the same holes. Back stitch worked between each stitch will help to cover the canvas and give added attraction.

method 1

method 2

alternating oblong cross stitch

114

Long-legged cross stitch

This strong stitch can be used as a filling, for backgrounds and as single lines. It is a stitch which flows rapidly once a rhythm is established. It is worked from left to right (right to left) to get a smooth surface, but if you work in rows from left to right and right to left alternately, you will get a plaited effect. For each movement the needle is inserted in an upright position under two horizontal threads of canvas. Start with a cross stitch over a square of two threads. Then working forward by two threads, insert the needle for the next stitch. This produces the 'long leg'. Next insert the needle back two threads, into the same holes as the end of the previous stitch. Repeat the last two moves continuously along the line. At the end of the line make a short stitch.

Smyrna stitch

The formation of Smyrna stitch gives a good texture against some of the flatter stitches and is very attractive on decorative work, but because the top stitch is considerably raised, it is unsuitable for use on stool tops, chair seats or kneelers. Not only can it be uncomfortable, but it is likely to wear out more quickly. Start by working a large cross stitch over a square of four threads. Then work the vertical stitch and finally the horizontal stitch before starting the next Smyrna stitch to the left (right).

Upright cross stitch

Worked over two horizontal and two vertical threads of canvas, from right to left (left to right), this small compact stitch is firm and hard wearing, and has a slightly textured surface. Each stitch should be completed separately and consists of one vertical stitch which is crossed with a horizontal stitch of the same length. The second and successive lines fit into the preceding row.

Tent stitch

This is a flat stitch which contrasts well with the more textured stitches. It is worked as a small diagonal stitch over one intersection of canvas. It is suitable for detailed work and for filling irregular shapes where larger stitches would not fit. It may be needed for outlining and for backgrounds. Use it also for covering threads where other stitches cannot necessarily be completed.

It can be worked horizontally or vertically, always with a long stitch appearing on the wrong side, to give both a good tension and extra strength to the work.

To prevent the canvas from pulling out of shape, particularly if worked in the hand, and to get a more even surface, tent stitch should be worked diagonally on large areas. If working in this way, the needle is passed under two horizontal threads of canvas, working downwards. To work upwards, the needle is passed under two vertical threads of canvas. On the wrong side the threads will show a woven effect.

Upright Gobelin stitch

This straight stitch could be called satin stitch as this is the method of working. The needle is inserted in a slanting position and is brought up in the hole next to the bottom of the previous stitch and in at the top immediately above, covering either two, three or four horizontal threads of canvas. To ensure that the canvas is well covered, use a stranded thread and do not pull the thread too tightly. If the canvas shows between the lines of stitches, work back stitches over one or two threads of canvas, using a fine thread.

Slanting Gobelin stitch

This is another version of satin stitch, and is worked in a similar way to upright Gobelin except that the needle is inserted in an upright position under two, three or four horizontal threads of canvas, creating a stitch which slants across one vertical thread of canvas. This tends to cover the canvas more satisfactorily than upright Gobelin. Back stitches may be worked between lines of stitches if necessary. Upright, slanting and wide Gobelin stitches are useful as filling stitches, in borders and motifs, and as backgrounds.

Wide Gobelin stitch

One line of stitches is slanted across two or three horizontal and vertical threads with each successive stitch lying parallel and close to the previous stitch. At the end of the line, the direction of the stitches of the next row may either be the same as the previous row, or reversed.

upright Gobelin

slanting Gobelin

116

Encroaching Gobelin stitch

This consists of long stitches worked over four, five or six horizontal threads of canvas and slanting across one vertical thread. When working the second and each successive row, the top of the stitch is taken down one thread above the bottom of the stitches in the previous row, thus each row encroaches on the row above by one thread. The stitches on the wrong side are upright. This is a flat stitch which covers the background rapidly.

Diagonal satin stitch

This is a versatile stitch which can be adapted by changing directions, varying its size, combining it with other stitches, and making unusual colour arrangements. To learn the basic stitch, work over a square of four single threads of canvas. Start by making the centre stitch which slants diagonally across four threads. Then work satin stitches on each side of it, to complete the square. The stitches will cross three, two and then one intersection in succession on each side of the centre. Then bring the needle up at the end of the longest stitch of the already worked square. Take this stitch across four threads diagonally to start an adjacent square and then complete the square stitch as before. The stitches of the adjoining square will be taken into the same holes as the one already worked.

This can be worked into an all-over pattern and it can be included in borders and motifs. It may be used in blocks of four squares among other stitches or to break up a large area of tent stitch. The changing direction of the stitches produces an interesting play of light. As an all-over pattern it may be padded slightly by passing a thread diagonally beneath the blocks of stitches in each direction.

The stitches can be worked entirely in one direction if this is preferred. To make variations in colour, either the whole square may be changed or attractive patterns can be made by changing the colour of half a square. Squares over two, three, five or six threads may also be worked. The number of stitches in each square will vary accordingly.

Chequer stitch

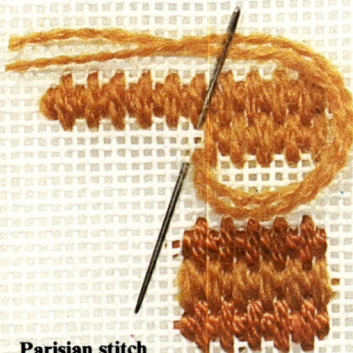

This is a combination of diagonal satin stitch and tent stitch. Squares of diagonal satin stitch alternate with squares of the same size which are composed of tent stitch. If the diagonal satin stitch is worked over a square of four threads, sixteen tent stitches will be worked in each of the adjoining squares. It provides a useful background stitch and is worked more rapidly than tent stitch alone.

Parisian stitch

Short and long upright stitches are worked alternately and continuously. Start by working over two and four horizontal threads of canvas alternately with the short stitch placed in the centre of the long stitch. The second row is worked over the same number of threads alternately, with the short stitch below the long stitch and the long stitch of the second row below the short stitch of the first row. Continue in this way to get a smooth all-over effect.

Hungarian stitch

This is a useful flat stitch. The upright straight stitches are worked in groups of three, over two, then four and two horizontal threads of canvas. Leave two vertical threads before working the next group of stitches. The second row is worked in the same way, fitting the top of the long stitch of each group into the holes left between the groups in the first row. The third row is worked immediately below the first row, with the top of the long stitch fitting into the hole at the base of the long stitch in the first row. All the short stitches are below one another, as are the long stitches. This may be worked in one colour, or by changing colour or tone alternately. It can also be worked into an all-over pattern.

Eyelet holes

These are worked in the same way as described in the section on drawn fabric work. Put the needle down into the centre hole and work straight stitches, radiating to complete the square. An eyelet hole cannot be worked with a thick thread. Use two strands of crewel wool if working a square of four or six threads on 16's single canvas. The stitches should lie side by side.

When the final stitch of each eyelet is worked, run the thread through the stitches on the wrong side to keep a good tension. When passing across the canvas on the wrong side, avoid covering the holes of the eyelets.

Eyelets may be worked in a small size, in scale with the rest of the work on practical pieces. Back stitching can be worked finely if the canvas shows between the eyelets. On decorative canvas work, large eyelets may be worked to give texture; part eyelets may also be included, and irregular eyelets may be made by not centring the holes.

chequer stitch

Parisian stitch

118

Turkey knot

This stitch, which gives a tufted effect, is worked on canvas with a needle and yarn. It may be used for small embroideries or for a needle-made rug.

Working from left to right (right to left), pass the needle from right to left (left to right) under one vertical thread of canvas. Do not start with a knot; leave an end lying on the front of the canvas, below the stitch, and hold it in place with the left (right) thumb. Next, pass the needle under the next vertical thread to the right (left) also pointing towards the left (right) with the thread above the needle. Repeat the first movement, allowing the thread to form a loop below the stitch. Hold the loop in place with the left (right) thumb while making the second movement. Repeat these two movements along the line. It may be helpful to take the thread round a pencil or stick of the required width, to obtain an even length of loop. Finally, cut the loops and trim.

'Waterfall' design using canvas stitches.

Samplers

Making a sampler is an excellent way to discover the sheer fun of canvas work. The astonishing variety of stitches, with their fascinating textures, will be a constant inspiration to you when you begin to plan more ambitious projects.

Start with a piece of single thread canvas having 14 or 16 threads to each 2·5 cm (1 inch) and measuring about 25 × 30 cm (10 × 12 inches). This is a good size to practise on. You can work the sampler in the hand, or – if you want to make sure of not distorting the canvas – use a simple stretcher frame, the kind sold in art shops. You buy the four strips of wood and slot them together. Then fasten the canvas to the frame – after covering the canvas edges with masking tape – by inserting drawing pins/thumbtacks at short intervals round all four sides.

Begin by working a group of several large stitches, each one over ten or more threads of the canvas, with some stitches larger than others, and place them either in the centre of the canvas or slightly off-centre. Continue by working some smaller, different stitches round the first group, and allow these to wander off at various angles from the centre in channels, some of which can continue to within 2·5 cm (1 inch) of the edge of the canvas. These channels will help to divide up the canvas into areas which can be filled with other stitches.

This carefree method of working can be great fun and helps in memorizing the stitches and learning how to get the correct tension, as well as providing an introduction to the problems of colour and textural contrast.

For your first sampler you might like to work all the stitches in one colour, or in two or three tones of the same colour. Then try using contrasting colours and a variety of threads. Interesting effects can be achieved by combining shiny and matt finish threads in the same stitch. For example, the large cross of rice stitch can be worked in crewel or Persian wool and the corner stitches in stranded cotton/floss.

Planning projects

When you are ready to move on to a more ambitious project, you must plan your work carefully before you start to stitch. If you are making a useful object, such as a chair seat, book cover or kneeler, you must take into consideration the amount of wear the object will receive. Choose stitches that cover the canvas well, and avoid those having long strands lying on the surface of the canvas. Some suitable ones include rice, Smyrna, small diagonal satin blocks and, of course, tent stitch, the most hard-wearing of all. This stitch is ideally suited to figurative designs, especially those including intricate details and subtle shading, but not a good choice for large areas of solid colour, as it lacks textural interest.

If you are making something purely decorative, such as a panel, you can give your imagination free rein. You can use any stitch you like, combining canvas work stitches with free stitchery, and you can mix threads and other materials freely. The surface of the canvas need not be entirely covered with stitches. It can be left bare in places, or holes can be cut out of it. Areas can be padded, and materials such as shells, stones, jewels, beads and pieces of metal or leather can be attached to the canvas and incorporated into the stitchery.

Pincushions

A pincushion is an excellent project for the beginner in canvas work. It's quick to work and makes a charming present. The pincushions shown opposite and on page 120 illustrate some of the many different forms this useful object can take.

Use single thread canvas in a medium gauge – 14 or 16 threads to each 2·5 cm (1 inch). You can use a variety of threads for the embroidery.

Pentagon pincushion
This pincushion uses a patchwork technique. Twelve pentagons stitched together automatically form a ball, which can then be filled with stuffing.

First make a pentagon template, tracing the pattern on page 164 and reducing or enlarging it if you like. Use this to draw 12 pentagons on the canvas. Make sure that the canvas threads run parallel with one side.

Work the embroidery in your chosen stitches and colours. The pin cushion shown uses a random combination of tent and cross stitches.

Cut the canvas to within 1 cm ($\frac{3}{8}$ inch) of the embroidery on all sides, press it to the wrong side and oversew the pentagons together along the folded edges, joining them first in two groups of six each – five round a central one – then joining the two halves.

Stuff the ball, close the opening edges and attach a loop of braid for hanging it.

Heart-shaped pincushion
This pincushion is designed to be worn on the wrist. The centre heart motif is worked in rice stitch in metallic yarn, outlined irregularly in tent stitch in black wool. More rice stitch, in red wool, is edged with tent stitch in black.

The back of the shape can be made of black felt, fine corduroy or velveteen. Stitch on a ribbon or a piece of black elastic for attaching the pincushion to the wrist.

Eyelet pincushion
A subtle and beautiful arrangement of eyelet stitches in shades of blue, turquoise, green, yellow and cream is combined here with blocks of oblong cross and upright Gobelin stitches and lines of tent stitch. A cluster of French knots and long straight stitches provides the focal point for this fascinating interplay of textures and light and dark tones.

Carnation pincushion (p. 120)
The border of this pincushion is worked in cross, tent and Smyrna stitches in a mixture of colours. The squares at each corner are outlined in cross stitch in light and dark green and contain groups of Smyrna stitch in white on a background of tent stitch in red and white. Bands of cross stitch in red surround the central motif of a carnation, worked in silk in tent stitch.

Black felt is used for the backing, with a bead sewn at each corner.

Round pincushion (p. 120)
The flower motif is worked in wheatsheaf stitch in gold wool, outlined in brown tent stitch, with a centre of tent stitch in orange. The background consists of alternating double rows of pink and red stem stitch.

Red velvet, slightly gathered, makes the base, and beads and decorative cord embellish the pincushion.

Tent stitch

Vertical

working down | working up

Horizontal

working left to right | working right to left

Diagonal

working left to right | working right to left

French knot

Oblong cross

Diamond straight stitch

Eyelet stitch

Smyrna stitch

Cross stitch

Rice stitch

Mosaic stitch

Stem stitch

A | B

Wheatsheaf stitch
A Even number of threads
B Uneven number of threads

Door fingerplates

Very attractive fingerplates for doors can be made by working pieces of embroidery on fine canvas and mounting them in plastic frames. As the work must be protected by a cover of transparent plastic, only flat stitches are suitable, and these are best worked in stranded cotton/floss, silk, or two strands of crewel wool. It's advisable to choose a subtle range of colours that will harmonize with the room's furnishings.

A suitable plastic cover and frame for a fingerplate can be purchased from specialist handicraft shops. They should be obtained before you plan the embroidery, in order to ensure that the dimensions of the work are correct. The frame can be painted a colour suitable for the embroidery.

After working the embroidery, trim the canvas to within 1 cm ($\frac{3}{8}$ inch) of the stitches; turn the canvas edges to the wrong side and glue them carefully in place.

Fit the embroidery into the frame, cover it with the plastic cover and fix it to the door with screws through the holes provided.

Two designs for fingerplates are given here. The lozenge design is worked in eyelet, small diagonal and tent stitches on a background of oblong cross stitch worked horizontally over four vertical threads and one horizontal thread of the canvas. The scroll design is worked in tent and mosaic stitches on a background of diamond straight stitch.

Left: *Cushion 1, top left; Cushion 2, middle; Cushion 3, right.*

1

15	14	7	6	7	8	9	8
15	5	16	12	6	9	11	10
14	12	4	3	1	3	2	2
16	4	5	13	2	1	4	11
16	4	5	13	2	1	4	11
14	12	4	3	1	3	2	2
15	5	16	12	6	9	11	10
15	14	7	6	7	8	9	8

2

3	1	1	3	2	13	16	12
2	11	13	5	4	5	16	12
10	9	8	6	7	7	12	5
11	10	9	8	14	16	6	14
11	10	9	8	14	16	6	14
10	9	8	6	7	7	12	5
2	11	13	5	4	5	16	12
3	1	1	3	2	13	16	12

3

13	2	3	1	1	7	14	15
5	16	12	5	3	2	13	14
16	11	8	4	4	6	15	7
12	10	9	8	9	10	11	6
12	10	9	8	9	10	11	6
16	11	8	4	4	6	15	7
5	16	12	5	3	2	13	14
13	2	3	1	1	7	14	15

Key for cushion charts
1 Maroon
2 Shocking pink
3 Cherry red
4 Dusty lilac
5 Pale blue violet
6 Lilac
7 Light purple
8 Light bright orange
9 Dark bright orange
10 Orange
11 Rust
12 Violet
13 Bright pink
14 Medium purple
15 Purple
16 Dark Mauve

Three cushions

Vivid colours in geometrical patterns worked in Smyrna stitch make three striking cushions.

Materials required
Double thread canvas with 10 holes to each 2·5 cm (1 inch), 1·4 m × 48 cm (1½ × ½ yards)

Cushion 1
Tapestry wool: 2 skeins each of maroon, shocking pink, dusty lilac, pale blue violet, light bright orange, violet, light purple, purple, medium purple, lilac, rust, cherry red, dark mauve; 1 skein each of bright pink, orange
3 cushion pads/pillow forms 35 cm (14 inches) square
Furnishing fabric for backs, 1 m (1⅛ yards)

Cushion 2
Tapestry wool: 2 skeins each of maroon, shocking pink, cherry red, dusty lilac, pale blue violet, purple, light bright orange, dark bright orange, orange, rust, violet, bright pink, medium purple, dark mauve; 1 skein lilac

Cushion 3
Tapestry wool: 2 skeins each of maroon, shocking pink, cherry red, dusty lilac, pale blue violet, light purple, light bright orange, dark bright orange, orange, rust, violet, bright pink, medium purple, purple, dark mauve

Working the embroidery
Cut the canvas into three 45 cm (18 inch) lengths and mark the centre in both directions. The three diagrams give the design for each cushion. The embroidery is worked in Smyrna stitch over two double threads of canvas. Each numbered square on the diagram represents a square of eight stitches. Begin working the design in the centre.

Making up the cushions
Trim the canvas to within 2·5 cm (1 inch) of the embroidery. Cut a piece of backing fabric the same size. Place the two pieces together with right sides facing and stitch them together close to the embroidery, leaving an opening of about 20 cm (8 inches) in one side. Turn the cover right side out and insert the cushion pad. Turn in the seam allowances along the opening and slipstitch the folded edges together.

Telephone pad cover

This attractive desk accessory in shades of green, yellow, white and beige is very quickly made. It uses only four stitches: cross stitch, oblong cross, diagonal satin and herringbone.

Materials required

Single thread canvas with 13 threads to each 2·5 cm (1 inch), 25 × 33 cm (10 × 13 inches)

Tapestry wool, 1 skein each of light olive green, emerald green, forest green, white, pale yellow, beige

Thin cardboard 40 × 15 cm (16 × 6 inches)

Stiff paper the same size, or

Cotton lining fabric 45 × 17·5 cm (18 × 7 inches) and more cardboard the same size as specified above

Fine wool for the backing 24 × 18 cm (9½ × 7 inches)

Dark green sewing thread

Fabric adhesive/glue

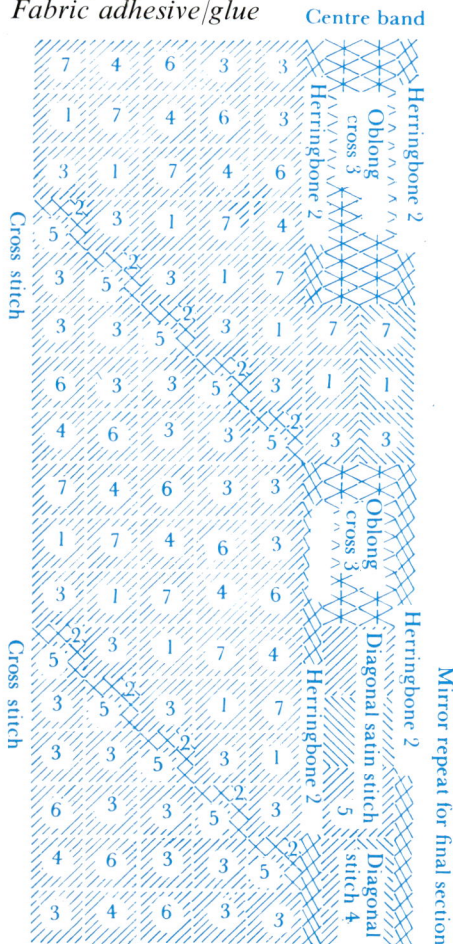

Centre band

Chart labels: Centre band; Herringbone 2; Oblong cross 3; Herringbone 2; Cross stitch; Oblong cross 3; Herringbone 2; Diagonal satin stitch 5; Herringbone 2; Diagonal satin stitch 4; Cross stitch; Mirror repeat for final section; Centre line

Key

1 Light olive green
1 Emerald green
3 Forest green
4 White
5 Pale yellow
6 Yellow
7 Beige

Working the embroidery

Mark the lengthwise centre of the canvas. Begin by working the centre band, at its upper right hand corner, starting 5 cm (2 inches) in from the top edge of the canvas. Count 6 threads to the right of the centre line. Using emerald green, work herringbone stitch (see page 33), going under 2 horizontal threads with each stitch and taking the wool over 2 vertical threads between each stitch. Continue the herringbone stitch over 30 horizontal threads.

Using forest green, work two rows of oblong cross stitch over 4 vertical and 2 horizontal threads, to the same depth as the herringbone stitch. Then work another row of herringbone to complete the width of the centre band.

Continue with two satin stitch blocks each in beige, light olive green and forest green, working each block over 6 thread intersections and slanting them as shown on the diagram.

Below this work oblong cross stitch in forest green over 18 horizontal threads. Work herringbone stitch in emerald green along side it and continue to the lower edge, over a total of 54 horizontal threads. Fill the spaces between with large diagonal satin blocks over 8 thread intersections using pale yellow wool. Slant the blocks in alternating directions.

Complete the centre band with satin stitch blocks in white, worked over 4 thread intersections.

Now work the right and left hand parts of the cover, following the diagram, noting that the right section is a mirror image of the left one. The cross stitches are worked over 2 canvas threads

Making up the telephone pad

Press or block the embroidery as required. Trim the canvas to 1·2 cm (½ inch) from the embroidery. Cut the cardboard into two pieces, each 20 × 15 cm (8 × 6 inches). Trim them slightly if necessary to fit comfortably within the embroidered area.

Place the back cover fabric and the embroidery face down on tissue paper. Centre the pieces of cardboard on both covers. Spread adhesive on the edges of each cardboard piece and fold the fabric edges over them, mitring the corners and gluing the two long sides first and then the short sides.

Line the insides of the covers with either stiff paper or lining fabric. If you are using lining fabric, first mount it onto thin cardboard as described for the covers, then glue it in place.

Join the back and front covers with two buttonhole cords, placed 2·5 cm (1 inch) from the side edges. Use ordinary sewing thread in dark green, fasten it to one cover and take it back and forth between the two covers several times, keeping the stitches close together and the strands even. Now work buttonhole stitch very closely over the strands.

Make a twisted cord using three strands of yellow tapestry wool, each 210 cm (83 inches) long. Fix the strands at one end and turn them clockwise until they are very tightly twisted. Fold them in half and give them a shake to form a double twist. Slipstitch the cord to the edges of the cover.

Glue a band of stiff paper inside the back cover to hold a tear-off note pad.

Florentine work

Although a form of canvas work, Florentine work (also known as bargello) is treated separately as it is dependent on the use of one straight stitch which is built into pointed and curved lines, by stepping at regular intervals. It is characterized by the skilful shading and blending of colours, usually in about three or four tones of two or more ranges of colour.

Use a single mesh canvas and a thread which will cover the canvas well. A stranded thread such as crewel wool or Persian wool is best as it lies flat, and another strand can be added if needed. Stranded cotton may be used on fine canvas if a sheen is required.

Florentine work may also be worked on an evenweave material such as hessian/burlap. On these, the stitches need not necessarily cover the material and not all the background needs to be covered with stitchery.

There are unlimited uses for Florentine work. Although it is not as hard wearing as some canvas stitches, it may be used for practical purposes such as chair seats, stool tops and cushions providing the stitches are not made too long. It is only suitable for kneelers if worked with a thread such as 2-ply rug wool, as most of the softer threads will wear thin too rapidly. Many small articles can be made and it can be used on clothing and accessories. Florentine stitch may be worked in with other canvas stitches when patterns created by this stitch, possibly worked in one colour only, are suited to the design being worked.

Florentine stitch can be worked either from left to right or from right to left. Start with a knot on the right side as in canvas work, allowing 3 cm (1¼ inches) of thread on the wrong side between the knot and the first stitch. Florentine stitch is worked by taking the needle down four threads above the point where it emerged. Then bring the needle up two threads lower than the top of the first stitch and one thread to the right (left). Take it down four threads lower and up on the same level as the base of the first stitch, one thread to

the right (left) each time. Repeat these two movements along the line. This is the basic Florentine stitch. The second line is worked immediately below the first row, bringing the needle out four threads below the base of the first stitch in the first row. Continue to the end of the row.

Untwist stranded threads to ensure that they lie flat. Do not pull the stitches too tightly: the thread should lie flat on the canvas without displacing the canvas threads.

From this basic stitch patterns are built up. To make peaks, work the first stitch over four threads, bringing the needle up two threads lower than the top of the first stitch. Take the needle down four threads higher. Repeat these two movements three times more, when you will have reached the top of a peak. Then set off downwards in the same way until you reach the level of the lower edge of the first stitch. Then start working upwards again. The second line is worked by starting four threads below the base of the first stitch in the first line. The tops of the stitches in the second line use the same hole as the bottom of each stitch in the previous row. It is usual to work the second line in a different tone to the first line, and the third line in yet another tone, working either from dark to light, row by row, or the reverse.

Once you are accustomed to the method of stepping the stitches, rising and dropping two threads each time, you will be able to vary the gradients. Sometimes you may wish to work over six threads; sometimes to rise and drop only one thread each time or to rise and drop

by three threads. The movement of the needle remains the same. Once the first row is worked it will act as a guide.

As a variation, the points can be flattened by working a series of stitches on the same level either at the top or at the bottom of a peak, or both. To get curved effects, work more than one stitch on the same level before stepping the next stitch. If canvas shows between blocks of stitches which are worked on the same level, a straight horizontal stitch may be worked.

By reversing a peak or a curved line, diamond or oval shapes can be produced. If this is done, it is best to work out the outline stitches of the shapes all over the canvas before filling in. It is easier to see a mistake in counting if this is done.

When working the first row of Florentine work, start from the centre of the canvas and work outwards. If working a large repeating pattern, it is worth spending a little time counting the threads of canvas, to decide whether the base or the top of a peak or curve should be centred.

To make your own patterns which are not regular or repeating, draw the freehand outline on graph paper, then work out the stitch arrangement by following this line. This is the same technique as is used for converting a design to cross stitch, see page 70.

Right *Early twentieth-century bag in Florentine stitch. The black stitches are worked horizontally.*
Below *A cushion in Florentine stitch.*

Florentine cushion

Curves and peaks are combined with tiny flower sprays in this design of Florentine stitches. The design is worked on only one side of the cushion; the other side is backed with a lining material. The repeating pattern enables you to make a cushion to any size and shape you require, although the instructions are for the 57 × 35.5 cm (22½ × 14 inches) cushion illustrated. The pad used is larger than the canvas design to give the cushion a good shape.

Because there is such a wide range of threads today, there may be a considerable choice of tones available within each suggested wool colour. Compare the effect of bolder tones used for the finished cushion in the photograph with the paler tones on the chart.

Materials required
½ metre (½ yard of 68 cm (27 inch) single mesh canvas with 18 threads to each 2·5 cm (1 inch)
Crewel wool – each skein weighs 4 grams (⅐ oz)
5 skeins black
3 skeins gold
3 skeins light tan
2 skeins dark tan
2 skeins pale pink
3 skeins deep pink
3 skeins rust
2 skeins beige
2 skeins pinky beige
2 skeins stone
1 skein green
A strong lining material, 3 cm (1¼ inches) larger than the finished stitchery; in this instance you will need a piece 60 × 38·5 cm (24 × 15¼ inches)
Cushion pad/pillow form 60 × 38 cm (24 × 15 inches)
Sewing thread for making up

Working the embroidery
Start working from the centre of the canvas. Each stitch is worked over six horizontal threads of canvas with the flowers in short stitches worked over two horizontal threads.

Work from the chart in the following order:
1 the outline of the pattern in black
2 the two outer beige tones
3 the flower spray
4 the stone-coloured stitches surrounding the flower

Making up the cushion cover
After stretching (see page 22), work Montenegrin stitch (long-legged cross stitch with bar) along the edge, over the spare canvas which is folded to the wrong side. Each stitch is worked over three horizontal and two vertical threads, to give a strong edging. Trim the canvas 1cm (½ inch) from the edge.

Turn in the raw edges of the lining and tack/baste it in place so that it is invisible from the right side. Hem into the back of the Montenegrin stitch on three sides. Insert the cushion pad and stitch up the remaining side.

Montenegrin stitch

centre

centre

1 line on the chart represents 1 thread of canvas

Far right *A variety of Florentine stitches have been used in this picture.*
Right centre *Two details from a canvas work sampler showing Florentine stitch and tent stitch.*

Right *Florentine stitches worked in stranded silk.*
Below *A spectacle case in canvas work with eyelet holes and cross stitch.*

Traditional techniques

Drawn thread work

One of the earliest methods of decorating material was done by drawing threads out of it and working on the remaining threads to form a pattern. Many different types of work have developed from this theme: in some instances threads are drawn in one direction only, in others threads are drawn in both directions.

One disadvantage of this type of work is that the material is weakened as a result of having so many threads withdrawn, even though extra stitching is added to the remaining threads in order to strengthen them. Much drawn thread work in large elaborate patterns was done during the first two decades of this century, usually for bed and table linen, but the method went out of favour because laundering the finely worked pieces proved detrimental and the threads were damaged. However, weaknesses need not occur, providing the added stitchery is compensatory, and nowadays drawn thread work can be done effectively using the stronger materials and threads which are available. Any strong material from which the threads can easily be removed is suitable, although an evenweave material is best for table linen.

Hemstitching

This is a means of neatening a hem in a decorative way. If the hem is to be 2 cm ($\frac{3}{4}$ inch) deep, plus 5 mm ($\frac{1}{4}$ inch) for the turning, allow 5 cm (2 inches) extra on the length and breadth of the finished article when cutting out the material. Measure in from each side at the corners, twice the width of the hem plus the turning allowance, i.e. 4·5 cm ($1\frac{3}{4}$ inches). Insert a pin at the point where these measurements meet. Using fine scissors, cut one thread in either direction. Lift up these threads with a pin, leaving the threads undisturbed towards the corner.

Repeat this process at the diagonally opposite corner, cutting and lifting the threads in the same way. Pull each cut thread gently towards the next corner. The crossing point of these indicates the two threads which need to be cut at each of the other two corners. Lift them slightly with a pin before cutting. Then pull out the single thread all round. Fold in the turning allowance to the wrong side. Turn the hem down all round to the place where the thread has been withdrawn, leaving it exposed. Pin the hem in place, mitring the corners (page 22).

To work the hemstitching, hold the work with the wrong side of the hem towards you. Use a fine tapestry needle and a thread which is about the same thickness as the threads of the material. Work from left to right (right to left) starting with a knot. Run the needle through the hem from the edge, to the point of starting. Work two back stitches into the fold. Pass the needle towards the left (right) under three or four threads in the space left by the withdrawn thread. Draw the needle through. Take a stitch into the fold only, not through to the right side of the material, pointing the needle towards you and with the working thread away from you. Pull up firmly. Continue all round in this way, securing the hem at the corners with one or two oversewing stitches. To fasten off, make two back stitches into the fold and pass the needle through the hem. Cut off the thread.

Above *Hemstitching.*
Right *Whitework sampler showing a variety of drawn-thread borders and corners (details far right).*
Facing page above *Mat in simple drawn thread work combined with pulled work.*

134

Neatening the ends of a border

Broader bands of drawn thread work, which need not necessarily be worked at a hem, will be neatened at each side with hemstitching before being strengthened with extra stitchery. The ends where threads are removed will need to be neatened.

For a border with six threads to be removed, snip and cut the end of the first and sixth thread, and pull these two out. Using a thread of the same thickness as the background, work a line of running stitch across the end of the border; then work close buttonhole stitch to cover the running stitch on the right side, with the looped edge against the open border. Now snip and remove the remaining four threads.

An alternative method is to cut the threads which are to be removed in the centre of the border; gradually remove each thread in turn to each end. Then thread each in a needle and darn it into the woven material for about 2·5 cm (1 inch) at the ends.

Spoke stitch

If more than one thread is withdrawn, the second side will need to be neatened with the same stitch but worked without a fold. To practise the stitch, remove two more threads alongside the one withdrawn. Work with the hem away from you. Start with a knot, on the wrong side. Bring the needle up one thread away from the opening, and 2·5 cm (1 inch) from the left (right) end of it. Carry the needle along to the beginning of the line and insert it two threads deep, pointing towards you. The hemstitching will enclose this starting thread. Work hemstitching, two threads in depth and picking up the same three or four threads as the first row. This groups the threads in straight lines. Fasten off by running through the stitches and cut off knots and long threads when work is complete.

Split group stitch

This is based on hemstitching. With three threads withdrawn from the background material, work the first side of the opening with hemstitch but pick up four threads for each stitch. On the opposite side, the same stitch is worked, picking up two threads from one group and two more from the next group. Continue in this way to the end of the line.

Twisted border

Work on a border which has been prepared, by hemstitching on both edges, into straight groups of threads, and which has the ends neatened.

Start by working back stitches into the material behind the buttonhole stitch at the middle of one end to secure the thread. Working from left to right (right to left), take the needle under the second group of threads, pointing the needle towards the left (right) and with the thread above the needle. Take the needle under the first and second groups of threads from left to right (right to left), and with the thread above the needle. Pull the thread tightly. Repeat these two movements along the line. Fasten off in the centre of the buttonhole stitches at the end of the open part. If you have an odd group left at the end of a row, divide the group and make a twist in the usual way.

spoke stitch

split group stitch

Double twisted border

The twists are made in overlapping pairs, with four groups of threads to each completed twist. To work this, make sure that the border contains a number of groups of threads which is divisible by four. If the border is short of a group of threads, divide the last one up into two, to complete the stitch.

Start on the first and second group as for the twisted border. Insert the needle from right to left (left to right) under the third group, with the thread above the needle. Pull it through. Take the needle under the first and third group from left to right (right to left), with the thread still above the needle. Pull the thread tightly. Take the needle under the fourth group then back under the second and fourth, pulling the thread up. Continue in this way to the end of the line.

Coral stitch border

Prepare a border by hemstitching on each side and by neatening the ends. Work coral stitch down the centre of the groups of threads. Hold the working thread with the left (right) thumb. Pass the needle under three groups and draw it out through the loop formed. Continue with this stitch to the end of the line.

Many variations of these borders may be made. For example, interesting results can be obtained by threading ribbon, strips of leather or cut strips of fabric as a twisted border.

Corners

If threads have been drawn in both directions at a corner, and a square hole is left, it is necessary to strengthen it. The simplest way to fill this is to work a woven wheel. It is worked after the borders.

Having worked a twisted border take the thread across the corner to the opposite side. Whip back to the centre of the square by passing the needle under the thread several times. Take the thread out at the adjacent edge and whip the thread back to the centre. At this stage insert the needle under the two threads with the working thread under the point of the needle, making a loop stitch. Continue the twisted border along the adjacent border until the next corner is reached. When the whole border is completed, return to one corner. Four extra diagonal spokes are added and whipped to the centre. It is not necessary to fasten these with a loop stitch until the last diagonal is worked. Using the same thread, work back stitch round and round the wheel, inserting the needle over one spoke and under two, then back over the second of these and forward under two. Continue until the wheel is wide enough. Fasten off into the stitches on the wrong side.

Needleweaving

Needleweaving is a type of drawn thread work. Stitching is worked to reinforce the threads left after others are withdrawn. It may be worked close to a hem, after it has been held in place by hemstitching. It may also be worked as a decorative border.

If the needleweaving is to be on clothing, linen and some woollens are good. A band of needleweaving on a pocket, yoke or at the hem of a skirt gives added interest. Use a thread which is similar in thickness to the threads of the material. Coton perlé/pearl cotton in different weights weaves well. So, too, do threads such as crewel or Persian wool. Use a fine tapestry needle.

Prepare a border by withdrawing about six threads in the position required, neatening the edges. Work hemstitching on each side of the border, to group the threads into bars. Generally bars made up of two threads will be best, although on fine materials three threads may be more practical.

To begin weaving, run the thread through the hemstitching towards the left for 2·5 cm (1 inch). Work on the wrong side. Then weave small blocks of colour on three bars. Pick up alternate bars, the first and third on one journey, and the second on the return. Press down each stitch while the needle is in position so that the threads of the material are entirely covered. Some bars may be left unwoven. Pass the needle under the hemstitching to the next group to be woven.

For a deep border, remove about twelve threads and work hemstitching to group the threads into bars. Weave a line of colour over six bars and continue weaving until you have covered one-third of the depth of border. Continue weaving over four bars, leaving out one bar at each end. Work the middle third of the depth of border in this way; then complete the border by weaving over two bars. Leave the thread hanging. Start with another colour or tone and repeat the motif in reverse, fitting the weaving over six bars into the section worked over two bars. When this is finished, continue with the first colour, by running through the hemstitching to the next group. Avoid joining a thread in the centre of a block of needleweaving.

At the ends of borders the thread in the needle may be woven in to avoid a gap occurring between the weaving and the neatening of the threads.

Many different needleweaving patterns can be worked out, either by experimenting directly on the material or by plotting on graph paper.

Below *Pocket in needleweaving.*
Right *Three panels showing different needleweaving effects.*

Needle lace

This type of lace is worked with a needle in contrast to the better known bobbin lace. To avoid confusion, needle lace is also known as needle-made or needlepoint lace. Traditionally needle lace was worked in fine white threads, many of which are not now available, and the result resembled the lace made with bobbins. The first examples of needle lace date back to the second half of the sixteenth century but the original complicated techniques have now been discarded.

It is a method which is suitable for working on a background material, as well as without a backing. It is best to learn the stitches by working on a fabric with threads that can be counted easily, but once the stitches become fluent almost any backing can be used. It is usually mounted on a frame for ease in working. Start by working in a thread which contrasts with the background. The stitches, which are based on buttonhole stitch, can be practised with coton perlé/pearl cotton no. 5. Use a crewel needle for the outline and a tapestry needle for the buttonholes as these do not mark the material.

As a basis for the filling, work stitches such as back stitch, chain stitch or couching round the outline of the shape, into which the button-holing is worked.

Right *Mobiles showing a modern interpretation of needle lace stitches worked irregularly to fill wire rings.*

Detached buttonhole filling

Work a back stitch edging. Bring the needle up just below the top edge at the left hand side. Work a stitch beneath the first back stitch with the working thread under the point of the needle from left to right. Continue working buttonhole stitch along the line to the edge, slipping the needle under the back stitch at the edge. Work buttonhole stitch in the opposite direction picking up the loop already made and passing the working thread under the point of the needle from right to left. Continue in this way all over the surface of the shape. On the last row, pick up the back stitch with the needle. Take the needle to the wrong side after the last stitch.

To work this filling within a circle, work back stitch or chain stitch all round the outer edge. Work the buttonhole filling continuously from the edge, in circles towards the centre.

Knotted buttonhole filling

This is worked in the same way as simple buttonhole filling but after each looped stitch, pass the needle under the stitch from left to right, with the working thread under the point of the needle.

Attractive large-scale buttonhole fillings can be worked as part of decorative hangings or panels. To work freely without a backing material these can be worked on a wire frame or within a hole cut out of a piece of fabric. It may also be worked downwards from a rod, with the first buttonhole stitches taken round the rod securely.

142

Edging stitches

These may be used for decorating hems. Turn up the hem and hold it in place with hemming or hemstitching. The stitches are worked on the right side.

Start each edging by running the thread into the hem and bring it out at the edge. Secure it with a shallow buttonhole stitch. All stitches taken into the hem should be as shallow as possible. To finish off, run the thread back through the hem.

Simple buttonhole edging

Make a buttonhole stitch slightly to the left of the holding stitch. Do not pull it tightly. Leave it just slack enough to form a scallop. Bring the needle up at the top of the stitch just worked. Then take the needle down through the loop which is made and pull it firmly. Make the next buttonhole stitch ready for the next scallop. At a corner, two stitches are worked diagonally to give a scallop on either side.

Antwerp stitch

This is similar to the previous stitch but is knotted after each scallop. After working the buttonhole stitch, insert the needle beneath two threads, with the working thread under the point of the needle. Pull the knot up, close to the edge of the hem. Continue with the next buttonhole stitch and work along the line. At a corner, make a small diagonal stitch.

Armenian stitch

This consists of triangles of knotted stitches repeated at intervals along the hem. Plan the position of the triangles so that they fall on either side of a corner. Make a row of six simple buttonhole stitches. Turn at the end and work back with five knotted buttonhole stitches into the loops of the previous row of stitches. Repeat this by reducing the number of stitches in each successive row. At the point, one stitch will be worked. Work whipping stitches up the side of the triangle to the hem; pass the needle through the fold ready to work the next triangle.

This stitch may also be worked in continuous lines without reducing the number of stitches as is necessary when forming triangles.

Many exciting variations of all these needle lace stitches may be worked. Experiment, for example, by working the stitches in groups or by using different thicknesses of threads.

Insertion stitches

Insertion stitches are sometimes called faggoting. They provide a means of joining together two pieces of material in a decorative way and are therefore particularly practical when inserting a contrasting fabric or piece of embroidery into clothing or accessories.

Turn under the raw edges of the two pieces of material to be joined. With the right side of the fabric upward, tack/baste the hems to a piece of strong paper which is contrasting in colour to the material in use. They should be about 6 mm ($\frac{1}{4}$ inch) apart and it may help to draw two parallel lines on the paper. Once the insertion stitch has been worked, the tacking/basting is removed to release the paper.

The thread used for insertion stitches will depend on the material. Coton perlé and coton à broder are suitable for most materials and soft embroidery cotton may be used where a thicker thread is required. If using a tweed or woollen material, wool can be used effectively. Avoid using a stranded thread.

Start and fasten off with back stitches under the hem. Work from top to bottom. If it is necessary to hold the two fabrics together at each end of the insertion stitches, work a buttonhole bar by laying three strands of thread between the two hems. Then work buttonhole stitch over these threads, pushing the stitches close together.

Right *A tea-cosy in pattern darning. The two sides are joined with knotted herringbone insertion stitches, and these have been threaded (in a second colour) for strength.*

Simple herringbone

With the thread at the top on the right, insert the needle down into the left fold from left to right with the working thread under its point. Repeat this movement by inserting the needle down into the right fold from right to left with the thread under its point. Repeat these two movements to the end.

Knotted herringbone

This is worked in the same way as simple herringbone with an additional movement after each stitch. Pass the needle from the top under the two threads, with the working thread under the point of the needle. Pull up tightly and repeat this knotting movement after each herringbone stitch is taken into the opposite fold.

Alternate buttonhole

This is worked in a similar way to knotted herringbone. Before making the knotted stitch, a group of two, three or four buttonhole stitches are worked on the same side.

Bullion bar

Start with the thread on the left. Insert the needle into the fold on the right immediately opposite; pull the needle through. Twist the thread round the needle, pull it through carefully to produce a firm twist. Take the needle into the left fold at the top of the twist, and bring it out below, ready for the next stitch.

Italian buttonhole seam

Worked closely, this forms a very good decorative join for cushions and garments and it is a useful way of joining leather or suede without turnings. It will be necessary to experiment to find out how far apart the hems should be tacked/basted as it takes up more room than other insertion stitches described above.

Lay a thread from right to left. Work four buttonhole stitches by inserting the needle behind the thread from the top and with the working thread under the point of the needle. Make a stitch into the fold on the right, slightly lower than the previous stitch and take the thread across to the left hand side, again slightly lower than before. Make three or four buttonhole stitches over the thread. Make a new holding stitch into the fold on the right. Take the needle to the centre and work a knotted stitch. Work two or three more stitches towards the left. Now take a new holding stitch into the fold on the left. Repeat in this way from the second line of stitches.

Knotted herringbone.

Bullion bar.

Simple herringbone.

Alternate buttonhole.

Italian buttonhole seam.

Whitework

As its name indicates this type of embroidery was traditionally worked in white thread on white material. However, the technique is now often worked by using colour and heavier threads than those used originally.

Whitework is based on satin stitch, worked on a closely woven material such as linen, lawn or cambric, and it can be adapted to fine closely woven wool for clothing. For the best results the design should consist of small shapes; long stitches are unsatisfactory. Many fine stitches using fine thread such as coton à broder or one strand of stranded cotton are better than a few worked in a heavy thread. For modern interpretations one strand of crewel wool can be used on a woollen ground. Use a fine crewel needle.

Satin stitch and its padding needs quite a lot of practice. Until the stitch becomes fluent, it should not be worked on a special piece as poor satin stitch is very disappointing.

Whitework should be worked on a frame.

Right *Details from a nineteenth-century christening robe in whitework.*

Satin stitch

This is worked over outline stitches or over padding. Start by working two back stitches within the shape to be worked. Then work small running stitches round the shape followed by herringbone stitch all over the shape. This constitutes the padding. Now work satin stitch from one end to the other, keeping the edge smooth and the stitches close to each other. The needle is brought up on one side and down on the opposite producing a long stitch on the wrong side. Fasten off on the wrong side. Do not take the thread across to the next shape, as it may show through from the right side.

An alternative method of padding, which will produce higher relief, needs a slightly coarser thread. Start with the running stitches. On curved lines work split stitch on the outline. Within this, lay straight stitches, filling the shape both across and lengthwise. Bring the needle up on the same side as it has been taken down, to avoid bulk on the wrong side. The top layer of padding stitches, which need not lie closely, should lie in the reverse direction to that of the final satin stitch which will be worked in the fine thread.

Trailing

This consists of close satin stitch worked over a bunch of an uneven number of threads which act as a padding; three or five is the usual number, depending on the thread being used and the thickness of trailing required. Bring the needle up on one side of the bunch of threads, and down on the opposite side, as with all satin stitch. However, in this instance the needle should be taken down at an angle towards the centre of the padding, to obtain a round corded effect with the stitches. Trailing needs practice and it is best done in long sessions to avoid breaking the rhythm. Interesting designs can be built up by combining satin stitch with trailing.

Traditional whitework stitches may be combined with patterns in any of the freehand stitches, such as chain, French knots, herringbone, Cretan and many others. Laid fillings can also be included.

Areas contained within an outline of trailing or satin stitch may have threads withdrawn. As an example, raise a thread in the centre of a shape with a pin, snip it. Lift this thread out to each side of the shape and cut it off with sharp scissors. The trailing will hold it firm. Extract threads in this way over the shape, drawing out two and leaving two or three in both directions. Using fine thread, the finest possible, overcast along the remaining threads in lines in both directions. Work fillings on this mesh.

Shadow work

Shadow work is worked on a transparent material such as organdie, lawn or muslin. The design should consist of narrow shapes with smooth edges. Transfer the design onto the wrong side of the material with a hard pencil. Use a soft thread such as stranded cotton/floss or crewel wool. Work herringbone on the wrong side of the area to be covered. The stitches on the right side look like continuous back stitch. Single lines should be worked in stem stitch which will also show up as back stitch on the right side.

If you find it easier to work from the right side, trace the design onto the right side and work one back stitch on the top outline, working from right to left (left to right). Then work one back stitch on the lower outline. Make the next back stitch on the top outline. Continue in this way along the line. If you turn the work to the wrong side, you will find herringbone stitch. Any single lines worked on the right side should be worked in back stitch.

Mountmellick

This type of whitework originated from the place of that name, near Waterford in Ireland, in the first half of the nineteenth century. It was worked there on a material known as white jean which resembles a cotton drill. The material used should be strong to hold the weight of the stitches. It consists of chunky stitchery worked in cotton threads, with a coarse cotton thread for padding. Its main characteristic is one of texture, with many bullion knots and French knots worked in solid blocks. Traditional designs were naturalistic, often of flowers, leaves and berries. Useful stitches include feather stitch, coral, seeding, ordinary satin stitch and padded satin stitch. Changes in tone, even though worked in one colour, are achieved by varying the different weights of stitch. Laid fillings may be used and these form an attractive contrast to the denser areas. No drawn thread or open work is included.

The edges of the work may be finished with a buttonhole fringe using a heavy thread. Turn down a single turning to the wrong side on the edge. Work buttonhole stitch with the looped edge at the edge of the fold. After one buttonhole stitch, bring the thread down under the left (right) thumb, for about 1·5 cm (1 inch) to form the first loop. Insert the needle at the top of the buttonhole stitch, alongside the previous stitch. Bring out as usual for the second buttonhole stitch. Hold the thread down again for the next loop. Make the next buttonhole stitch and continue. A pencil can be inserted into the loop of the fringe as you work to make it even in length. The loops of the fringe should not be cut.

Right *Detail of a cushion cover in Mountmellick.*

Cut work

Cut work is an embroidery method where parts of the background materials are cut away from the design. Traditionally, cut work was done on a fine closely woven linen in white or a natural colour. However, today it can be worked in any colour on a non-fraying material which may be as fine as organdie or on a heavier woollen material or cotton and wool blend.

Coton à broder works well on most fabrics. For decorative work such as on a garment which can be dry cleaned, one strand of crewel, Persian or tapestry wool is effective, depending on the scale of work being done. Use a crewel needle.

There are certain restrictions on design for cut work. In simple cut work, the background spaces must not be too large or they will fail to support the embroidery, although in Richelieu embroidery, the spaces are strengthened with decorative bars. In both methods, buttonhole stitching is worked on the right side of the material, over a pair of parallel lines, generally about 3 mm ($\frac{1}{8}$ inch) apart, with the looped edge against the space to be cut out.

Right *Cut work mat in Richelieu.*

Simple cut work

Prepare the design with a double outline. Work small running stitches all round and just within both lines of the design. Do not pull them tightly or the work will twist. They will act as a slight padding for the buttonhole stitches. Cover the running stitches by working buttonhole stitches from left to right (right to left). Insert the needle into the material on the inner line, pointing towards you. Place the working thread under the point of the needle from left to right (right to left). Repeat this stitch along the line, so that the stitches lie closely side by side. Each stitch should lie at right angles to the double outline, except at corners and points, when the stitches will have to be spaced out or lengthened.

When the buttonholing is finished, use a pair of small sharp-pointed scissors, and carefully cut away the material close to the looped edge of the stitches. If the outer edges are buttonholed, trim away the material close to the looped edge of the stitches.

In order to avoid cutting the wrong area by mistake, it is a wise precaution to colour a drawing of the design, indicating the areas to be cut. Once cut in error, the material cannot be repaired.

151

Richelieu

The decorative bars worked to strengthen spaces are worked before the buttonhole stitching. Plan the position of the bars on paper before you start work. Mark these lines on your material. They should be arranged so that the spaces between them are about the same size. If there is a point or sharp corner on the design which is included in the area to be cut out, a bar should be worked from it. In Richelieu, the bars may be twisted, buttonholed or woven. When working any type of bar, work the holding stitches within the double lines to avoid them showing and to prevent them from getting snipped during the cutting out of material.

Buttonholed bars

Start by working the running stitches as in simple cut work. When you reach the position for the first bar, carry the thread across to the position of the bar opposite. Pick up a small piece of material near the inside of the outer line; return to the first end of the bar and pick up a small amount of material, then return back to the opposite end and repeat the small stitch. Work close buttonhole stitching over these three threads, taking the needle under the threads but not through the material. At the end of the bar, continue working the running stitches until the next bar is reached. Work another bar, continuing in this way until all the bars are worked. Finish working the running stitches.

Darned bars

To work darned bars, work running stitches as for buttonholed bars; lay four or six threads from one end of the bar to the other; then weave under and over two or three threads at a time, depending on the number laid, until you reach the opposite side.

Twisted bars

To work twisted bars, work the running stitches. In the position for the first bar, take the thread across to the opposite side, picking up a small amount of material. Pass the needle under the thread several times, to obtain a twist. Pick up a small amount of material at the beginning of the bar and continue with the running stitches. Twisted bars are less strong than the other methods, and should be kept short.

Branched bars

In order to keep the buttonholed bars relatively short, it is sometimes necessary to work branched bars. Lay the threads for a bar. Work buttonhole stitch up to the position for the adjacent bar. Lay the threads for this bar, work buttonhole stitch along these back to the join. Complete the original bar.

Picots

Bars may be embellished with picots. For a loop picot, work part of the buttonholing on a bar, then insert a pin into the material beneath the bar to hold the loop of the last buttonhole stitch in place. Insert the needle under the loop on the pin, and twist the working thread once round the point of the needle. Pull through and pull up tightly to secure the picot. Remove the pin and continue with the bar as before.

A bullion picot is worked by buttonholing to the position of the picot. Take the needle under the loop just made. Twist the working thread round the needle about six times. Pull the needle through carefully, keeping the twisted thread near the bar. Continue the buttonhole stitching, pushing the next stitch close to the one before the picot.

Buttonholed ring

As a change from the bars, another filling can be used. A buttonholed ring worked independently gives added decoration and is a means of filling a larger space. Make a small ring by winding thread about six times round a pencil or rod of the required size. Slide the thread off, leaving the end hanging. Thread this up in a needle and work buttonhole stitch all round it. Darn the end into the stitches on the wrong side. Pin the ring into position on the material. Work twisted bars out from the design outline to the ring and back again. At least four or five twisted bars are needed to hold a buttonholed ring in position.

Once all the bars and rings are worked, complete the work by buttonholing round the double outline of the design, as in simple cut work. Finally, carefully cut away the material round the edges and behind the bars.

Baby's dress in Richelieu

Any of the motifs on this baby's dress would be suitable to work on other garments such as a blouse, dress or on lingerie. As a variation, the motifs could be worked in freehand stitchery. If you line the yoke, it will not be necessary to have a scalloped edge.

Materials required
1·70 metres (2 yards) of 90 cm (36 inches) lawn or other fine, closely woven material in white or a pastel colour
4 skeins stranded cotton/floss
3 tiny buttons
Fine sewing thread

Draw up the pattern to full size, allowing 1 cm (½ inch) turnings as indicated. To avoid having a seam through the centre of each side motif on the skirt, the pattern must be positioned so that the warp threads run round the hem of the skirt. It is best to work tacking/basting all round the outline of the pattern pieces, and work the embroidery before actually cutting out and making up.

Once you have practised the method of working Richelieu, you will find that you only need one line of running stitches. Work the running stitches on the outer edge of the buttonholing, i.e. on the outlines of the design. The threads laid for the bars must be worked so that they are enclosed in the tiny buttonhole stitches. Leaf veins should be worked in stem stitch.

The ladder-like openwork is done by working the bars first; then work buttonhole stitch on each side before removing the material.

When all the buttonholing is completed, carefully cut away the open areas with fine scissors.

Make up the dress according to standard dressmaking principles, easing and gathering as indicated.

Turn in the raw edge at the hem by 1 cm (½ inch), then fold it again, positioning it just below the decorative stitching. Work hemming stitches all round.

To do the scalloping, work running stitches close to the raw edges, then work buttonhole stitches at right angles to the edge.

Back skirt cut 1 — gather — opening — fold
Front yoke cut 1 — fold
Back yoke cut 2
Sleeve cut 2 — ease
Front skirt cut 1 — gather — centre front fold
area for cut work motifs

1 square = 4cm (1½ inches)

fold — 1 — 2

1. Base of skirt motif*
2. Sleeve motif
3. Yoke motif*

Motifs are shown actual size.
*When tracing, place fold of paper
along lines indicated to obtain
complete motifs.

fold

Patchwork and quilting

Patchwork

In the late eighteenth century the idea evolved of using up spare pieces of material by stitching them together to form coverlets. At that time, the material was folded and cut into simple shapes such as diamonds, triangles, rectangles and squares. Later, when more unusual shapes were used, the template was developed.

From the old patchwork quilts which still exist, we can see the materials and types of print from which dresses were being made at the time. In the eighteenth century, cotton prints were used whereas during the nineteenth century, silk and velvet were fashionable, and the remnants of these were used for patchwork. Some of the early examples were combined with quilting for warmth, hence the expression patchwork quilt.

Today we have a wealth of materials from which to draw and since many people nowadays do their own dressmaking and soft furnishing at home various scraps are often readily available. The patchworker becomes a collector of pieces of material, however tiny, for this is essentially a thrift craft which uses up left-over materials. Patchwork is a form of needlework which often appeals to those who do not enjoy other decorative methods. Only a few small items of equipment are needed for even the most complicated patchwork.

The different methods of working patchwork which are described here are template patchwork (including clamshell), block construction, log cabin, cathedral window and Suffolk puffs. They can be worked on a large scale, but equally well, tiny items such as pincushions, spectacle cases and insertions for paper weights can be made from patchwork. A garment may be made entirely in patchwork, or it may have a motif or border applied to its hem or sleeve. A piece of patchwork can, in fact, be substituted for a piece of material for most purposes, providing you plan the shape of the area required as it is not wise to cut through the joined up patches.

Generally the same type and the same weight of material should be used within one piece of work. Avoid using springy, fraying materials which are made from man-made fibres. Pure cotton is the easiest to use but the more expert you become, the greater will be your choice of material; lightweight woollens, fine tweeds and silks can all be made into enchanting patchwork. Corduroy may be used and an interesting play of light will result if these materials are used with the grain in different directions.

Patchwork does not consist of joining up pieces of material in a haphazard fashion. The materials available should be planned into a purposeful pattern and each scrap of material used with thought. A patch of dotted material, for example, could be cut out with the dot centred rather than just cut out at random.

Some patchwork, although beautifully made, lacks the sparkle of other pieces. Sometimes this is due to lack of planning, more often it is because the colouring tends to be without variation in tone. Include materials which are of light, medium and dark tones: unbleached cotton provides a light tone and the inclusion of some white in a piece of pale patchwork will give contrast.

Sewing thread for patchwork should be fine and of the same type as the material used – for example, cotton thread on cotton fabric. Some people like using white cotton throughout, or black if the patches are predominantly dark. No. 50 is generally the finest cotton thread available. If you want to use a thread which matches the patches being joined, mercerized cotton comes in a wide range of colours. For joining patches of silk, use a pure silk sewing thread. If using synthetic materials, or mixtures of synthetic and natural fibres, join patches with a synthetic thread. Tacking/basting thread may be used when tacking/basting. Use sewing silk when tacking/basting silk material or glazed cotton which would retain thread marks if any other thread were used.

Right *A mid-nineteenth-century American patchwork quilt in the Star of Bethlehem design.*

Sewing needles will be fine sharps or crewel, size 8 or 10. The choice of needle will depend on the thread you are using. Pins can be brass, lace or dressmaker's steel pins.

Sharp scissors are needed for cutting out pieces of material and a second pair of scissors used exclusively for cutting paper (or a craft knife) will be needed for cutting out templates. A cutting board will be needed if you use a craft knife.

The underside of both template and log cabin patchwork should be protected by lining.

Template patchwork

Templates are metal, plastic, or cardboard shapes and may include different sizes of hexagon, long hexagon, diamond, triangle and square. Many people prefer to use professionally made templates to be sure they are accurate. When buying a template, the measurement given indicates the length of one side.

Window templates are not essential but are often sold as a pair with the template. A window template is made of transparent plastic which has an opaque frame 6 mm ($\frac{1}{4}$ inch) wide. The width of the frame is the turning allowance for each patch. It enables the patchworker to select a certain area of material, making sure, for example, that a flower sprig falls in the centre of a patch. It is also helpful to be able to see the grain of the material when cutting out. A window template is not needed when cutting patches of plain or all-over patterned materials.

Papers are needed to mount each patch, before joining up. The paper should be thin enough to take a needle through comfortably, but strong enough to support a patch of material.

For the following method of working template patchwork, the 2·5 cm (1 inch) hexagon has been used. This is a good average size but larger or smaller hexagons could be used. Other shapes are worked in the same way except when making turnings of the material over the paper.

Cutting out

Place the template on a piece of the paper. Hold the two together and cut round with paper-cutting scissors. If you prefer to use a craft knife, place the paper on the cutting board. Put the template flat on the

Constructing a hexagon.

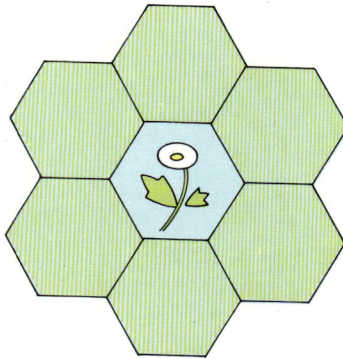

Making a rosette, keeping the grain vertical throughout.

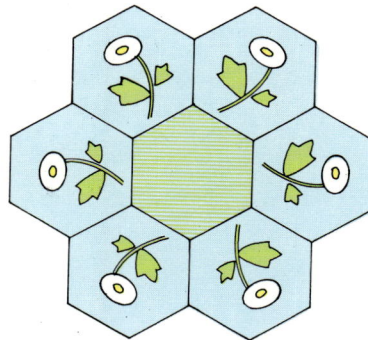

Making a rosette, radiating the fabric pattern from the centre.

Combining hexagons and diamonds.

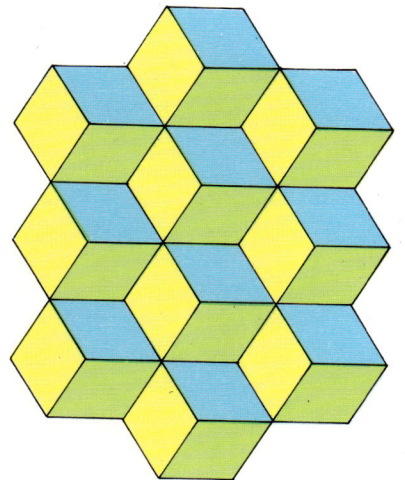

'Baby block' patchwork pattern using diamonds.

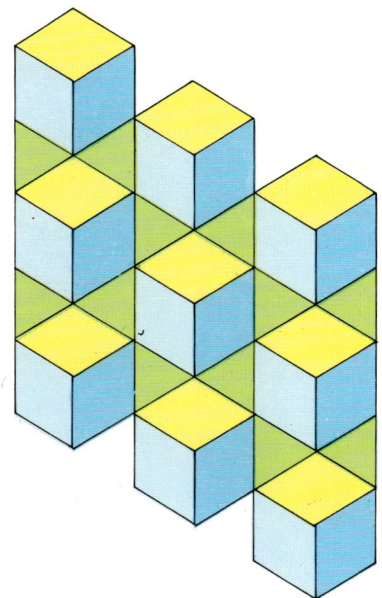

Combining diamonds and triangles.

paper and, holding it firmly, cut round it. Do not draw lines round the template as this may result in papers of uneven sizes. It is not wise to cut more than two papers at once. Cut out a batch before starting work. Throw away any which are not cut accurately.

Patchwork is usually best if the grain of the patches is constant. Try to plan the patches so that the warp threads run from top to bottom throughout. However, once the method has been learnt, striped materials can radiate from a centre hexagon, or be matched sideways.

Cut out each patch with turnings 6 mm ($\frac{1}{4}$ inch) larger than the template. It may be necessary to allow more on some materials. If using a window template, the extra turnings are already included.

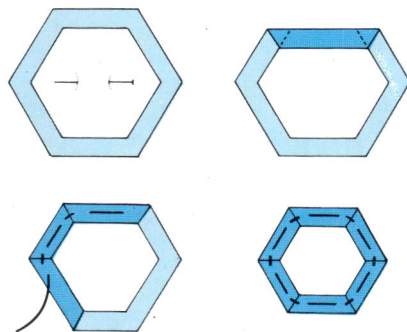

Making patches

Place one paper in the centre of the wrong side of a patch. Pin it in the centre. Fold one edge over the paper and tack/baste it in place. Start with a knot on the right side of the patch. Work one stitch towards the end of the first side. Turn down the second side and take the needle down into the double fold at the corner. Make another stitch working towards the next corner. Repeat this on the following four sides, with holding stitches at each corner. Fasten off with a back stitch. A hexagon with sides longer than 2.5 cm (1 inch) will need more than one tacking/basting stitch at each side; the edges of the material should be held down flat on the paper.

Joining patches

Do not start joining until you have a large number of patches made and you are sure of their position. Place the right sides of two patches together. Start by working three or four oversewing stitches from left to right (right to left) towards the corner before working over them from right to left (left to right) up to the end of the seam. Fasten off by stitching back over a few stitches already worked, or leave the thread ready for joining the next patch. Open up the patches so that they lie flat, pick up the next patch, place it in position and continue oversewing. The stitches should be fine and the patches should be placed with the corners matching or gaps will occur. Make about seven stitches to 1 cm ($\frac{1}{2}$ inch), keeping a smooth tension so that when the patches are opened out they lie flat without puckering, and they are firmly held together. The oversewing stitches should skim through the top of the fold and should not pierce the paper which can be used repeatedly so long as it is not damaged.

To practise the method make a single rosette from seven hexagons, one of which should be in a plain or in a contrasting tone to the remaining six and will be used for the centre. The rosette can be the start of a larger article or it can be applied to a background material with hemming stitches, as a decoration for a cushion, garment or bag.

The removal of papers which are required for more patches should be done at intervals. Do not remove any papers from patches which are still to be joined to other patches. Alternatively, all the papers can be left in until the work is finished.

When making up a piece of hexagon patchwork, you will be left with an irregular line at the sides. Either fill in the spaces with half a hexagon to obtain a straight edge, or back each hexagon with another at the edges before making up the article. Piping makes a good edging for a patchwork bedcover.

Using diamonds

The preparation of the papers and the cutting out of the patches is the same as for hexagons. To make a diamond the points need careful handling and a different treatment.

Place a paper in the centre of the wrong side of the patch, turn down one side and tack/baste in place. Before tacking/basting down the point make an extra fold there by turning down the projecting piece. Fold over the turning on the next side and hold it in place. Fold over the third side before making another extra fold at the lower point. Tack/baste the last side in place, using back stitches at each point. To make a star from six diamonds join three together, then another three, before joining each group in one seam. This method avoids having a tiny hole in the centre of the star. Another pleasing arrangement of diamonds is the box pattern, which requires materials in dark, medium and light tones.

Hexagons and diamonds may be worked independently, or they may be used in patterns which combine the hexagon and the diamond providing the sides of each are the same length.

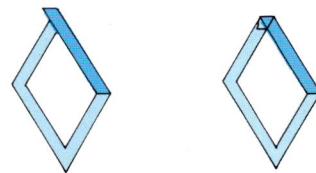

Unusual shapes

The preparation of square, long hexagon and triangle patches is based on that of the hexagon and diamond. If you wish to make patchwork in shapes not available commercially, make a firm cardboard template with straight edges and accurate corners.

To work a free design in patchwork, prepare a copy of your design on strong paper; cut out the pieces. Tack/baste each piece of material onto its paper shape and join it to the next piece with oversewing stitches. Any curved patches should be clipped at the edges as in dressmaking methods.

Suede and leather can be used for patchwork but instead of mounting the patches onto paper with turnings, the edges are joined with oversewing stitches. When cutting out the patches use a craft knife against the template.

Making patches.

Joining patches.

Planning patchwork designs

One of the delights of patchwork is the astonishing number of designs that can be constructed from only a few basic shapes. Even a patchwork made of one repeated shape, such as a hexagon, can take many different forms, depending on the arrangement of the fabrics and the shape of the design. Often arranged in rosettes, as in the bedspread opposite, hexagons can also form borders, lozenges and garlands, as shown in Fig. 1. But once you start combining squares and triangles, for example, or octagons and squares, you find that the design possibilities are virtually endless.

Traditional American patchwork shows an amazing ingenuity in devising patterns mainly from squares, triangles and diamonds. Three examples are shown in Fig. 2. (The middle design uses appliqué for the diagonal strip.) Star shapes are popular motifs in American patchwork. The Eight Point Star (Fig. 3, page 164) is made of parallelograms – or, viewed another way, lopsided diamonds – in squares and triangles. Expanded as shown in Fig. 4, it becomes the Star of Bethlehem design. Diamonds on their own, using three fabrics in contrasting tones, can be joined to make the fascinating, 'three-dimensional' Baby Blocks pattern (Fig. 5).

Simple projects in patchwork

To learn patchwork techniques, begin with a small object. A potholder, for example, is quickly made. Try using the same design on both sides, altering the placement of fabrics.

Some patchwork trimming on a plain garment will give it a lift. Pockets, a border for a skirt or a yoke are some of the possibilities.

A cushion cover is also a relatively easy project. You can make an elegant one using two or three shades of silk, cut in squares or rectangles and stitched together with plain seams, as in the block method described below.

Block construction

Block construction is the traditional method used for American patchwork, in which patches of different shapes, or of the same shape in different sizes, are joined together in a regular sequence to make square blocks, which in turn are joined to make the complete pattern.

The individual patches are cut out as already described on pages 160–161, but are joined with ordinary seams, stitched along the seamline (now usually by machine) with right sides together. The sequence of joining depends, of course, on the block's design, but the principle is always that all the smaller units are joined before going on to join the larger ones. Fig. 7 shows the method of joining patches for the Whirlwind design. When all the blocks are completed, they are joined, again with plain seams, into strips (Fig. 8). Finally, the strips are joined to make the complete patchwork.

Many variations can be made on a single block design. Sometimes blocks are separated by strips of plain fabric or alternated with plain blocks chequerboard fashion, which has the effect of giving the design a

Fig. 1

Fig. 2

Fig. 3

Fig. 4

Fig. 5

more subdued character. Blocks can also be joined in a diagonal pattern. Different effects can be created by altering the positions of the fabrics within the blocks – for example, by placing the darker-toned fabrics towards the centre of a block instead of at the edges.

Clamshell patchwork

The clamshell is the most difficult of the patchwork shapes to handle, but well worth mastering in order to make the pretty fish scale pattern shown in Fig. 9.

Before you attempt a fish scale pattern, try using the shape separately, as part of an appliqué. Four clamshells made in pretty printed fabrics and applied to a table napkin with their lower corners touching make an attractive 'clover' motif – and will give you good practice in working with the shape.

Use purchased clamshell templates – a window template and a solid one. Cut the patches using the window template, then use the smaller solid one to mark the seamline centrally on the wrong side. Using the solid template, cut patches from lightweight interfacing. Pin the interfacing patch inside the seamline on the fabric patch (Fig. 10), and tack/baste the turnings over it, as you would over a patchwork paper. When going round the top edge make the tacking/basting stitches very small and gather up the turning allowance to fit smoothly. Clip the side edges so that they will lie flat when tacked/basted in place. Press

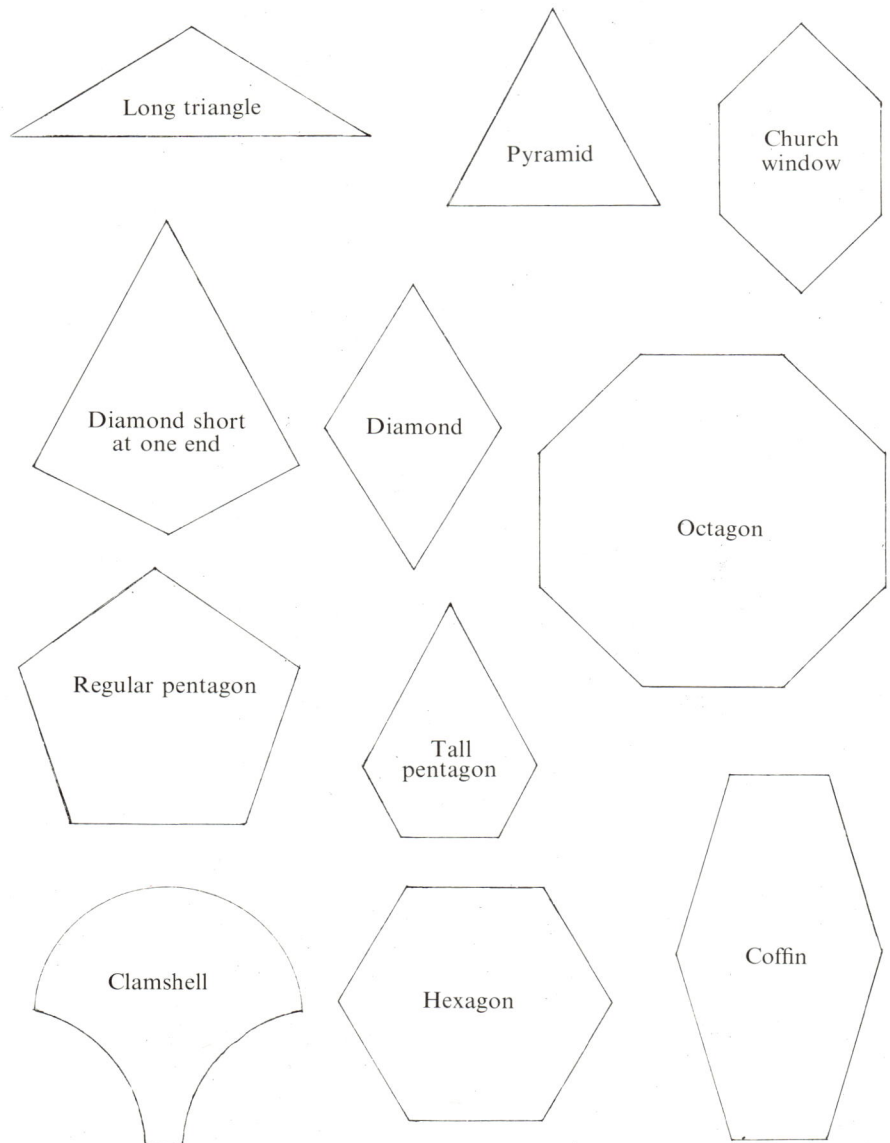

Fig. 6 The traditional shapes used in patchwork

164

the patches and slip stitch them to the background fabric.

To make the fish scale pattern, use paper patches and turn under only the top edge of the patch. Gather it to fit, using tiny stitches without going through the paper. Leave the remaining turnings flat. When you have made the required number of patches, join them in rows, starting at the top and working downwards. The top edge of each shell overlaps the side edges of two shells just above it, exactly on the seamlines. Make sure that the patches are aligned exactly horizontally (check this with a ruler). Tack/baste them together along the curved edges, then slipstitch them together with tiny stitches.

Fig. 7

Fig. 8

Row 1

Fig. 9

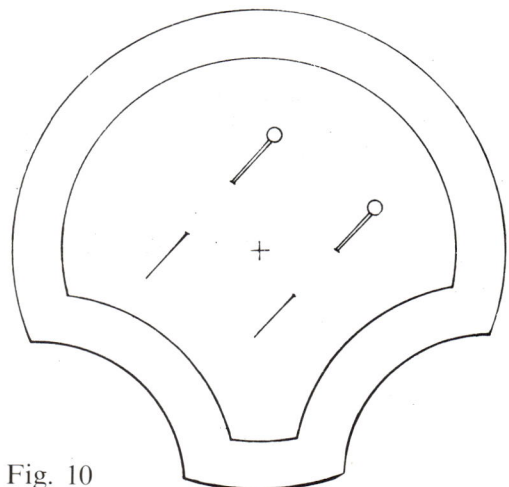

Fig. 10

165

Patchwork bedcover

This attractive single bedcover is made in template patchwork, using 57 mm ($2\frac{1}{4}$ inch) hexagons, half-hexagons, diamonds and triangles.

The design is built up of thirteen large hexagonal motifs, each of which is itself built up of seven hexagon patches and twelve triangles. A star made of six diamond patches is at each point of the large hexagon motifs. Between each star are two half hexagons.

Materials required
Cotton fabrics for the patches
5 metres ($5\frac{1}{2}$ yards) of 90 cm (36 inch) cotton material for the lining
Templates: 57 mm ($2\frac{1}{4}$ inch) hexagon, diamond and triangle
Sewing thread

The diagrams show one complete quarter of the bedcover. Make up the whole of the centre rectangle first. Then make up four strips for the border, two for the long sides and two for the short sides. Make up four squares for each corner piece.

Join the borders to each side with oversewing stitches, right sides together, then attach the corners.

Cut the lining into two lengths and join them down the centre with a plain seam. The lining should be 18 cm (7 inches) longer and wider than the piece of patchwork made. Turn under 1 cm ($\frac{1}{2}$ inch) along all four edges and tack/baste in place.

Place the wrong side of the patchwork to the wrong side of the lining, matching the centres. Pin and tack the two together all over, working on a flat surface. Fold the side edges of the lining over the patchwork, tack/baste them in place, and hem with closely worked slip-stitching. Repeat this at the top and bottom edges.

To avoid ballooning, work tying stitches through the two thicknesses of material at intervals of about 30 cm (12 inches) all over the work. Use a double thickness of sewing thread. At a point where there is a join of patches, bring the needle from the wrong side to the right side and back. Tie the ends of thread firmly in a knot at the back and leave an end of about 5 mm ($\frac{1}{4}$ inch) before cutting off.

centre

centre

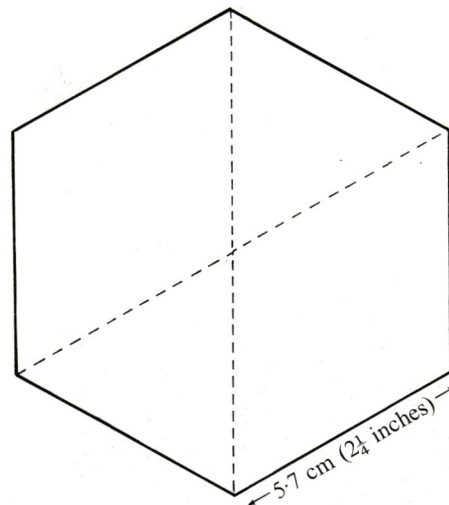

5·7 cm ($2\frac{1}{4}$ inches)

Making a diamond, triangle and half hexagon from a hexagon

Detail of patches of one quarter

centre

Log cabin patchwork

This is a completely different way of using up left-over pieces of material. Strips of cotton material are stitched in rotation onto a square backing material, built up around a small centre square. Calico/unbleached muslin is a cheap, suitable backing.

The size of the backing square may be up to 30 cm (12 inches) for a large article such as a bedcover. Several of these squares will then be joined together. A cushion can be made up of a single square, or it can be built up of several smaller squares. Make a paper pattern and cut out the backing squares. Press one backing square and fold it in half diagonally in both directions, to mark its centre point. Open it out and lay it flat. For a 10 cm (4 inch) square, cut out a 3 cm (1¼ inch) square of patterned or plain material following the warp and weft. Place it in the centre of the backing square and work running stitches close to the edge. This small square does not need to have any turnings. From now on, straight strips will be stitched on in a clockwise direction, lapping over one another.

Draw a diagram on paper to show the lengths required for each successive strip. Four pieces of each length are needed. The width of each finished strip on the diagram, in this instance, is 2·5 cm (1 inch), less the width of two turnings each 5 mm (¼ inch). Cut out the strips following the grain of the material.

Pin one of the shortest strips in place, with the right side of the strip to the right side of the centre square. Work running stitches 5 mm (¼ inch) from the edge. Turn the strip over to expose the right side, and press flat. The second strip is then attached in the same way, over the folded end of the first. Continue in this way gradually building up until you reach the edge of the backing square, each strip covering the raw edges of the previous round of strips.

Traditionally each complete square was built up of light-coloured strips on two adjacent sides with dark colours on the other two sides. Plain materials mix well with patterned ones. More patterns can be created by placing the squares in different positions.

To join up squares, place two squares together, with the right sides facing. Pin and work running stitches along the seam, or use a sewing machine. The raw edges of the last round of strips will be enclosed.

Right *A log cabin patchwork bedcover. The strong diagonal lines are created by using dark strips on adjacent sides of joined squares.*

1. Draw a diagram on paper showing the lengths of each strip.

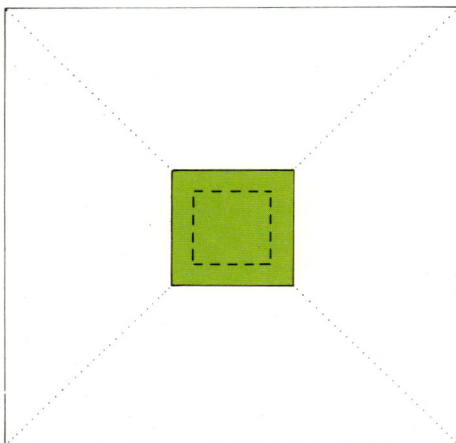

2. Work running stitches round the centre square.

3. Pin and stitch one of the shortest strips in place.

4. Pin and stitch a second short strip in place.

5. Continue stitching strips in place.

6. A finished square.

Cathedral window patchwork

This type of patchwork is so called because the all-over pattern formed resembles the tracery of a cathedral window. It consists of folded squares of material which, when joined, envelop squares of a contrasting material, giving a considerable amount of body. Once joined, no further lining is needed. It takes a long time to make a bedcover with this method but smaller pieces may be made into cot covers, cushions, bags, or be applied to a garment.

Accurate cutting, folding and stitching is essential, so it is necessary to choose a material which maintains a crease when folded. A cotton material such as natural or white calico/muslin for the main squares is very suitable if the contrasting fabrics used are pieces of non-fraying cotton with small-scale prints.

The patches may be made of any reasonable size. Press the material before cutting out. A useful size for practising the method is obtained by cutting out a 15 cm (6 inch) square from a piece of unbleached cotton, following the warp and weft threads. Crease or press the diagonals of the square to find the central point. Turn in narrow turnings of about 5 mm ($\frac{1}{4}$ inch) on all sides. You will now have a square of about 14 cm ($5\frac{1}{2}$ inches). Fold each corner to the

centre point and pin in place. The measurement of each side becomes about 10 cm (4 inches). Then repeat the folding movement by placing each point to the centre. Pin these folds into place and remove the first set of pins. Secure the corners firmly in the centre by working small stitches through two points at a time. The square measures about 7 cm ($2\frac{3}{4}$ inches). Make a matching second square with the same measurements, also in unbleached cotton. To join the two squares, place the right sides together. The flat sides will be outside. Work oversewing stitches to join one side, using a matching sewing cotton.

Cut out a square of the contrasting material, following the warp and weft threads. It should be just smaller than the diagonal square obtained by joining two folded squares. Place it in position over the seamed edge of the two main squares, and pin it carefully.

Take one folded edge of the cotton which is alongside the raw edge of the contrasting square. Turn it back over the square, holding it in place with the thumb and first finger of the left (right) hand. Stitch the folded edge down with small running stitches, worked with up and down movements, taking the needle down through to the back of the cotton, so that the folded fabrics are

held firmly together. Hemming stitches may be used if preferred. At each corner, work two back stitches to hold adjacent folds together firmly.

At the edges of a piece of cathedral window patchwork, half squares will be left. There are two ways of dealing with these. Firstly, continue the pattern, make a fold down the centre of a square of printed fabric, with the wrong side of the material inside. Trim off to within 5 mm ($\frac{1}{4}$ inch) of the fold through one thickness. Pin the material in place. Turn down the folds onto the print on two sides of the square, and stitch into position. Work oversewing stitches along the edge, to hold together the folded edge of the cotton square and the folded print.

The second method is to leave the triangles of cotton plain at the edges. Stitch down the folds on two sides of each square to make the edges firm in a simple way.

To maintain the charm of this patchwork it should not be pressed with an iron after the squares have been formed.

Right *A floor cushion in cathedral window patchwork, showing a careful combination of soft-coloured prints on calico/muslin. Small circles of suede emphasize the joins.*

1

2

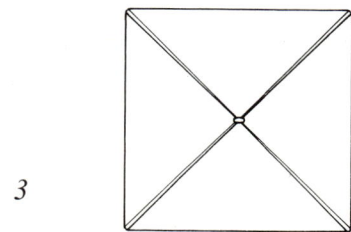

3

1. Make turnings on all sides of the square.
2. Fold the corners to the centre.
3. Fold the corners to the centre a second time.
4. Pin a contrasting square on two joined patches.
5. Turn back folded edges and stitch.

4

5

Suffolk puffs

This delightful form of patchwork consists of circles of material which are gathered up and joined. It needs no making up or lining, although it can be mounted on a background material if wished. Suffolk puffs can be made into a full-size bedcover or a cot cover or cushion. They make an attractive decoration on clothing, where they can be used as separate motifs on a background fabric, or they may be built up in clusters.

To make Suffolk puffs you will need a circular paper template. This can be made from strong brown paper or fine cardboard. For general use, a template of 9 cm (3½ inches) in diameter resulting in a patch of about 3·75 cm (1½ inches) across is suitable. For smaller patches of very fine material, a template of 5 cm (2 inches) in diameter will make a puff patch of about 2 cm (¾ inch).

Avoid using heavy material which will not gather up well. Cotton prints and plain cottons are the most suitable. Soft woollens, including Viyella®, gather into well-formed puffs and have the added advantage of providing warmth. Georgette and muslin, if worked on a small scale, are a charming form of decoration on special clothing. Silk material gathers up beautifully and will make up into a bag, yoke of a dress, or a cushion.

The thread used for the gathering should be strong and of a matching colour as it will remain permanently in the puffs. Use mercerized sewing cotton, buttonhole twist, or one of the man-made threads on most cotton or synthetic materials. On fine georgette or silk, use pure sewing silk for gathering.

To sew the puffs together, use mercerized sewing cotton, except for silk materials which should be sewn with pure silk, and synthetics which require a man-made thread.

Pin the circular template onto well-pressed material and cut it out with sharp scissors. Remove the paper.

Pin down a single turning of 6 mm (¼ inch) onto the wrong side. Using strong thread, make a double back stitch at the edge, through the double material. Work gathering stitches all round the edge of the circle, through double material. Pull up tightly and fasten off by taking the needle through to the back of the puff. Fasten off with several back stitches. When cutting off the end of the thread at this stage, leave about 6 mm (¼ inch) so that it is secure. By taking the thread through to the back, any possible 'ballooning' of the puff is avoided. It is essential to start and fasten off firmly, to avoid problems with the gathering at a later time. The gathered side of the puff is the right side of the work; the flat side is the wrong side.

To join up the puffs, place two together, gathered sides together and the flat sides outside. Work several oversewing stitches, securing the end firmly, as described for joining patchwork hexagons. It is not necessary to fasten off. Instead, slide the needle through the fold, to the next side to be joined. Practice will show how many stitches are needed at each join. Too few will result in an insecure, flabby piece of work, too many will pull the work unnaturally out of shape. The circular shape of each patch is bound to be slightly lost, but remember that the shapes that show between the joined patches form an integral part of the finished piece. The work should not be pressed after the gathering is done.

Right *A detail of Suffolk puff patchwork.*
Right below *Individual Suffolk puffs decorate a skirt.*

1. Circular template.

2. Work gathering stitches.

3. Gather up puff.

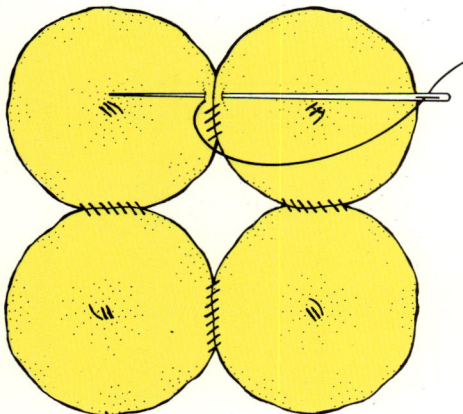

4. Oversew the puffs together.

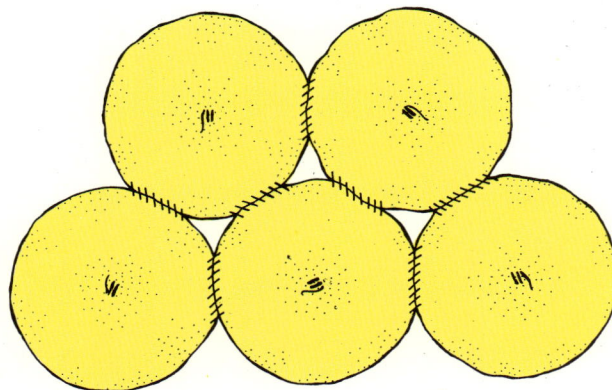

5. Alternative arrangement for joining puffs.

Quilting is an age-old craft which grew out of the need for warm garments in times when even indoors there was little heating. Two layers of cloth, with wool sandwiched between them, helped to keep out the chilly air. In time the stitching used to hold the layers together began to be worked in decorative patterns. Inspiration for some of these patterns came from natural objects – leaves, flowers, feathers and shells. Some examples can be seen on pages 176–177. Patterns also acquired regional characteristics, so that quilts made in one area could be distinguished from those made in another.

Many traditional British regional patterns crossed the Atlantic to America with the early settlers, who also devised new patterns. In America quilting came to be closely associated with patchwork and was used mainly for patchwork quilts. A woman would make a number of blocks of patchwork and join them together, then her friends would gather in her home to help her work the quilting stitches. These quilting 'bees' were popular social occasions.

Hand-quilting on a large scale is less frequently done today, though in America it is enjoying a revival. Small items such as cushions, handbags and articles of clothing readily lend themselves to hand quilting and can be worked relatively quickly. And with a sewing machine quilting can be worked literally in minutes.

But machine quilting, though it has its uses, lacks something of the charm and quality of hand stitching.

Besides wadded or padded quilting, there are two other kinds: trapunto, in which a design is stitched through two layers of fabric and parts of the design filled with stuffing inserted through the underside, and corded quilting, which is essentially the same as trapunto, except that the design is made of parallel lines through which yarn is inserted. These methods are more fully explained on pages 182–184.

Frames
A traditional quilting frame consists of two long bars of wood called rails, over which the fabric is rolled when

not being stitched, and two others called stretchers, to which the sides of the quilt are attached with woven tape to keep the fabric taut. Relatively lightweight collapsible frames, which can be adjusted for different sizes, are available. A full-size frame can also be constructed at home, using two trestles, the rails and stretchers and some G-clamps/C-clamps.

For small quilted projects you can use a slate/scroll frame, as used for canvas work, or a standing ring frame. Large oval ring frames are very useful for quilting. The frame must be free-standing, as you will need both hands for the stitching.

Machine quilting
No frame is required for machine quilting, which is a good way to quilt simple designs, especially on children's clothes, where the effect is more important than subtlety of workmanship. Avoid quilting very large items by machine, as they are difficult to manoeuvre on the small working surface.

For stitching the lines of a grid pattern, you can use a quilter guide-bar attachment, which runs along the previous line of quilting, helping you to keep the new line parallel to it. With a little practice you can also work curved designs by machine, though very complex designs involving continual turning are best avoided.

The machine can also be used in making perforated patterns for quilting. Enlarge the design to the correct size, then stitch over the lines with an unthreaded machine. Apply the design to the fabric using pounce powder, as explained on page 180.

In machine quilting, as for hand quilting (explained fully on pages 178–181), it is important to tack/baste the layers together firmly before working the design. Place the lines of tacking/basting about 5 cm (2 inches) apart, in a grid pattern.

Finishing the edges
There are three methods of finishing the edges of a quilted object.

The edges of the top and backing can be turned in and a line of running stitches worked as near to the edge as possible. A second row of stitching is then worked 6 mm ($\frac{1}{4}$ inch) inside the first one.

A piped edge is used on cushion covers, on the edges of quilted gar-

ments and sometimes on babies' quilts.

On coverlets the backing material is cut slightly larger than the top. It is then turned over the top and hemmed in place. Alternatively, the edges are trimmed and bound with a bias strip cut from the same fabric as the top, or from a contrasting fabric.

Points to remember
In planning a quilted bedcover, avoid placing a seam down the centre. Instead, use a full width of fabric for the centre, cut another width in two lengthwise and stitch these pieces to the sides of the centre piece.

When making a quilted garment, remember that the process of quilt-

Tapestry and embroidery frames can be used for quilting small items.

ing will cause the fabric to shrink slightly. Allow generous turnings on all quilted pieces. Plan your quilting design on the paper pattern, matching the lines at seams and avoiding darts.

Child's quilt

For your first quilting project, try a simple quilt for a baby's cot, worked by machine in a square pattern, following the lines of a checked fabric (shown on page 174). The finished quilt measures about 82×62 cm ($32 \times 24\frac{1}{2}$ inches).

Materials required

Cotton gingham 90 cm (36 inches) wide, 1·5 m ($1\frac{5}{8}$ yards)
Synthetic wadding/batting 90 cm (36 inches) wide, ·5 m ($\frac{5}{8}$ yard)
Fine sewing thread

Making the quilt

Cut two pieces of gingham, each 70×50 cm ($27\frac{1}{2} \times 19\frac{1}{2}$ inches), for the top and backing of the quilt. From the remaining fabric, cut and join 10 cm (4 inch) wide strips to make a strip 3·6 m (4 yards) long. Join the ends of the strip to make a ring; this will be used for the frill.

Cut the wadding to the same size as the fabric pieces and tack/baste it to the wrong side of one piece (the backing).

Fold the frill in half and press the two folds. Run two lines of gathering stitches 1 and 1·2 cm ($\frac{3}{8}$ and $\frac{1}{2}$ inches) from one edge, beginning and ending at the folds. Pin the frill to the right side of the backing, matching raw edges and placing the pressed folds at the centres of the short ends. Pull up the gathering threads until the frill fits round the quilt, adjust the fullness evenly, and tack/baste the frill in place. Pin and tack/baste the top piece to the backing piece, right sides facing, so that the frill lies between them. Stitch through all the layers, 1·2 cm ($\frac{1}{2}$ inch) from the edge, leaving a gap of about 20 cm (8 inches) on one side.

Turn the quilt right side out. Fold in the turnings along the opening and tack/baste and slipstitch them together.

Using pins as markers, plan the positions of the lines of quilting. The lines should be about 6.5 cm ($2\frac{1}{2}$ inches) apart.

With the machine set for a fairly long straight stitch, work straight across the fabric in both directions, using the fabric strips as guides. Begin and end the stitching just at the frill, and when the quilting is complete take the ends to the wrong side and fasten them off securely.

Quilting patterns

Elongated Diamonds

Double Diamonds

Circular patterns are easily made using wine glasses or teacups. A variety of patterns can be created by combining circles as shown here.

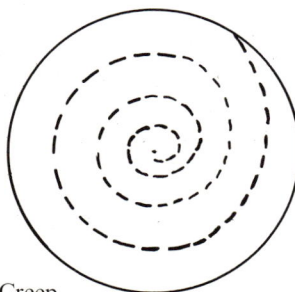

Snail Creep

Here are some traditional quilting patterns. In every case the pattern outlines should be marked onto the fabric before stitching is begun. On the left are two patterns based on straight lines. Use the patterns on this page same size or enlarge them. Mark only the outline on the fabric; the dotted lines are stitched while working.

Rose

Shell

Fan

Star

Feather Circle

Thistle

Banana

Welsh Tulip

Paisley Flower

Goose Wing

Paisley Pear

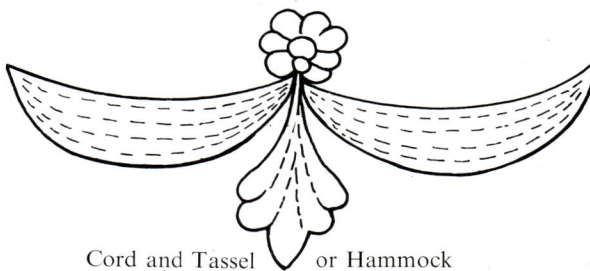

Cord and Tassel   or Hammock

Tulip

Lined Twist

177

In quilting, two or more layers of materials are sewn together by stitching patterns, in order to raise the surface of the top material. The high and low relief of the surface provides the decoration. Traditionally quilting was worked for warmth on clothing and bedcovers or as a protection under armour. There are several ways of achieving this type of work. Three methods are described here: wadded quilting which gives an all-over padding, corded quilting which consists of padded lines, and trapunto quilting where certain areas only are padded.

Wadded quilting by hand

This consists of three layers of material, the middle one of wool or some other warm filling. It is used when warmth or weight is needed. The stitching on the wrong side is the same as on the front. It may be used for quilted bedcovers or cot covers, bags, cushions and headboards, as well as for quilted clothing such as the bodice of a dress, a housecoat or skirt. A band of wadded quilting at the hem of a long skirt will give added weight and is delightful if used for part of a garment such as a yoke or pocket.

Material for quilting should ideally be closely woven and plain coloured, cotton, fine wool such as Viyella® or lightweight linen. Silk can be quilted but is more difficult to handle. Suede and leather also quilt well in this method but require a fabric backing. Some knitted fabrics quilt successfully and, being uncrushable, are practical for everyday use. Carefully chosen patterned material can be quilted, although the printed pattern should not dominate the quilting. A fine cotton print is easy to work but not a harsh fabric.

If making a quilted bed or cot cover, it is best to use the same material for the backing as for the top so it is reversible. This decision will, however, depend on the choice of top material. You may decide that you need a finer one, or one of a contrasting colour. If your quilting is part of an article which will not be seen from the wrong side, a muslin or scrim may be used for the backing.

There are several fillings available and the choice will depend on what is being made. Fillings which will need to be dry cleaned include soft wool fabric which is easy to handle, cotton wadding or batting, or one or more layers of a flannel-type material. Carded lamb's-wool may also be used. For an article which is to be washed, use a synthetic filling such as polyester wadding or batting. This is available in several weights and is particularly suitable for bedcovers.

For the stitching, use a fine sharp or crewel needle and a thread which is similar in type to the top fabric. It is best to use cotton on cotton materials, silk thread on silk materials, and synthetics on materials of man-made fibres. The colour of the thread should be of a slightly deeper tone than the top material. Although it is the stitches which create the high and low relief of the quilting, they themselves should not be predominant.

Wadded quilting may be done in the hand, but it is best worked on either a ring or a slate/scroll frame. A large qilting frame is advisable for working a full-size quilt.

When choosing a design, consider the whole area to be covered. Traditionally a quilt would consist of a centre motif, borders with corners and an all-over background filling. However, there are no rules and the design may equally well be a simple geometric pattern built into an all-over design, or a non-repeating design with subjects such as landscapes, flower shapes, a simplified aerial view or an idea from a photograph. Bear in mind that the function of the quilting lines, which may be curved or straight, is to hold together three layers of material, so there should not be too much distance between the stitching. If the lines are too close, the quilting effect will be spoilt. Generally the stitches should not be more than 3 cm (1¼ inches) apart, but it is impossible to be specific as each instance will vary.

Right *Quilted hot-water-bottle cover.*
Below *A linear quilting design.*

178

An experimental piece of work will show the varying effects obtained from stitches enclosing areas of different sizes. A good way of practising wadded quilting is to prepare three layers of material, with the top one of a lightweight patterned material. By stitching round the pattern you will be working the basic method and see the effect.

An important part of quilting is transferring the design onto the material. It may be put onto the top material by means of running stitches through tissue paper (page 18), before or after framing up. This is the method to be used for a non-repeating pattern.

A geometric repeating pattern may be transferred to cotton or linen by the use of a metal or cardboard template. When the materials have been framed up and tacked/basted together, use a blunt needle to scratch the material round the template. Each part of the design should be scratched just before stitching, as the marks will disappear even overnight.

The two methods of transfer for the design described are suitable for quilting done in running stitch. If, however, back stitch is to be worked, the prick and pounce method may be used for greater accuracy as the painting line will be covered. Alternatively, if using a muslin backing, the design can be painted onto that and the quilting can be worked from the back, in running stitches.

If using a slate/scroll frame, first stitch the backing, wrong side uppermost, to the frame and lightly lace the sides. Lay the filling on top of this, spreading it outwards so that it lies flat. Then lay the top material, right side uppermost, on the filling, matching the grains of all the materials. Smooth the top material outwards from the centre. With the frame slack, work tailor tacking/diagonal basting (page 65) from the centre outwards towards each side. This will blend the three layers together as one.

If working in the hand or in a ring frame, lay the three layers flat on a table with the backing at the bottom, wrong side upwards, the filling, and then the top material with its right side upwards.

The preparation for quilting takes some time, but the project will only be a success if all these preparatory stages are carried out carefully.

Work running stitches through all three layers. The stitches should be even and regular, to obtain the same-sized stitch on the back. It is a help to work with a stabbing action, down and then up in a separate movement. Keep your eye on the back, particularly at first, to ensure that you are enclosing all three layers. Start and fasten off with back stitches, running the end of the thread into the filling. Snip the tacking/basting stitches as you come to them, so that they do not get stitched in with the running stitches.

When the quilting is finished, remove it from the frame; no further stretching or pressing should be done. To make up, treat the quilting as if it were a single fabric and use standard dressmaking or soft furnishing methods. To neaten the edges of a bed or cot cover, trim away the wadding to the required size. The front and back materials should be about 1 cm ($\frac{1}{2}$ inch) larger all round than the required size. Turn this allowance to the inside, and hold the two edges together with running stitches. Piping may be inserted if desired.

Above *Tailor-tacking/basting through three layers.*
Right *Working running stitch with a stabbing action – down and up in separate movements. The cross-section shows the stitches passing vertically through the layers of material.*
Facing page *Designs suitable for wadded quilting.*

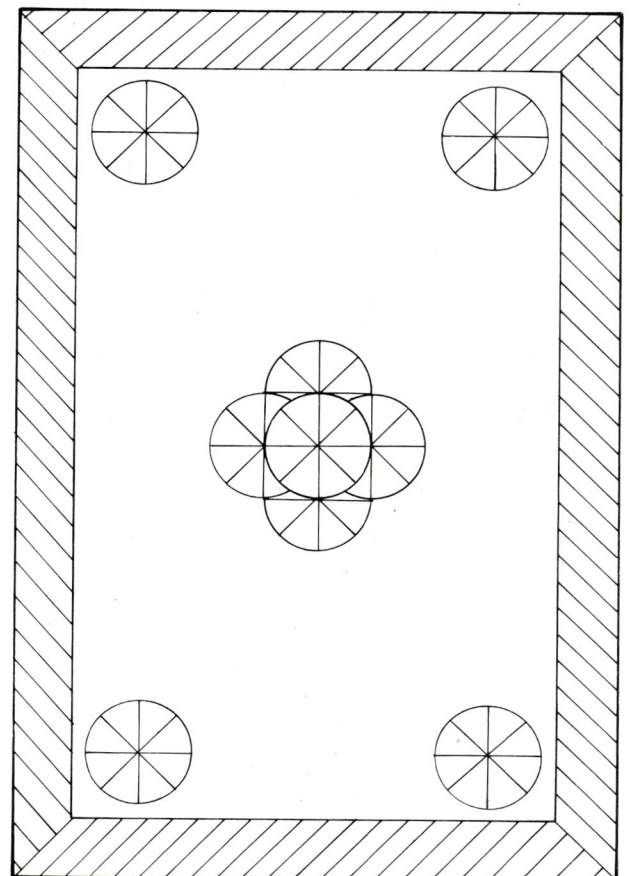

181

Corded quilting

Only two layers of material are used for corded quilting. They are joined by means of pairs of parallel lines of stitching, through which cord or yarn is threaded to give a raised quilted effect and create a linear design. This type of quilting is mainly used for decoration on clothing or accessories, or on items for the home such as curtains or cushions. Corded quilting can also be combined with trapunto quilting which is described on the following page.

The material for the top layer should be a smooth, closely woven cotton, linen or lightweight wool. Suede and soft leather may also be used. For the backing, use fine muslin or scrim. The filling, which is inserted after the stitching is done, is usually white and should be either quilting wool or a thick yarn such as two strands of double knitting worsted. These provide a soft pliable padding. If a harder padding is required, use a cotton piping cord which is available in a good range of thicknesses. For general purposes, size 3 or 4 are suitable. The piping threads used for padding should be pre-shrunk (soaked in hot water and dried) before inserting into the work

if the article is likely to be laundered.

Corded quilting is usually worked without a frame. Before starting work, experiment to see that the distance between the parallel lines of stitching will be correct for the filling thread you are using. The sewing thread should be similar in type and colour to the top material; use a fine sewing needle for the stitching and a large tapestry or darning needle for threading the yarn or cord.

Corded quilting can be worked in regular or interlacing geometrical patterns of squares, stripes or circles. Free designs may also be used. Each line must be repeated with a second parallel line which should be about 3 or 4 mm ($\frac{1}{8}$ inch) away, to allow for the filling thread.

Attractive patterns may be created by pinning cords onto a soft board. They can be overlapped or interlaced. Place a piece of tracing paper over the cord, trace the design and draw it out carefully before transferring it to the back layer of material. Paint the design onto the backing, using the prick and pounce method, or tack/baste the design through tissue paper. The latter is less satisfactory for accurate results.

Press the top material. Place it flat on a table with the wrong side

upwards. Lay the muslin over this, matching the grains of the two materials, smoothing it carefully. Pin into position and work tailor tacking/diagonal basting all over, from the centre outwards.

Work running stitches along all the pairs of parallel lines, with the backing towards you. Start and fasten off with back stitches, taken through the muslin only. When the whole design has been stitched, thread up the yarn or cord into a tapestry needle or bodkin, and, with the muslin uppermost, make a small hole in the muslin and run the needle between the parallel lines. Be careful not to go through the top material. Leave an end of 3 mm ($\frac{1}{8}$ inch) protruding at the beginning and end. Work the needle gradually through the channel. Bring it out at a point or curve in order to leave a small loop of cord before re-entering the needle in the same hole of the muslin. The cord is acting as a padding and the small loops allow for movement and prevent the material from twisting. If threading cord into a circle, start and finish at the same point, to get a continuous padding.

Corded quilting should be lined, to protect the looped padding on the wrong side.

Leave a loop at points and curves when threading cord through parallel lines.

Above *Three designs suitable for corded quilting.*
Above right *Miniature cushion in corded quilting.*
Right *'Waves' in corded quilting worked on organdie with coloured cord.*

183

Trapunto quilting

This form of quilting is sometimes known as padded quilting. Usually, two thicknesses of material are used, and the areas of the design which are enclosed with stitching are filled with padding from the underside. It may be used on clothing or accessories and it is the method used to pad areas on a panel or wall hanging. It can also be used for appliqué and it combines well with freehand stitches.

Most closely woven materials will quilt in this way. Use fine muslin or scrim for the backing. For the padding, you can use lamb's-wool, wadding/batting or cotton wool/absorbent cotton. Use a fine sewing needle, and a thread similar in type and colour to the top fabric. Other threads may be needed for additional freehand stitches. A frame will be helpful for a large piece of work.

Designs may be geometrical or free; the raising of the surface of the material will give a three-dimensional effect and will create light and shade which is unique to this method. When planning the design, keep the shapes simple and avoid sharp points where possible. Large areas of design may need to be divided up into smaller sections. To experiment, try working circles or squares of different sizes from 1·5 cm ($\frac{5}{8}$ inch) upwards.

Press the top fabric. Tack/baste or paint (with fine lines) the design onto the right side of it. If working in the hand, lay the two fabrics flat on the table, the muslin below the top material. Smooth the two together and match the grains, then work tailor tacking/diagonal basting to hold them in place. If using a frame, frame up the top fabric with the right side at the top. Turn the frame and lay the muslin on the wrong side of the top material. Join the two with tailor tacking diagonal backing.

Using sewing thread, work back stitch all round the outlines of the design. Start and fasten off with back stitches into the muslin. Once the design is completely outlined, turn the work to the wrong side. To pad small areas up to about 2·5 cm (1 inch) square, push the threads of the muslin aside in the centre of the area to be filled. Poke in a small amount of the padding and push it to the edges with the pointed end of a knitting needle. Repeat this, putting in a small amount at a time to avoid lumps; turn the work to make sure a smooth padding is being produced on the right side. Once you have filled it sufficiently, work the muslin threads back into place to cover the wool.

Large areas are padded by another method. They are similarly filled with wool, but it is necessary to slit the muslin carefully with small sharp scissors in one direction down the widest point of a shape and following the woven thread. Cut to within 5 mm ($\frac{1}{4}$ inch) of the stitching. Pad the area, using the knitting needle, pushing the wool to the edges first and gradually filling the shape. When the area is padded, sew the edges of the slit together, inserting the needle under the muslin to left and right alternately.

1. Slit the backing and pad.

2. Sew the edges of the slit together.

For small areas, push the threads of the backing aside and poke in the stuffing.

Left Simple designs suitable for trapunto quilting.
Right 'Green Dorset' design. Trapunto quilting is combined with fabric-covered cardboard and embellished with straight stitches.

184

Smocking

Smocking

Smocking is worked on gathered material as a decorative means of controlling fullness. When fashion demands loose fitting and full garments, it is an attractive and functional embroidery method. If straight close-fitting clothing is in fashion, smocking may be used as a textured decoration set into an otherwise plain garment.

The smock is of Anglo-Saxon derivation, a shift-like garment without decoration worn in England for many centuries. Decoration on smocks came into general use by countrymen in the mid-nineteenth century and was usually in self colour on smocks of heavy natural hand-woven linen.

Smocking in the first half of the twentieth century became associated with children's wear, when material in pastel shades was delicately smocked beneath a yoke. Nowadays, however, fashion and colour are more important than the age of the wearer and the traditional method of smocking has been adapted to suit the fabrics, colours and styles of the present time. Not only is it possible to use smocking on clothing, but also on accessories and furnishings for the home. A curtain heading may be smocked, if it is not to be drawn across the window. Pelmets/valances can also be made with smocking instead of gathers or pleats. Many variations of bags may have smocking as part of their construction. Wherever material is gathered, it can be held in place with smocking stitches, some of which will allow the material to stretch more than others.

As the decorative stitches are worked entirely on material which is to be gathered, it is helpful at first to choose a material which lends itself to gathering. Generally, fabrics of natural fibres gather better than those of man-made fibres. Materials which smock well include cotton ginghams and lawn, fine woollens and wool-cotton blends and pure silks. Corduroy, fine tweed, hessian/burlap and some lightweight furnishing fabrics can be used and soft leather and suede are effective with self-coloured smocking. Some fine synthetics such as polyester and cotton mixtures and lawn are delightful to work on, and, having drip dry qualities, are practical in use. Remember to consider the washing or dry-cleaning properties of fabrics before starting to make a garment.

When choosing fabric, try and visualize the effect that gathering will have on the pattern of a material. For example, gathering a two-coloured striped material may bring one colour to the top of the fold on the right side, or the effect can be completely changed by bringing the second colour to the top. However, if the stripes are wider than the gathers, you will not end up with a particular colour lying at the top of each fold.

A dotted material may appear to be ideally suited for gathering but it should be studied carefully to ensure that the printed dots follow the weft threads of the fabric. Often they slant in one direction, away from the true weft. To overcome this, it is possible sometimes to turn the material so that the gathering will lie along the warp threads. Avoid turning the material in this way if the garment being made will rely on the natural stretch of the weft threads.

The width of material to allow will depend on the fabric selected and on the depth of fold taken up by the gathering. As a general guide, most fine materials need three to four times the finished width. Small experiments will soon show how the depth of gathering will influence the final result.

For the gathering, use a strong mercerized sewing thread preferably in a contrast to the material. For the smocking stitches, the choice of thread will depend on the material being used. On clothing, coton perlé and coton à broder are effective. Coton perlé no. 5 is used on Viyella or gingham; finer material such as lawn may need no. 8. Soft embroidery cotton is attractive on furnishing fabrics and hessian. A twisted silk or buttonhole twist is sympathetic to suede or leather and does not damage the skin. Use a sewing needle for the gathering and a crewel needle for the smocking.

If smocking plain material, self-coloured thread is attractive, as it is the folds of material which form the characteristic of this technique. One contrasting colour may also be used. Different coloured threads result in confused smocking and, if working on a fine print, it is best to emphasize just one colour.

Smocking is done before a garment is made up. Cut out the pieces, allowing the required width for smocking, and neaten any edges which may fray.

Gathering

On striped, checked or some dotted materials, do the gathering visually. On plain or patterned material mark out dots on the wrong side with a transfer or pencil and ruler, keeping straight with the threads of the material. Do not use a transfer on fine material as it will show through to the right side and spoil the finished result. A transfer may be cut and splayed out if required for a curved area. The first row of dots should be 1 cm ($\frac{3}{8}$ inch) above the position required for the first row of smocking stitches. An average spacing is 1 cm ($\frac{3}{8}$ inch) both between each dot and between lines.

To gather, use a thread long enough to go across the width without a join. Start with a knot on the wrong side, pick up the first dot on the right (left) hand side, of the top line. Make a double back stitch for strength. Take the needle down half-way between the first and second dot, and up into the second dot. Continue this to the end of the line. Leave a loose end of thread, about 8 cm (3 inches) long. Start again at the right (left) hand side and repeat these lines of gathering until all the dots are used up. Done in this way, the folds above and below the gathering threads will be equal in depth. On striped or checked material, work gathering stitches in the same way.

When the gathering stitches are finished, place the material flat on the table in front of you. Carefully pull up all the gathering threads in the left (right) hand. At the same time, ease the folds into place with your right (left) hand. Pull up the gathering thread tightly to help the folds to form clearly. Now ease out the folds to about two-thirds of the width required finally. The tension of the stitching as well as the stitches used will affect this measurement. Do not fasten off the gathering threads with a needle, as these holding stitches are awkward to remove. Instead, place the material flat on the table, twist the gathering threads together in pairs down the side of the gathering, starting at the top. As you reach the second pair, join them into the twist. Continue in this way until the last pair are included. Tie a simple knot just below the twist. Oversew the threads to the fabric just above the knot to stop it from slipping. Cut off the surplus gathering threads 2·5 cm (1 inch) below the knot. If a very deep area of smocking is to be worked, this process can be divided into sections to avoid too long a twist. Turn the material to the right side and spread out the folds evenly. This completes the preparation.

Above *Working gathering stitches.*
Top right *Gathering up and twisting thread.*
Right *Splaying out a transfer for curved areas.*
Below left *Regular checks can be used as a guide for gathering.*
Bottom left *Use even stripes as a guide for gathering. The dots indicate a suitable positioning.*
Below right *Dots are needed on some printed fabrics.*
Bottom right *Gather alternate lines on spotted fabrics.*

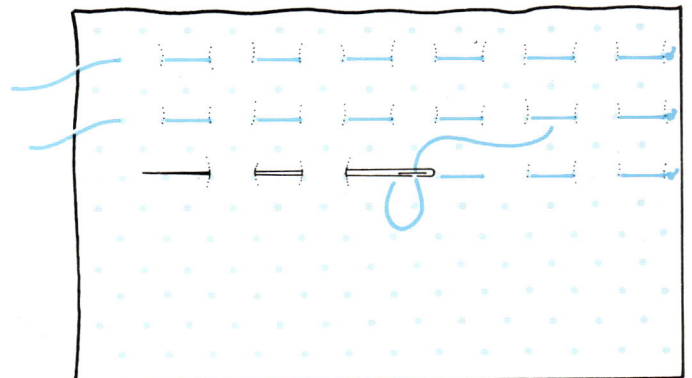

Smocking stitches

The gathering threads, which are visible between the folds on the right side, act as guide lines on which to work. The first line of the gathering controls the position of the folds, during smocking; the first line of smocking should be on the second line of gathering. If it is to be used below a yoke or as an inset, it is best to start with one of the outline smocking stitches such as stem stitch or double, alternate, or double alternate stem stitch. Any of these control the gathers firmly. However, if more elasticity is required, use one of those with stretch such as diamond, chevron or honeycomb stitch.

Freehand stitches which may be used for smocking include *herringbone* which is worked on folds and *feather stitch* worked by picking up one new fold for each movement.

To start working, use a knot at the end of the thread. Bring the needle up from the wrong side to the left of the first fold on the left, working from left to right. Make a small back stitch through the top of the first fold to secure the thread. You are then ready to start working the stitches.

To fasten off, take the needle down to the wrong side, through the outside of the last fold. Turn the work to the wrong side and sew several times over the embroidery thread which is visible on the underside of the last fold. Leave 5 mm ($\frac{1}{4}$ inch) of thread before cutting off.

Whenever possible, use a thread which is long enough to smock across the whole of one line. If a join is essential, fasten off as described above and start again, making the join as inconspicuous as possible. Only the top of each fold is picked up for each stitch. The needle should be inserted at right angles to each fold, parallel to the gathering threads, unless working a stitch which uses slanting movements.

Once the smocking is finished, remove the gathering stitches. If the smocking is to be used for an insertion it will need to be lined.

Stem stitch

This is worked from left to right. Secure the thread in the first fold. Pick up the second fold, with the thread below the needle. Work along the line, picking up each fold in turn, with the thread below the needle each time. If you prefer to work from bottom to top, you can turn the work so that the folds lie in a horizontal position.

Double stem stitch

Work one line of stem stitch as above. The second line is worked from left to right, picking up each fold close to the previous line of stitches, but with the thread kept above the needle each time.

An attractive variation can be built up of a solid band of double stem stitch, but it should only be worked where little stretch will be required.

stem stitch

double stem stitch

Alternate stem stitch

This is worked from left to right. As with stem stitch, the top of each fold is picked up once but the thread is placed above and below the needle alternately.

Double alternate stem stitch

Work one row of alternate stem stitch. A second row of alternate stem stitch is worked closely to the first so that the top stitch of the second row lies alongside the lower stitch of the first row. Spaced rows of this stitch may be worked following the gathering guide lines. As a variation, bands of several rows may be worked close together, providing a mass of stitching, but restricting the amount of stretch in the folds.

alternate stem stitch

double alternate stem stitch

Chevron stitch

This combines the working of stem and alternate stem stitches. Work from left to right. Make stem stitches on different levels, inserting the needle parallel to the gathering threads. The stem stitches worked downwards should have the thread placed above the needle, whereas when working upwards, the thread should be below the needle. At the top and base of each chevron an alternate stitch is worked to change the position of the thread. One row of chevron stitch will usually cover half the distance between two rows of gathering threads.

To make a diamond pattern from chevron stitch, reverse the second line of stitches, by working upwards towards the lowest stitch of the previous row, so that the top stitch of the second row lies alongside the bottom stitch of the previous row. To obtain an all-over diamond pattern, repeat the pairs of rows of chevron stitch.

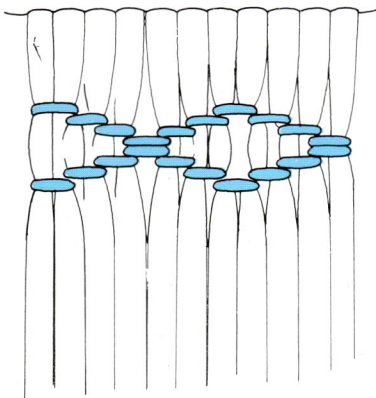

Diamond stitch

Work from left to right. Every stitch is made by picking up a new fold, with the needle pointing from right to left for each stitch. The variation is created by the position of the needle on the fold and the position of the thread.

First row 1st stitch: having made a starter stitch into the first fold on a gathering guide line, pick up the second fold with the thread above the needle. 2nd stitch: half-way between two gathering stitches, pick up the third fold with the thread above the needle. 3rd stitch: on the same level, pick up the fourth fold with the thread below the needle. 4th stitch: back to the gathering line at the top, pick up the fifth fold with the thread below the needle. Repeat these four stitches on two levels, to the end of the line.

Second row Start on the level of the next line of gathering stitches. The rotation of the four stitches made in the first row is repeated, with the top stitch of the second row lying alongside the lowest stitch of the first row. Continue in this way to the end of the line.

Another row of diamond stitch may be worked either by starting on the same level as the first stitch of the second row previously worked, or by starting on the next line of gathering, leaving a space. A band of all-over diamond stitch is very attractive and simple to work.

Honeycomb stitch

This stitch has good elasticity and if short of material for smocking, it will be the best to use. Start working on a line of gathering. With the thread on the left side of the first fold on the left, point the needle towards the left, pick up the top of the second and first folds. Pull the folds together. Then slide the needle diagonally from the right of the stitch just formed, to the left of the same fold, half-way between two lines of gathering. Pick up the third and second fold, with the needle pointing from right to left. Pull these folds together. Slide the needle upwards diagonally through the fold, to the top and to the left of the third fold. Repeat these movements along the line. If you wish to emphasize the dots made with the stitches, the first movement of each stitch can be repeated before proceeding to the next stitch. The second row is worked in the same way, starting on the next line of gathering and working each dot stitch immediately below the previous row. An all-over effect of a honeycomb is obtained by working several rows.

Vandyke stitch

This is worked from right to left. Bring the needle up on the first pleat on the right, halfway between two gathering threads, pass it through the first two pleats together and work another stitch over them; go up to the first gathering thread and work a stitch over the second and third pleats; go back down to the level of the first stitch and work a stitch over the third and fourth pleats. Continue in this way to the end of the line.

Practice piece

Polka dot fabric makes an ideal background for smocking, as you can use the dots as a guide for the gathering. Practice the smocking on a piece of dotted fabric about 25 cm (10 inches) wide and 50 cm (20 inches) deep, using these three basic stitches: *1st row* stem stitch; *2nd row* alternate stem stitch; *3rd row* stem stitch; *4th and 5th rows* diamond stitch; *6th row* stem stitch; *7th row* alternate stem stitch; *8th row* stem stitch.

You could use several different colours of thread for variety, as shown here, or just one colour.

Checked and striped fabrics are also well-suited to smocking. In gathering the fabric, pick up threads on the same part of the check or stripe with each stitch. Make your own original sample using combinations of the stitches given on this and the preceding pages.

Little girl's sundress

This charming sundress will fit a child about five years old, but it can be adapted for other sizes.

Materials required
Cotton fabric 90 cm (36 inches) wide, 1 m (1⅛ yards)
2 skeins of stranded cotton/floss
Matching bias binding (optional)

Cutting out and smocking
Cut two pieces of fabric, each 54 × 90 cm (21 × 36 inches), with the short sides along the selvedges. Cut four pieces 30 × 4 cm (12 × 1½ inches) for the ties. Cut curves for the armholes by cutting out quarter circles at the upper corners of the two large pieces, making them 7·5 cm (3 inches) deep and 5 cm (2 inches) wide.

Make a small hem, by hand or machine, along the top edge of each piece. Trace off the smocking dots opposite onto the wrong side of the front and back, 2·5 cm (1 inch) down from the hemmed edges and 2 cm (¾ inch) in from the armhole, repeating the tracing as often as required.

Gather up the fabric and secure the gathering threads.

Using three strands of embroidery thread, work the smocking pattern shown opposite. The sequence is: *1st row* double alternate stem stitch; *2nd row* half a row of diamond stitch, with another just below it; *3rd row* as second row; *4th row* alternate stem stitch; *5th row* half of chevron stitch.

1

2

Making up the dress
Press the smocking lightly under a damp cloth, taking care not to flatten the pleats. Remove the gathering threads.

Join the front and back pieces with French seams. Face the armholes, using either bias binding or

bias strips cut from the fabric. Turn up the hem to the desired length; tack/baste it in place and hand-hem. Press.

Fold the ties in half lengthwise, right sides together, and stitch along the long edge and one short edge, taking a 1·2 cm ($\frac{1}{2}$ inch) seam. Turn the ties right side out. Turn in the raw edges and slipstitch them together. Stitch the ties in place.

Baby's dress

This little dress uses a variety of stitches and is easy for a beginner to make.

Materials required
Fine fabric 90 cm (36 inches) wide,
  1·6 m (1$\frac{3}{4}$ yards)
Smocking transfer with about 30 dots
  per 2·5 cm (1 inch) square
Stranded cotton/floss, 1 skein each of
  pale pink, mid-pink, rose
Three buttons

Cutting out
Enlarge the pattern (page 194). Cut the pieces out in the fabric adding 2 cm ($\frac{3}{4}$ inch) all round for turnings; a 10 cm (4 inch) hem is included. Place pieces on the fold where indicated

Pattern diagram labels: Dress front Cut 1, Place on fold, Sew to here, Centre back, Dress back Cut 2, Straight grain, Grain, Collar Cut 4, Centre back, Straight grain, Yoke back Cut 4, Centre front, Yoke front Cut 2, Place on fold, Gather from dot to dot, Centre Shoulder seam, Straight grain, Sleeve Cut 2, Front, One square = 12mm

and on the straight grain of the fabric.

Smocking
Join the front and back sections.

Transfer the smocking dots to the backs and front, on the wrong side of the fabric, placing the first row of dots 2 cm ($\frac{3}{4}$ inch) below the top edge. Gather each row, picking up dots. Tie the threads in pairs and spread the pleats. Using two strands of embroidery thread, work as follows:

1st row stem stitch in rose; *2nd row* double alternate stem stitch in mid-pink and pale pink; *3rd row* diamond stitch in rose; *4th row* diamond stitch in mid-pink; *5th row* diamond stitch in pale pink; *6th row* alternate stem stitch in rose; *7th and 8th row* diamond stitch in rose; *9th and 10th row* diamond stitch in mid-pink; *11th and 12th row* diamond stitch worked into points in pale pink.

Remove the gathering threads.

Making up the dress
Collar and yoke Stitch one front yoke section to a pair of back yokes at the shoulders. Repeat with the remaining yoke (facing) pieces.

Pin two collar sections, right sides facing, and tack/baste and stitch the outer edges. Trim and clip turnings. Turn the collar right side out. Repeat with other collar section.

Tack/baste the collars to the yoke, right sides facing, matching centre fronts and placing back collars 1.2 cm ($\frac{1}{2}$ inch) in from the centre back opening. Tack/baste the yoke facing, right side down, over the collars. Stitch along the neck edge, grade the turnings, and turn the yoke right side out. Press.

Attaching the yoke Turn up 2 cm ($\frac{3}{4}$ inch) on the lower edge of the main front yoke section and press. Pin it in place over the skirt front, tack/baste and stitch it by hand, using tiny hemming stitches. Repeat with the yoke facing on the inside of the skirt.

Join the skirt sections at the centre back with French seams, stitching only to the dot. Attach the back yoke and yoke facings as instructed for the front yoke.

Sleeves Join the underarm edges with French seams. Work two rows of gathering stitches round the lower edges and draw up the sleeve to fit the baby's arm, plus 1.2 cm ($\frac{1}{2}$ inch)

for ease. Cut two 2 cm ($\frac{3}{4}$ inch) wide bias strips of fabric, slightly longer than the gathered edge. Pin and tack/baste them to the right side of the sleeve, right sides facing and edges matching. Stitch the ends of the strip together. Stitch round the edge of the sleeve, between the rows of gathering. Press the strip away from the sleeve. Turn under the raw edge and slipstitch to wrong side of sleeve. Remove gathering thread.

Gather up the sleeve heads/caps to fit the armholes. Pin and tack/baste the sleeves into the armholes, right sides facing, matching the centre mark to the shoulder seam and the side to the underarm seam. Distribute the fullness evenly. Stitch. Remove the gathering threads, trim the seam and cover with bias strips.

Hem the back neck opening. Make three buttonholes and stitch buttons to other edge.

Finishing
Turn up a double 5 cm (2 inches) hem and tack/baste it in place. Using deep pink embroidery thread and small running stitches, top stitch the hem. Work running stitches round the sleeve to match.

Traditional smock

This present-day version of the traditional smock is made of linen, but other closely woven materials suitable for a dress or blouse which will gather up well could be used.

Materials required

3 metres (3¼ yards) of 90 cm (36 inch) material
2 balls coton perlé/pearl cotton no. 5 in each of three tones of colour (light, medium and dark)
Sewing thread for making up
5 domed button moulds for covering

Draw up the pattern to full size. The diagram is for size 86 cm (34 inch) bust but being a full garment it can be readily adapted to other sizes. Turnings of 1·5 cm (⅝ inch) are allowed everywhere except at the lower edge of the front and back, where 3·5 cm (1½ inches) are allowed.

Pin the pattern on the material and mark out the shapes with tacking/basting. Do not cut out the pieces before smocking as the material may fray while working.

To work the smocking, mark out dots or use a transfer with holes about 4 mm (⅛ inch) apart to make stitches and spaces each 4 mm. The rows of gathering should be spaced 1 cm (⅜ inch) apart.

Gather to the following lengths:
Smocking area A front smock, to 10·5 cm (4¼ inches)
Smocking area B back smock, to 28 cm (11 inches)
Smocking area C top of sleeve, to 10 cm (4 inches)
Smocking area D lower edge of sleeve, to 7 cm (2¾ inches)

Work stem, alternate, double alternate, and diamond smocking stitches in the three tones.

Make up the garment, following standard dressmaking principles, before working the freehand stitches. These consist of ten spaced rows of back stitch, whipped back stitch, twisted chain, coral and feather, in any arrangement. The pockets should be decorated before setting into position.

To cover a button, mark out on the material the circumference of the button with tacking/basting. Work a star stitch in embroidery thread, to fill this circle. Leaving adequate turnings for the size of your button, cut out the material. Remove the tacking/basting and make up the button. Then work back stitch on the spokes of the star stitch, as for a woven wheel (see page 36).

Collar cut 1
fold
place to shoulder seam
Back yoke cut 1
c.b. fold
buttonhole
centre front
smocking
Front yoke cut 2
Pocket cut 2
smocking area B
smocking area A
yoke seam
yoke seam
smocking area C
underlap
fold line
Back cut 1
centre back fold
Front cut 1
centre front fold
Sleeve cut 2
smocking
fold line
Cuff cut 2
buttonhole
slash for opening
smocking area D
pleats
pleats
fold line
buttonholes
Front opening tab cut 2
1 square = 4 cm

Smocking

Back yoke

Front yoke

Smocking

Front

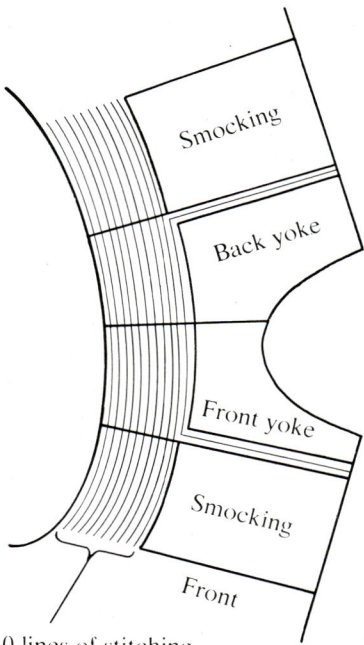

10 lines of stitching
evenly spaced

Pocket

Collar

Cuff

position of
freehand stitches

Fabric craft

Fabric craft is not strictly a craft; the term covers a group of needlework techniques. Its special characteristic is the imaginative use of fabric – choosing exactly the right fabric for the project and using the colour and the design to develop the basic idea. Often the inspiration for a toy or an accessory comes from the fabric itself.

To enjoy fabric craft fully it is essential to have a rich collection of fabric scraps. Buy end-of-season remnants, choosing them for pattern, colour and washability. Collect dressmaking remnants from friends, and hoard scraps of trimmings and ribbons.

Tie and cravat

Make this elegant necktie using a purchased pattern; for the matching cravat, follow the simple instructions below.

Materials required
For the cravat
Patterned crease-resistant fabric 70 × 36 cm (27½ × 14 inches)
Lining fabric, the same amount
For the necktie
Patterned fabric 90 cm (36 inches) wide, ·8 m (⅞ yard)
Interfacing, ·6 m (¾ yard)

Making the cravat
Enlarge the pattern as indicated. Cut the pattern from a double layer of printed fabric; repeat with lining fabric. Mark the pleats on the patterned pieces with tacking/basting.

Pin the patterned pieces together with right sides facing; tack/baste and stitch them together along line A–B. Press the seam open. Repeat with the lining.

Pin the patterned and lining pieces together with right sides facing; tack/baste and stitch them together round the edges, leaving an opening on one neck edge. Trim the seams, clip the corners and turn the cravat right side out. Slipstitch the opening edges together and press.

Fold the broken lines to meet the solid lines and tack/baste the pleats in place. Stitch from C to D and from A to B. Press.

Cravat   Scale: 1 square = 1·2 cm (½ inch)   Cut 2   Straight grain   Stitch across here   Pleat   Pleat

Hot pot holders

Brightly printed fabric makes these attractive kitchen accessories (shown on page 200).

Materials required
Oven glove
Printed fabric 90 cm (36 inches) wide, ·3 m (⅜ yard)
Plain fabric, the same amount
Matching bias binding
Stranded cotton/floss (optional)
Synthetic wadding/batting
Oven mitt
Printed cotton 90 cm (36 inches) wide, ·5 m (⅝ yard)
Plain fabric, the same amount
Matching bias binding
Synthetic wadding/batting

Making the oven glove
Enlarge Fig. 1 as indicated and cut it twice in patterned fabric, plain fabric and wadding. Embroider round a motif on one piece, if you like. Place both wadding pieces between the bottom patterned piece and a lining piece, with the right sides of the fabric outwards, and tack/baste round the edges. Tack/

Fig. 1   Glove   One square = 1·2 cm (½ inch)

Fig. 2   Mitt   One square = 1·2 cm (½ inch)

baste the remaining two pieces together, wrong sides facing. Bind both wrist edges. Join the layers with zigzag stitch and cover the edges with binding.

Making the oven mitt

Enlarge Fig. 2 as indicated and cut it out twice in patterned and plain fabric. Placing wrong sides together, tack/baste and stitch a patterned piece to each plain piece. Bind the edges.

Cut two pieces of plain fabric, each 68 × 20 cm (27 × 8 inches), and

one or two pieces of wadding the same size. Pin them together with the wadding inside and right sides facing outward. Pin the mitt sections on top. Join the layers with zig-zag stitch. Trim and bind the edges.

Breakfast set

Sunny yellow fabric is ideal for brightening the breakfast table.

Materials required

Printed cotton 122 cm (48 inches) wide, ·5 m ($\frac{5}{8}$ yard)
Synthetic wadding/batting, the same amount
Double-edged broderie anglaise/eyelet lace 2 cm ($\frac{3}{4}$ inch) wide, ·5 m ($\frac{5}{8}$ yard)
Gathered broderie anglaise/eyelet lace, the same width and amount
Narrow broderie anglaise/eyelet lace, 1·3 m (1$\frac{1}{2}$ yards)
White bias binding, ·5 m ($\frac{5}{8}$ yard)
Narrow elastic, ·3 m ($\frac{3}{8}$ yard)

Making the tea cosy

Using a compass, draw a 23 cm (9 inch) diameter circle (Fig. 1) and mark the centre (A). Draw a vertical line through A. Mark point B, 6 cm (2$\frac{1}{2}$ inches) below A and draw a horizontal line (C–D) through it. Mark point E, 2 cm ($\frac{3}{4}$ inch) from the top edge of the circle and draw a horizontal line (G–H) through it.

Extend line E–F to 2·5 cm (1 inch) (point J) and draw a 15 cm (6 inch) horizontal line (K–L) through it. Join points K–G and L–H. With the compass point at A, draw an arc from K to L. Cut out the pattern, omitting the shaded section. Draw a 12·5 cm (5 inch) diameter circle for the base.

Cut the main pattern four times and the base twice from printed fabric, adding 1·2 cm ($\frac{1}{2}$ inch) turnings. Cut the main pattern twice more and the base once from wadding, without turnings.

Tack/baste a double wadding piece to the wrong side of each lining piece and to the wrong side of one base. Place each lining piece on an outer piece, right sides facing. Tack/baste and stitch all round, except for the straight edges. Trim the seams, clip the curves and turn each piece right side out. Turn in the raw edges and tack/baste them together. Pad and stitch the base piece

EGG COSY

RIGHT SIDE

Fig. 2a

Fig. 1

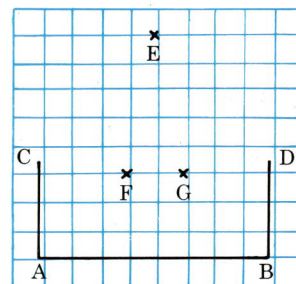

Fig. 2 One Square 1·2 cm ($\frac{1}{2}$ inch)

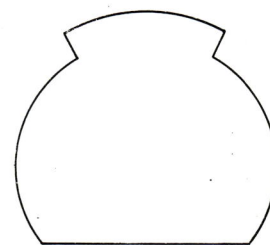

the same way. Slipstitch the opening edges together. Tack/baste the two side pieces to the base with corners touching and oversew the lower edges together.

Stitch bias binding to the wrong side of the broderie anglaise. Thread elastic through it and join the ends of the lace. Draw up the elastic to fit the neck of the cosy. Insert the teapot, then slip the ring over the sides.

Making the egg cosy

Enlarge Fig. 2 as indicated, including all markings. With the compass point at F, draw an arc from E to D; with it at G, repeat from E to C.

Cut the pattern in fabric four times, allowing 1·2 cm ($\frac{1}{2}$ inch) for turnings, and twice in wadding, without turnings.

Tack/baste the wadding to the wrong side of each lining piece. Stitch the two lining pieces together, right sides facing, leaving the lower edges open.

Stitch gathered broderie anglaise on the seamline of one outer piece (Fig. 2a). Place the other piece on top, right sides facing, and stitch again, leaving the lower edges open. Trim the seam and turn the cosy right side out.

Slip the lining into the cosy. Turn in the lower edges and slipstitch them together.

Making the napkin

Cut a 30 cm (12 inch) square of fabric. Neaten the edges with zig-zag stitch and trim them with narrow broderie anglaise.

Striped bathmat

Diagonal stripes in bright colours make a handsome bathmat (shown on page 202).

Materials required

Terrycloth towelling, 1 m (36 inches) wide, 1·3 m (1$\frac{1}{2}$ yards) of dark blue, ·3 m ($\frac{3}{8}$ yard) each of pale pink and turquoise, ·2 m ($\frac{1}{4}$ yard) of orange

Thick crochet cotton in orange, 50 g (2 oz)

Making the bathmat

Cut a piece of the dark blue terrycloth 50 × 65 cm (19$\frac{3}{4}$ × 25$\frac{1}{2}$ inches) for the underside of the mat. Cut another dark blue piece to the measurements given in the diagram.

Cut the strips to the measurements given. Each strip is 10 cm (4 inches) wide, and all measurements include 1·2 cm ($\frac{1}{2}$ inch) turnings. Join the strips on the long sides as shown. Seam the turquoise strip to the dark blue piece.

Tack/baste the top and bottom pieces together, right sides facing. Machine stitch all round twice, taking 1 cm ($\frac{3}{8}$ inch) turnings and leaving a 15 cm (6 inch) gap in one side. Trim the seam and turn the mat right side out. Slipstitch the opening edges together.

Cut the crochet cotton into 23 cm (9 inch) lengths. Tie ten strands together at the middle. Repeat to make 22 bunches, and stitch them to the short ends.

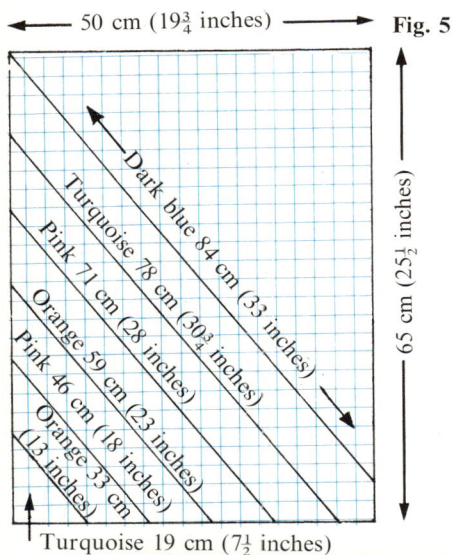

Emmeline

Fig. 5

← 50 cm (19¾ inches) →

Dark blue 84 cm (33 inches)
Turquoise 78 cm (30¾ inches)
Pink 71 cm (28 inches)
Orange 59 cm (23 inches)
Pink 46 cm (18 inches)
Orange 33 cm (13 inches)
Turquoise 19 cm (7½ inches)

65 cm (25½ inches)

This delightful rag doll would be treasured by any little girl.

Materials required

Calico/unbleached muslin 90 cm (36 inches) wide, ·3 m (⅜ yard)
Printed cotton 90 cm (36 inches) wide, ·4 m (½ yard)
White cotton 90 cm (36 inches) wide, ·3 m (⅜ yard)
Black felt 30 cm (12 inches) square
Broderie anglaise/eyelet lace with insertion slits 2·5 cm (1 inch) wide, ·3 m (⅜ yard)
Narrow satin ribbon, ·3 m (⅜ yard)
Narrow elastic, the same amount
White ric-rac, 1 m (1⅛ yards)
Velvet ribbon 2·5 cm (1 inch wide, 1 m (1⅛ yards)
Gold bead
Double knitting/knitting worsted yarn in black, 25 g (1 oz)
Scrap of narrow black braid
2 buttons with 4 holes in each
Button thread
Stranded cotton/floss in black and pink
Synthetic stuffing
Thin cardboard

Making the doll

Enlarge the pattern (Fig. 1) as indicated and cut them out. Transfer the markings to the fabric.

Body Pin the printed fabric and calico together along one long edge, right sides facing, stitch and press the seam open. Pin the arm and body patterns to the fabric with the broken lines along the seam (Fig. 2). Cut four pieces of each in this way, reversing two of them and adding 1·2 cm (½ inch) turnings all round. Join the felt to a piece of calico in the same way and cut four leg/shoe pieces. Cut four head pieces from calico, reversing two of them. Cut two soles from black felt and glue these to cardboard.

Join the head and body pieces at the centre fronts and backs, right sides facing. Join each head piece to a corresponding body piece at the printed fabric end, then join the two head/body sections at the sides, leaving the straight edges (A–B) open.

Legs Join two pairs of leg pieces, leaving the tops and sole edges open. Clip the turnings and turn the legs right side out. Turn in the upper edges and place them together, matching centre seams, and oversew them (Fig. 3).

Arms With button thread, sew a button on two inner arm pieces at the X, on the wrong side (Fig. 4). Place each pair of arm pieces together with right sides facing and stitch round them, leaving a small gap on the back of each sleeve. Trim the seam closely round the hand, and clip elsewhere. Turn the arms right side out.

Stuffing Fill the body firmly with stuffing. Fold in the turnings at the lower edge and oversew them together, matching centre seams. Fill the hands and lower arms very firmly, the sleeves a little less firmly. Turn in the opening edges and slipstitch them together. Fill the legs firmly and oversew the soles to the feet, matching C and D.

Attaching the arms Using button thread and a long darning needle, fasten the arms to the body (Fig. 5). First mark points 4 cm (1½ inches) down from the neck edge on the side seams. Take the needle under the crossed stitches, attaching the button on one arm, then straight through the body between the points, then under the stitches on the other arm. Go back through the

body and repeat. Pull the thread tight, tie the ends together firmly and trim the ends.

Hold the doll upside down and oversew the legs to it, holding them in a sitting position and working on the back.

Making the clothes

From the printed fabric cut a skirt, 12 × 54 cm (5 × 21 inches), a frill, 85 × 5 cm (33½ × 2 inches) and two sleeve frills, 23 × 5 cm (9 × 2 inches).

Press under 6 mm (¼ inch) on one edge of each frill and zig-zag stitch it in place. Join the short ends of the skirt and the frills. Press under 1·2 cm (½ inch) on the top edge of the skirt and the remaining raw edges of the frills and run gathering stitches close to the folds. Gather the frills to fit the skirt edge and the arms. Pin the skirt frill to the lower edge of the skirt, overlapping it slightly, and topstitch it in place. Stitch ric-rac over the join. Draw up the skirt to fit the waist and oversew it in place. Oversew the sleeve frills to the sleeves and stitch ric-rac over the join.

Trim 15 cm (6 inches) from the velvet ribbon and tie the remaining length round the waist, with a bow at the back. Slipstitch the ribbon in

place. Stitch narrow black braid round the neck and stitch the bead to the front.

Cut two pantalette pieces on folded white cotton, adding 1·2 cm (½ inch) turnings. Join both centre seams (E–F). Thread narrow ribbon through the broderie anglaise. Stitch the lace to the lower edge of each leg, then stitch the inner leg seams with right sides facing. Turn under and stitch a 1·2 cm (½ inch) hem at the waist edge and thread elastic through it.

Hair and features

Cut 55 strands of yarn, each 50 cm (20 inches) long. Lay the strands across the head, starting and finishing 4 cm (1½ inches) from the side seam, and back stitching them in place at the centre. Arrange the strands evenly and back stitch them all round the head at eye level. Cut more strands, 70 cm (27 inches) long. Lay them across the head, along the parting, with the centre of the strands placed as shown in Fig. 6. Back stitch across the strands at this point. Fold back the strands and tie them together about 7 cm (3 inches) from the front. Stitch them to the head. Arrange the rest of the velvet ribbon over the stitching.

Using pink thread and stem stitch, embroider the mouth, making it a little less than 2 cm (¾ inch) wide. Embroider the eyes in black stem stitch, making them 2·5 cm (1 inch) wide. For the irises work a solid area of stem stitch in black, with a single line of white down the centre for 'sparkle'.

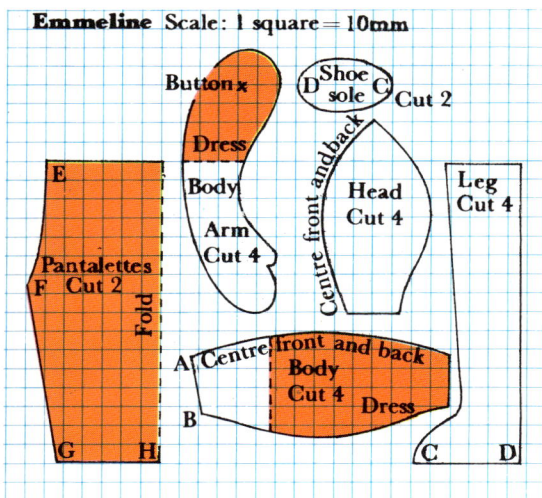

Emmeline Scale: 1 square = 10mm

Button x

Shoe sole D C Cut 2

Dress

Body

Centre front and back

Head Cut 4

Leg Cut 4

Arm Cut 4

E

Pantalettes F Cut 2

Fold

A Centre front and back Body Cut 4 Dress

B

G H

C D

Dress material Right side

Body

Arm

Body material

Fig 1

Oversew

Fig 2

Fig 3

Sewing thread

Fig 4

Tie here

Fig 5

Stitch here for fringe

Fold this part back

Macramé

An ancient craft, macramé was practised many centuries ago by the Egyptians and the Chinese, among others. The origins of the name are obscure, but it may be derived from Turkish or Arabic. The Arabs introduced it into Europe during the Middle Ages, when it flourished. After a long period of neglect it has once again become a popular craft, especially in Italy. Macramé can be used to make a variety of attractive household and fashion accessories, including handbags, wall hangings and room dividers.

Materials and equipment

Any string can be used for macramé, depending on the effect desired. The most successful are smooth, firm twines, which knot easily and do not fray or slip. Ordinary string is also very suitable. If a crisp finish is desired, a firm material such as string, nylon twine or cotton cord should be used. For a softly textured look, rug yarn is excellent. Knitting yarn may also be used, though it tends to be rather elastic.

Few pieces of equipment are needed, but a convenient-sized surface to work on is essential for small items. A piece of wood or cork can be used for this, or several sheets of cardboard. If you are using a wooden board, pad it with a sheet of plastic foam.

You will also need some pins, scissors, a tapemeasure and, for some projects, fabric adhesive/glue.

Preparing the cord

Before beginning to knot, cut the cord into suitable lengths and mount it onto another cord. This is called 'setting on' or 'mounting cords'. The holding cord is sometimes used as part of the design and sometimes withdrawn later.

It is not always easy to join in new cords, so make sure to cut lengths long enough for the complete design. As a general guide, if you are setting on each cord double, the cord should be cut eight times the length of the item. If setting on cords singly, cut them four times the length.

Setting on cords

For practice, cut a holding cord of about 20 cm (8 inches) and ten lengths of string, each 1 m (1 yard) long. Knot one end of the holding cord by taking the end over and round itself and through the loop formed to make an *overhand knot*. Pin the knot to the surface near the upper left-hand corner. Stretch the cord across the working surface, knot it near the other end, and pin it down (Fig. 1).

Now double the first working cord and insert the loop under the holding cord from top to bottom. Bring the ends over the holding cord, through the loop. Draw them tight. This is called a *lark's head knot*. Repeat with each cord, placing them close together (Fig. 2).

More basic knots

Half hitch Work on the first two cords. To tie the knot from the left, hold cord 2 taut and bring cord 1 over and then under it, then over itself (Fig. 3). Pull the knot tight. On cords 3 and 4 work a half hitch from the right, keeping cord 3 taut and reversing the knotting procedure (Fig. 4).

On cords 5 and 6 tie half hitches from left and right alternately (Fig. 5). This is called a *single alternate half hitch chain*.

Working on cords 7, 8, 9 and 10, tie half hitches alternately as before, using the cords double to make a *double alternate half hitch chain* (Fig. 6).

Flat or square knot Work on cords 11, 12, 13 and 14. Hold the middle cords taut and take cord 11 under

Fig. 1

Fig. 2

Fig. 3   Fig. 4   Fig. 5   Fig. 6

Fig. 1 Holding cord pinned down.
Fig. 2 Lark's Head knots mounted on holding card.
Fig. 3 Half hitch knots tied from left.
Fig. 4 Half hitch knots tied from right.
Fig. 5 Single alternate half hitch chain.
Fig. 6 Double alternate half hitch chain.

them and over 14. Take cord 14 over the middle cords and under 11. This is the first half of the knot – known as a *half knot* (Fig. 7). Worked continuously, the half knot forms a spiral, sometimes called a *sinnet* (Fig. 15). To complete the flat knot, bring cord 11 (now at right) back under 12 and 13 and over 14, and take cord 14 over 12 and 13 and under 11. Draw the knot tight (Fig. 8). Flat knots worked continuously make a chain, sometimes called a *Solomon's bar* (Fig. 9).

Alternate flat knot pattern This can be worked on any number of cords divisible by 4. Begin with a row of flat knots. Then, omitting the two cords at each end, work another row of flat knots (Fig. 10). Repeat these two rows alternately. The knots can be positioned loosely or densely, depending on the desired effect.

Cording This is a method of working horizontal and diagonal ridges in the work. Set on some cords, then tie

an additional cord to the left of them (Fig. 11) and take it across the mounted cords. This is called a leader cord. Keeping it taut (with a pin if necessary), work double half hitches (Fig. 16) closely over it with the mounted cords (Fig. 12). To work a second row, take the leader cord round a pin, and work from right to left as before. This is known as *horizontal cording*.

For *diagonal cording*, place the leader cord at an angle across the others (Fig. 14). Cording may be worked either with a separate cord, as shown, or with one of the mounted cords used as leader.

Fig. 7

Fig. 8

Fig. 9

Fig. 10

Dog lead

Macramé is ideal for making dog collars and leads as it produces a strong hard-wearing fabric. The quantity of twine specified will make a lead about 38 cm (14 inches) long.

Materials required

Macramé twine, 12·3 m (13½ yards)
1 dog lead clip

Making the lead

Cut two threads 4.8 m (5¼ yards) long and two 1·2 m (1⅜ yards) long. Set these cords onto the clip, with the short threads in the middle. Work four flat knots using the two long threads on either side over the central four short threads.
*Leave 2·5 cm (1 inch) unworked and then work one flat knot. Push this knot up to lie against previous knots, forming a picot.

Make three more flat knots. **
Repeat from * to ** three more times.

Leave 5 cm (2 inches) unworked, then work 14 more flat knots. This should bring the work to within 7·5 cm (3 inches) of the end of the short threads. Fold the lead so that these short ends lie over the 5 cm (2 inches) gap. With the outside threads work four flat knots over all the cords to make the hand loop. Trim short ends close to the last knot and glue them in place. Glue the last four ends behind the flat knots.

Fig. 7 The half knot. **Fig. 8** The flat knot completed. **Fig. 9** Chain of flat knots. **Fig. 10** Alternate flat knot pattern. **Fig. 11** Leader cord in position. **Fig. 12** Double half hitch cording. **Fig. 13** Horizontal cording. **Fig. 14** Diagonal cording. **Fig. 15** Sinnet formed by continuous half knots. **Fig. 16** Double half hitch. **Fig. 17** Overhand knot. **Figs. 18, 19** Centre cords pulled over three knots and through knot to make button.

Fig. 11

Fig. 12

Fig. 13

Fig. 14

Fig. 15

Fig. 16

Fig. 17

Fig. 18

Fig. 19

Plant holder

Macramé plant holders look fresh and summery whether used indoors or in the garden. This one hangs to a depth of about 137 cm (54 inches).

Materials required
String, twine or cord 54 m (59 yards)
Wood or brass ring 5 cm (2 inches) in diameter.
Flowerpot 23 cm (9 inches) in diameter.

Making the plant holder
Cut four cords 7·3 m (8 yards) long. Fold them in half and bind together 5 cm (2 inches) from the loop for 4 cm (1½ inches).

Starting 5 cm (2 inches) down, work 12 half knots, treating each pair of cords as one to form a spiral about 6 cm (2½ inches) long.

Cut four cords 6·1 m (6⅔ yards) long. Fold in half and set onto the ring with lark's head knots.

Between each lark's head, attach two cords of the original work to the ring with a double half hitch, leaving 5 cm (2 inches) unworked below the spiral.

With each pair of cords make an overhand knot close underneath the ring. Using two cords from a lark's head and two from a double half hitch, work one flat knot 2·5 cm (1 inch) down from the ring. Repeat to make four flat knots in all. (See the detail photograph.)

*Leave an unworked portion of 1·2 cm (½ inch). Taking two cords from each flat knot, work another flat knot. Repeat to make four knots in all.**

Repeat from * to ** once again. Leave 5 cm (2 inches) unworked and make another 6 cm (2½ inches) spiral.

Leave another 5 cm (2 inches) unworked. Work five flat knots. Take centre two cords back over last three knots and take through the knot itself. Pull threads down to make a 'button'. Make two flat knots underneath it.

Leave 2·5 cm (1 inch). Take centre threads of each set to outside and work one flat knot. Repeat until five flat knots have been worked on each sinnet.

From this point the net which will hold the pot is worked. Leave 7·5 cm (3 inches) unworked. Take two cords from two adjacent sinnets and on these four work two flat knots.

Repeat to make four flat knots in all.

*Leave 6 cm (2½ inches) unworked. With two cords from each group, work two more flat knots all round.** Repeat from * to **.

Leave 4 cm (1½ inches) unworked. Work two flat knots all round.

*Leave 2·5 cm (1 inch) unworked. Work one flat knot all round.** Repeat from * to **.

A gradually narrowing net has been formed which will hold the pot. Leave 2·5 cm (1 inch) unworked. Using one cord as a leader, work a row of horizontal cording all round. Take the third thread from the leader and work a second row. Take any thread as leader and work a row of diagonal cording from left to right.

With the next thread as leader, work diagonal cording. Again take any thread and work horizontal cording. Repeat.

Cut all cords to about 20 cm (8 inches). Knot and fray the ends.

Fringe for a bag

Make a fringed bag in a textured furnishing fabric with nylon twine in a harmonizing colour. The fringe shown is 45 cm (18 inches) wide and 18 cm (7 inches) deep.

Materials required

Spun nylon twine 64 m (70 yards)
Large wooden or glass beads

Making the fringe

The fringe can be made any width, so long as the number of ends on the holding cord is divisible by 4. The number in each repeat is 16. Cut each cord 80 cm (32 inches) long. Set on the cords with reversed lark's head knots so that the bar of the knot is on the wrong side. Using an extra cord as leader, make a row of double half hitch knots.

Leave the two left-hand cords free. Work the next four cords in an over-hand knot. Continue knotting each group of four to the end, leaving last two cords free. Make an overhand knot in the first four cords at left. Repeat to the end. Leave first group of four cords free.

Make a braid with the next four cords as shown below. Finish braid with a knot. Repeat on next two groups of four threads. Knot a bead onto each of the unbraided cords, level with the knotted ends of the cords. Repeat to the end, alternating one group of beaded threads with three braids. Weave the ends of the holding cord back into the work. Stitch the fringe to the bag.

Fig. 20 Working a braid with four threads.

208

Wall sampler

Work this attractive wall hanging as a sampler to practise macramé techniques. It measures about 55×25 cm ($21\frac{1}{2} \times 10$ inches), excluding the fringe.

Materials required
Sturdy parcel string
Assorted glass and china beads

Making the wall hanging
22 cords, each 4·8 m ($5\frac{1}{4}$ yards) plus length of fringe required, onto a holding cord of about 60 cm (24 inches).

With cord on left as leader, work a row of horizontal cording.

1st pattern panel With first four cords, work a chain of four flat knots. Work on next eight cords: with cord 1 as leader slanting right, work diagonal cording with cords 2, 3 and 4. Similarly slant cord 8 down to the left and work diagonal cording with cords 7, 6 and 5. Link the two leaders by looping one round the other. Cord 1 continues as leader and is slanted left with diagonal cording worked over it. With cord 8 as leader, work diagonal cording slanting right.

With next four cords work a chain of four flat knots. Work on next six cords: work three rows of diagonal cording slanting left. The first row will have cord 4 as leader and cords 3, 2 and 1 knotted over it. In the second row, cord 5 is leader and cords 3, 2, 1 and 4 are knotted, and in the third row, cord 6 is leader, and cords 3, 2, 1, 4 and 5 are knotted.

Complete remainder of panel to correspond, reversing direction of triple row cording motif.

Divider row With cord on left as leader, work a row of horizontal cording.

2nd pattern panel Work in alternate flat knot pattern for seven rows. After the first row, drop two cords on each row at outside edges. After the third row, leave centre four cords unworked, then drop four more cords in the centre with each subsequent row to create a 'W' shape. The final row should have only two flat knots one in each tip of the 'W'.

With cord on far left as leader, slanting right, work diagonal cording with all cords coming from left-hand side of the 'W'.

With four cords now lying in centre of work (two each cording row), work a sinnet of 16 half knots. With four cords on left of this spiral, work a spiral of eight half knots; repeat with four cords on the right. Now with the same leaders as before, work diagonal cording beneath spirals to complete the diamond motif. Complete pattern panel to match upper section, first working a row of diagonal cording at each side of panel with original leaders, then filling in remaining area with alternate flat knots.

Divider row as previous divider row.

3rd pattern panel With centre four cords work a half knot sinnet of 24 knots. Now go back to top left-hand corner of work. With cord second from left as leader, slanting right, work diagonal cording with all cords on left-hand side of work, including the two left-hand cords of central spiral.

Work a second row of cording just below the first one, using cord on far left of work as leader and same knotting cords as in previous row.

Similarly, work a double row of diagonal cording down right-hand side of work.

Tie the four leader cords, now lying in centre of work, in a single flat knot. Return to cords on left-hand side of work. Work on first six cords: work a four-row zigzag of diagonal cording, using cord 6 as leader throughout. End of fourth row of the zigzag should line up with point of central 'V' of cording.

Work on next four cords. With central two cords as the knot-bearing core, work a chain of reversed double half hitches – called a tatted bar – as follows: keep central knot-bearing cords taut and tie a half hitch from the left across them with cord 1.

Take cord 1 under the knot-bearing cords, then up and across them from right to left, then down through the loop formed. Draw tight. This completes one reversed double half hitch worked from left.

To work the knot from the right, use cord 4 as the knotting cord and work as given above, working half hitch from the right across knot-bearing cords, then taking knotting cord under, up and across them from left to right.

Work nine reversed double half hitches altogether, which should bring chain level with zigzag of cording already worked.

Similarly work diagonal cording down the right-hand side, using cord on far right as leader. Work rows of diagonal cording down the inside edges of the 'W', using left-hand central cord as leader for left-hand row and right-hand central cord as leader for right-hand row.

Now work on next eight cords:

209

with first four cords tie a chain of two flat knots; with second group tie one flat knot. Now link these two sets of cords by tying a multi-end flat knot with double knotting cords over a knot-bearing core of four cords.

Divide into two groups of four cords each again, and work a single flat knot with each group. Link group as before in one multi-end flat knot. Complete right-hand side of work to correspond with left-hand pattern.

Divider row as first divider row.

4th pattern panel On first four cords, work a tatted bar with 12 reversed double half hitches. Work a similar tatted bar with last four cords in row.

Now work on central cords: work one row of flat knots across all cords. Now divide cords into two equal groups and continue in the alternate flat knot pattern on each group, dropping two cords at each end of every row to form a 'V'. Work diagonal cording down each side of the 'V' shapes, using outside cords as leaders.

Work on cords in centre from two centre rows of diagonal cording. Weave these cords over and under each other to form a lattice pattern, as shown in the photograph.

With same leaders as before, reverse their directions and work a row of diagonal cording below lattice pattern to form a diamond motif.

Work two final rows of diagonal cording, using same leaders as before, to the left and right of central diamond motif, and reversing their directions.

Divider row As first divider row.

5th pattern panel Divide cords into groups of four each. On each group work a half knot sinnet with 20 half knots in each spiral.

Divider row as first divider row.

Finishing the wall hanging

Thread a bead onto each cord end in the desired position and tie an overhand knot below it. Trim cord ends as required and fray them. Untie knots in holding cord, and tie ends together for hanging the work.

Shoulder bag

The two sides of this attractive bag are alike. It measures about 25×21 cm (10×8 inches) excluding the fringe and handle.

Materials required
Heavy weight parcel string
Lining if required

Making each side of the bag
Set 26 cords, each 2·2 m ($2\frac{1}{2}$ yards) long onto a holding cord of about 36 cm (14 inches). With left cord as leader, work a row of horizontal cording.

First pattern panel With first four cords, work a chain of six flat knots. Work on next eight cords: slant first of eight cords down to the right and work diagonal cording with remaining seven cords over the first cord as leader. Arrange slant so that end lines up with base of chain just worked. With next four cords work a sinnet of half knots. Stop spiral at same depth as chain and cording row already worked. With next two groups of four cords, work chains of seven flat knots. With next four cords, work a spiral of half knots to the same depth as previous spiral.

With next two groups of four cords, work chains of seven knots. With next four cords, work a spiral of half knots.

Work on next eight cords: slant last of the eight cords down to the left and use as leader for a row of diagonal cording.

With last few cords, work a chain of six flat knots. Cross each pair of adjoining flat knot chains and pin them in place.

Divider rows With cord on far left as leader work horizontal cording. Reverse direction of leader, and work a second row of horizontal cording.

Second pattern panel Work on first eight cords: Work a chain of three flat knots with each group of four cords. Link the two chains by knotting two adjacent cords from each in a single flat knot. Work a further three flat knots with each group of four cords. Work on next 16 cords: work in alternate flat knot pattern, keeping left-hand edge straight, and dropping two cords from right-hand edge on each row until only one flat knot remains. Now work from right to left, working two chains of linked flat knots, followed by alternate flat

knot pattern over 16 cords, right-hand edge kept straight with a slanting left-hand edge.

Central panel With cord 17 as leader slanting to the left, work diagonal cording across all cords from alternate flat knot section. With cord 18 as leader, work a second row of diagonal cording below. With cords 19 and 20, work two rows of cording slanting to the right.

Fill in central diamond with half knot spirals. Use two cords from each diagonal cording section for central spiral. Work three more spirals of four cords each on either side, leaving a single unworked cord at each end.

The central spiral will have 32 knots. Allow spiral to twist round itself after every fourth knot. The first spiral on either side will each have 28 knots; the next 24 knots; and the last, 16 knots.

Cord 18 continues as leader. Reverse its direction and slant it down to the right. Work diagonal cording over it with all cords on left-hand side of diamond. Work a second row of diagonal cording below it.

Similarly, work a double row of diagonal cording down right-hand side of diamond with cords 19 and 20 as leaders. Complete lower part of pattern panel to correspond with upper part so that there are linked chains of flat knots, and triangles of alternate flat knot patterns. Link the single knot of the alternate flat knot triangle to the flat knot chains next to it by tying a single flat knot with two cords of each.

Divider rows Work as previous divider rows.

Third pattern panel On first four cords, work a chain of six flat knots. Work on next eight cords: work a crossover of diagonal cording thus – with cord 1 as leader slanting right, work diagonal cording over it with cords 2, 3 and 4. With cord 8 as leader slanting left, work diagonal cording over it with cords 7, 6 and 5.

Now link the central point of the crossover by tying a flat knot with the four central cords. Re-number cords in the position in which they now lie from one to eight. With cord 4 as leader slanting left, work diagonal cording over it with cords 3, 2 and 1.

With cord 5 as leader slanting right, work diagonal cording over it with cords 6, 7 and 8. With next two groups of four cords, work chains of two flat knots. Tie two adjacent cords from each chain in a single flat knot. Then continue with chains as before, making two flat knots in each. Work on next six cords: with cord 6 as leader slanting left, work diagonal cording over it with 5, 4, 3, 2 and 1.

With cord 5 as leader slanting left, work a second row of diagonal cording below the first, knotting over it cords 4, 3, 2 and 1.

Now reverse direction of cord 5 and work diagonal cording slanting right, knotting over it cords 1, 2, 3 and 4. Similarly, reverse direction of cord 6 and knot over it cords 1, 2, 3, 4 and 5. Complete rest of pattern panel to correspond with first part, reversing direction of patterns as required.

Divider rows as first divider rows.

To make handle

Cut two cords, each 5 m (5½ yards) plus eight times the length of finished handle. Double these cords and pin them to the working surface. Begin knotting about 23 cm (9 inches) below top loops. Work a flat knot chain about 25 cm (10 inches) long. Work in half knot spirals to the required length. Finish with a 25 cm (10 inch) chain of flat knots.

Finishing the bag

Trim leader cords to within about 2·5 cm (1 inch) of knotting. Press under work, and secure with a few stitches. Place both sides of bag together, wrong sides facing. Position handle so flat knot chains form sides of bag. Stitch firmly in place.

Divide cords along lower edge into groups of eight (four from back and front). Tie these groups into tassels: take one of the cords, and form a loop over other cords in group. Take it around the group from left to right and then down through loop. Draw tight. Repeat four more times. Trim cord ends evenly.

Tatting

Tatting is a way of producing lace-like work with only thread, a small shuttle and your two hands. It is generally worked in white or natural-coloured cotton thread and is used on linens and delicate clothing.

Materials

Crochet cotton is available in several thicknesses, the choice depending on the delicacy of the work. Tatting can also be done with string.

Shuttles are made in various materials including bone, steel and plastic. Choose one that is no longer than 7 cm ($2\frac{3}{4}$ inches) for ease in working. Some shuttles have a bobbin, for winding the thread, and a hook for joinings.

Beginning work

Wind the thread round the centre of the shuttle. If there is a hole in the centre of the bobbin, insert the thread through it and tie a knot. Do not wind the thread beyond the edge. The instructions that follow show how to work the basic stitch – called double stitch – rings and chains, and other techniques.

The directions apply to both right- and left-handed people. If left-handed, work from right to left. Hold a mirror to the illustrations below to see the method of working.

Holding shuttle and thread

1 Hold the shuttle horizontally between thumb and forefinger. Allow a short length of thread to hang free.

2 Grasp the free end of the thread with the left thumb and forefinger. The diagrams up to 8 show how thread and shuttle are held before beginning tatting.

3 Spread out the middle, ring and little finger of the left hand and pass the thread over them.

4 Bring the thread round the fingers to form a circle and hold it between thumb and forefinger.

5 Raise the middle finger of the left hand to 'open' the circle.

6 Bend the ring and little fingers of the left hand to catch the thread against the palm.

7 Adjust the thread so that the fingers are comfortable and draw the shuttle thread straight.

8 Pass the shuttle thread round the right little finger. You are now ready to begin tatting.

Double stitch

9 Pass the shuttle under the shuttle thread and through the circle.

10 Bring the shuttle back over the circle of thread and under the shuttle thread.

11 Relaxing the left fingers, drop the thread from the right little finger and draw it taut.

12 Raise the left middle finger and slide the loop between thumb and forefinger, so completing the first half of the stitch.

13 Move the shuttle forward, dropping the shuttle thread and passing the shuttle over the circle.

14 Move shuttle back, between the circle and the shuttle thread.

15 Drop the middle finger of the left hand.

16 Relaxing the fingers of the left hand, draw the shuttle thread taut with a sharp jerk.

17 Slowly raise the left middle finger to slide the loop into place next to the first half of the stitch – completing the second half.

18 Hands and shuttle are shown in position for the next double stitch. Once this stitch has been mastered it will be possible to work any design in this chapter.

Rings, picots and joinings

19 First ring As each double stitch is formed, slide it along to meet the preceding one. Hold them between thumb and forefinger. Make four

double stitches. Then make the first half of a stitch, sliding it to within 6 mm ($\frac{1}{4}$ inch) of the preceding one.

20 Complete the double stitch.

21 Slide the stitch along to meet the first four double stitches. The small loop formed between the last two stitches is a picot. Make three more double stitches, a second picot and four double stitches. Make a third picot and four double stitches.

22 Holding the stitches between thumb and forefinger, draw the shuttle thread tight so that the first and last stitches meet, forming a ring. In general instructions the ring just completed would be written: R of 4ds, 3ps sep by 4ds, 4ds, cl.

Second ring

23 (i) Wind the thread round the left hand. Leaving 6 mm ($\frac{1}{4}$ inch) from base of last ring, make four double stitches. (ii) Insert a hook through the last picot of the last ring and pull the circle thread through. (iii) Pass the shuttle through the loop. Raise the left middle finger to draw up the loop, completing the first half of a double stitch. (iv) Work the *second* half. Work 3 ds, 2ps sep by 4ds, 4ds, cl. (Second ring completed.)

Using ball and shuttle

Most designs include both rings and chains. For these you must use both the shuttle and ball threads. First tie the two threads together and make a ring.

24 Chains are made with the thread held across the left fingers, winding it round the little finger to control the tension.

25 A chain consists of double stitches, and sometimes pleats, worked over the ball thread.

Reversing

26 Normally, the rounded end of the working ring or chain faces upwards, but for some designs you must sometimes reverse the work.

27 To reverse, turn the ring or chain just completed face down. Work the *next* ring or chain in the usual way.

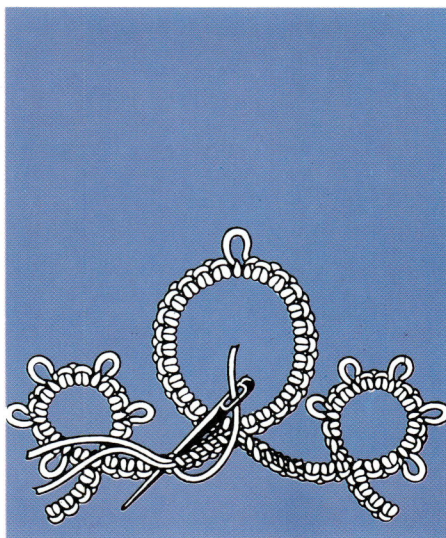

Finishing off ends

28 Make a flat or square knot close to the base of the last ring or chain. Do not cut off ends, as the strain during working may loosen the knot. With a single strand of cotton, oversew the ends to the wrong side.

To join threads

(a) When ball and shuttle threads are used, avoid a knot at the beginning of the work by filling the shuttle and beginning the ring without cutting the thread.
(b) Make a flat or square knot close to the base of the last ring or chain. Do not trim the ends, as the knot may need re-tying.

Tatting abbreviations

r(s)	ring(s)
sr	small ring
lr	large ring
ds	double stitch
p(s)	picot(s)
smp	small picot
lp	long picot
sep	separated
cl	close
RW	reverse work
sp	space
ch(s)	chain(s)
tog	together
rep	repeat

Handkerchief edging

Add a simple edging to a ready-made handkerchief (shown on page 212).

Materials required
Crochet cotton No. 40, 20 g (1 oz)

Working the edging
*R of 2ds, 7ps sep by 2ds, 7ds, cl. Join shuttle thread to last p, making sure that thread lies at back of work. (To do this, insert hook into p, catch shuttle thread and draw out into a loop, pass shuttle through loop and adjust knot.)**
Start next r immediately. Repeat from * to ** for length required.

Corner
Lr of 2ds, join to last free p of previous r, 2ds, 12ps, sep by 2ds, 2ds, cl. R of 2ds, join to last p of previous lr, 2ds, 6ps sep by 2ds, 7ds, cl. Join shuttle thread to last p. Cont edging from * to ** as required.

Making up
Press and oversew to handkerchief.

String belt

This belt in twine will be an attractive addition to your wardrobe.

Materials required
Fine parcel twine or string
Pair of toggles

Making the belt
Use shuttle and ball thread. R of 9ds, p, 3ds, cl. RW. Ch of 5ds. R of 9ds, p, 3ds cl. RW. *Ch of 3ds. RW. R of 3ds, join to p of last r, 6ds, p, 3ds, cl. RW. Ch of 5ds. R of 3ds, join to p of facing r, 6ds, p, 3ds, cl. RW. Ch of 3ds. RW. R of 3ds, join to p of last r, 6ds, p, 3ds, cl. RW. Ch of 5ds, R of 3ds, join to top facing r, 6ds, p, 3ds, cl. RW**. Repeat from * to ** for length required.

Fastening
Work a r of 12ds and enclose a toggle while closing r. Ch of 6ds. R of 12ds and enclose second toggle while crossing r.

Finishing
Divide the strands and weave in the ends. Press with a damp cloth and a hot iron to set the waxy surface of the string.

Pillowcase edging

Decorate a plain pillowcase with this attractive edging and matching insertion.

Materials required
Crochet cotton No. 20 20 g (1 oz)
A plain pillowcase

Working the panel
1st row: Tie ball and shuttle threads together. *R of 8ds, 2ps sep by 4ds, 8ds, cl. Ch of 8ds; rep from * for length required, having an even number of chs between rs and joining last ch to base of first r, without twisting work, RW. **R of 8ds, 2ps sep by 4ds, 8ds, cl. Ch of 8ds, join by shuttle thread to base of next r; rep from **, joining last ch to base of first r. Tie ends, cut and oversew on wrong side.
2nd row: Tie ball and shuttle threads tog. R of 5ds, join to p at right of any r on lower edge of previous row, 5ds,

join to next p of next r, 5ds, cl. RW. * Ch of 3ds, 4ps sep by 3ds, 6ds, join by shuttle thread to next p. Ch of 3ds, join by shuttle thread to next p. Ch of 6ds, join to last p of adjacent ch, 3ds, 3ps sep by 3ds, 3ds, RW. R of 5ds, join to next p, 5ds, join to next p, 5ds, cl. RW; rep from * skipping r at end of last rep and joining last ch to base of first r. Tie ends, cut and oversew on wrong side. Work other side to correspond.

Edging
1st row: Work as for first side of working the row for length required.
2nd row: Work as for first side of panel second row.

To make up
Pin panel in place 9 cm ($3\frac{1}{2}$ inches) from edge of pillowcase. Cut away surplus leaving 6 mm ($\frac{1}{4}$ inch) underneath for hems. Sew hems and panel in place, attaching 2ps of each ch, as shown. Sew on edging, attaching at base of each r. Press.

Making up
Baste the edging in place; buttonhole-stitch along the inner edge, catching the picots. Cut away raw edges of linen. Tack/baste the motif panels in place and attach them with continuous lines of buttonholing. Cut away linen behind each motif.

Traycloth

The edging on this pretty traycloth is approximately 18mm wide with the motif/panel approximately 37mm square. About 3mm should be left between each ring throughout the pattern.

Materials required:
Linen fabric 45cm × 36cm
Coats Mercer-Crochet No. 20 (20gr) or J&P Coats 'Knit-Cro-Sheen' No. 20, 1 ball
Tatting shuttle.

To work the edging
R of 4ds, p, 4ds, p, 4ds, p, 4ds, cl. RW. * Sr of 5ds. p, 5ds, cl. RW. R of 4ds, join to last p of first r, 4ds, p, 4ds, p, 4ds, cl. RW. Lr of 4ds, join to p of sr, 10ds, p, 4ds, cl. RW. R of 4ds, join to last p of facing r, 4ds, p, 4ds, p. 4ds, cl. RW. Sr of 5ds, join to last p of lr, 5ds, cl. RW. R of 4ds, join to last p of

facing r, 4ds, p, 4ds, p, 4ds, cl. RW. ** Rep from * to ** for 40cm or length required.

Working the corner
Sr of 5ds, p, 5ds, cl. RW. R of 4ds, join to last p of facing r, 4ds, p, 4ds, p, 4ds, cl. RW. Lr of 4ds, join to p of sr, 10ds, p, 4ds, cl. RW. R of 4ds, join to last p of facing r, 4ds, p, 4ds, p, 4ds, cl. Join shuttle thread to last p of r just made. (To do this, insert hook into p, catch shuttle thread and draw out into a loop, pass shuttle through loop and adjust knot). Sr of 5ds, join to p of facing lr. 5ds, cl. Work a second sr of 5ds, p, 5ds, cl. Join shuttle thread to next p on r to which it was previously joined. Lr of 4ds, join to p of sr just made, 10ds, p, 4ds, cl. RW. R of 4ds, join to p already connecting the two facing rs, 4ds, join to remaining p of facing r, 4ds, p, 4ds, cl. RW. Sr of 5ds, join to last p of lr, 5ds, cl. RW. R of 4ds, join to last p on facing r, 4ds, p, 4ds, p, 4ds, cl. RW. Repeat edging from * to ** for 300mm or length required, work another corner, then complete the remaining trimming similarly.

Working the motif panel
Sr of 5ds, p, 5ds, cl. RW. R of 4ds, p, 4ds, p, 4ds, p, 4ds, cl. RW. Lr of 4ds, join to p of sr, 5ds, p, 5ds, p, 4ds, cl. RW. R of 4ds, join to last p of facing r, 4ds, p, 4ds, p, 4ds, cl. RW. * Sr of 5ds, join to last p of lr, 5ds, cl. RW. R

of 4ds, p, 4ds, p, 4ds, p, 4ds, cl. RW. Lr of 4ds, join to junction of sr and lrs, 5ds, join to centre p of lr, 5ds, p, 4ds, cl. R.W. R of 4ds, join to last p of facing r, 4ds, p. 4ds, p. 4ds, cl. R W. **
Repeat from * to ** twice more to complete the square. Tie first and last rs tog to finish off. Work six squares altogether.

To make up
Baste the edging into position and buttonhole-stitch along the inner edge, catching the picots. Cut away raw edges of linen afterwards. Baste the motif panels into position so that they are aligned and attach so that the lines of buttonholing continue from square to square. Then cut away linen behind each motif. Press with a damp cloth and a warm iron on the wrong side.

Rugmaking

Rug making

Rug making is a satisfying craft – a restful activity that produces beautiful, practical furnishings for the home at relatively little cost. There are several ways of making rugs; two of the most popular are the latch hook method, which produces a thick pile, and the cross stitch method, which is essentially canvas work on a large scale.

Rug canvas and yarns

Both latch-hooked and embroidered rugs are made on rug canvas, which is available in a variety of different widths. The most frequently-used rug canvas has four threads and three holes to each 2·5 cm (1 inch). Some canvas has coloured lines dividing it into squares for ease in following a pattern. If you cannot obtain the width of canvas specified by a pattern, buy wider canvas, turn hems at the sides, and tack/baste the hems in place before beginning to work the design. Then work over both thicknesses.

The yarn normally used is a coarse, 6-ply yarn sold in both pre-cut packs, balls and skeins. Rya yarn, which is thinner than rug yarn, can also be used, with two or more strands being used at a time, depending upon the gauge of the canvas.

The latch hook method

A latch hook is easy to use, but it takes a little practice to develop a smooth rhythm of working. Work with the rug lying flat on a table and a few strands of yarn close at hand. Follow the steps shown in Fig. 1, always working in the same direction – i.e. with the worked portion toward the body – so that the pile will lie smoothly.

First loop the yarn round the shaft of the hook, then slip the hook under one double canvas thread.

Pull the ends of the yarn up and into the curved end of the hook.

Now pull the hook back towards you. As it goes under the canvas thread, the latch will close, holding the yarn in place and pulling it through the loop. Pull the yarn ends to tighten the knot thus formed.

The cross stitch method

For this method you will need a rug needle, which is a size 13 or 14 tapestry needle. Use rug yarn in skeins, cut into lengths about 35 cm (14 inches) long; longer lengths tend to tangle and become frayed. Work cross stitch (see page 114) throughout, beginning and ending as instructed on page 112.

Marrakesh rug

The design of this luxurious pile rug was inspired by North African tile motifs. The rug is worked with a latch hook, but if you prefer you could embroider it in cross stitch. The finished rug measures about 137 × 68 cm (54 × 27 inches).

Materials required

Rug canvas with 3 holes to each 2·5 cm (1 inch), 68 cm (27 inches) wide, 1·6 m (1¾ yards)
Pre-cut rug yarn in 240-strand packs: 20 packs dark tan, 18 cream, 10 beige, 8 burnt orange, 7 old gold, 4 scarlet, plus 3 50 g (2 oz) balls dark tan for binding
Latch hook
Rug needle

Working the rug

Fold under about 10 cm (4 inches) across one cut end of the canvas and,

Marrakesh rug

Centre row ▶

Centre stitch ▲

Key

Cream background

✶ Dark tan
• Beige
× Burnt orange
∨ Old Gold
○ Scarlet

Fig. 1

Fig. 2

Fig. 3

Fig. 4

Fig. 5

1   Latch technique
2   Single cross stitch
3   Binding stitch
4   Fringing
5   Braid stitch

219

skipping the thread on the edge of the fold, work the first few rows over a double thickness. Use the latch hook method shown in Fig. 1, page 219. Work each row of the design from left to right, following the chart and colour key on page 219 and starting at the bottom. When you have worked the whole chart (one quarter of the rug), reverse the pattern vertically and horizontally to complete the design. Note that at the right-hand edge one canvas hole will be left empty.

When the rug is almost complete, count the remaining rows to be worked, fold the canvas under along the last thread (left unworked) and work the last few rows over a double thickness.

Using dark tan yarn work binding stitch (Fig. 3) over the selvedges. Oversew the short ends.

Oriental mask

Work this wonderfully fierce Chinese theatrical mask using the latch hook method to make an unusual rug or wall hanging. The finished rug measures about 90 × 68 cm (35½ × 27 inches).

Materials required

Rug canvas with 3 holes to each 2·5 cm (1 inch), 68 cm (27 inches) wide, 1·1 m (1¼ yards)
Pre-cut rug yarn in 240-strand packs: 17 packs dark plum, 8 scarlet, 7 mimosa, 8 marigold, 3 pale purple, 2 black, 4 white, plus 2 50 g (2 oz) balls for binding
Latch hook
Rug needle

Key

Dark plum background

× Scarlet	◆ Pale purple
• Mimosa	+ Black
∕ Marigold	■ White

Fig. 2 Oriental Mask

Working the rug

Fold under about 10 cm (4 inches) across one cut end of the rug and, skipping the thread on the edge of the fold, work the first few rows over a double thickness. Work from left to right throughout, using the latch hook method shown in Fig. 1.

The chart gives one lengthwise half of the design. Follow the colour key and, when you reach the centre, repeat the pattern in reverse to complete the right-hand side.

When the rug is almost complete, count the number of rows remaining, fold under the canvas along the (unworked) thread that will form the edge, and work to the end over a double thickness.

Using plum yarn, work binding stitch (Fig. 3) over the selvedges. Oversew the short ends.

Rose rug

Pink roses on white and old gold backgrounds make a rug with a traditional flavour. If you prefer, you could use different colours, first planning the new colour scheme on graph paper with felt-tip pens. The design is worked in cross stitch, and the finished rug measures about 130×60 cm (51×60 inches), excluding the fringe.

Materials required
Rug canvas with 3 holes to each 2·5 cm (1 inch), 60 m (24 inches) wide, 1·5 m ($1\frac{5}{8}$ yards)

Rug yarn in 50 g (2 oz) balls: 7 balls each of old gold and white, 5 of moss green, 4 of black, 3 of light green, 2 of pink, 1 each of wine, dark rose, dark tan

Rug needle

Large crochet hook

Working the rug
Fold under 8 cm ($3\frac{1}{2}$ inches) across one cut edge and, skipping the thread on the edge of the fold, work the first few rows over a double thickness. The design is worked in cross stitch throughout, using a rug needle. Follow the chart and colour key on page 222, and work across the width of the rug until you have completed the whole repeat of four motifs. Work two more repeats, each time omitting the first row.

When you are within several rows of the end, turn under the canvas, as at the beginning, and work over a double thickness.

Using black yarn, work binding stitch (Fig. 3) along both selvedges. Cut the remaining black yarn into 18 cm (7 inch) lengths and work a fringe over the folded edges, as shown in Fig. 4.

Press the rug on the wrong side with a warm iron over a damp cloth.

Key White background

Cardinal × Moss Green • Light Green ∨ Dark Rose ■
Old Gold ╱ Black ◢ Pink ○ Dark Tan ✗

and colour key opposite. After completing one repeat (20 rows), work five rows of mid-blue. Continue until you have completed five repeats and four intervening bands of blue. At the end, work over a double thickness, as at the beginning.

Work the vertical lines on each soldier in back stitch, using a split length of black yarn. Work the mouth and eyes in red and blue.

Using white yarn work binding stitch (Fig. 3) along both selvedges. Cut the remaining white yarn into 15 cm (6 inches) lengths and fringe the ends (see Fig. 4).

Press the rug according to the type of yarn used.

Soldiers in a row

Ideal for a playroom, this rug features five smart Guardsmen at attention. The design is worked in cross stitch, and the finished rug measures about 90 × 45 cm (36 × 18 inches), excluding the fringe.

Materials required
Rug canvas with 3 holes to each 2·5 cm (1 inch), 45 cm (18 inches) wide, 1·1 m (1¼ yards)
Rug yarn in 50 g (2 oz) balls: 6 balls white, 5 mid-blue, 4 each of black and scarlet, 1 each of pink and gold
Rug needle
Large crochet hook

Working the rug
Fold under about 10 cm (4 inches) of canvas across one cut end and, skipping the thread on the edge of the fold, work the first few rows through a double thickness. Work the design in cross stitch following the chart

Fig 4 Soldiers rug
Key
White background

Dutch tile rug

Shades of blue, cream and beige are used for this charming cross-stitched rug suggesting Dutch tiles. Squares containing a floral design are alternated with cream-coloured squares and joined in two rows of four squares each. The finished rug measures 136 × 68 cm (54 × 27 inches).

Fig 4 Soldiers rug
Key
White background

Blue	v
Scarlet	∕
Black	•
Pink	o
Gold	×

Fig 5
Dutch-tile rug

Key   Cream background

v Royal blue   ∕ Medium blue
o Marble   × Light blue

Materials required

Rug canvas with 3 holes to each 2·5 cm (1 inch), 68 cm (27 inches) wide, 1·6 m (1¾ yards)
Rug yarn in 50 g (2 oz) balls: 14 balls cream, 7 royal blue, 6 beige, 4 mid-blue, 3 light blue
Rug needle

Working the rug

Fold under about 10 cm (4 inches) of canvas across one cut end and, skipping the thread on the edge of the fold, work the first few rows of the design over a double thickness. Work in cross stitch, following the chart and colour key. Each square represents one cross stitch. Work from arrows A to C, then continue to the right-hand edge, working from C to B, so forming a mirror image of the left side of the plain square.

Knitting

Knitting

Knitting is one of the most enduringly popular of all crafts – relaxing, practical and capable of producing garments of great style and individuality. In this chapter are clothes for men, women and children, each featuring an interesting combination of colours.

Tension/gauge

It is most important, in any knitting but especially in garments, to obtain the same tension/gauge as that obtained by the pattern designer. That is, you must obtain the same number of stitches (and sometimes rows also) per centimetre (inch). Even a slight variation may produce a significant difference in the size of the garment.

Before beginning to knit the garment, make a tension/gauge sample at least 10 cm (4 inches) square, using the needles and stitch pattern specified in the pattern. Pin the sample to a flat surface and count off the specified number of stitches;

mark the outer edges of the first and last stitches with pins. Measure the distance between the pins; it should be the measurement given in the pattern. If it is smaller, make another sample using needles a size larger. If it is larger, change to smaller

needles. Repeat as necessary until the measurement is correct. Row tension (generally less important) is measured in the same way.

Abbreviations

The knitting abbreviations used in the patterns in this section are as follows:

alt	alternate
beg	beginning
cont	continue, continuing
dec	decrease, decreasing
foll	following, follows
g st	garter stitch (knit every row)
inc	increase, increasing
K	knit
m1K	make 1 knitwise (by picking up the strand in front of the next stitch, placing it on the left-hand needle and knitting into it)
P	purl
patt	pattern
psso	pass slipped stitch over
rem	remain, remaining
rep	repeat, repeating
RS	right side
sl	slip
st(s)	stitch(es)
st st	stocking/stockinette stitch (knit 1 row, purl 1 row)
tog	together
tbl	through backs of loops
WS	wrong side
yo	yarn over needle (sometimes called 'yarn forward' or 'yarn round needle' in British patterns)
* *	repeat instructions within asterisks as later directed

Girl's Tunic Dress

Sizes
To fit 56 (61:66:71) cm (22 [24:26:28] in) chest
Length: 41 (46:51:61) cm (16 [18:20:24] in) (adjustable)

Tension/Gauge
15 sts and 19 rows to 5 cm (2 in) measured over st st on 3 mm/size 2 needles.

Materials
80 (100:120:160)g (3 [4:5:6] oz) of 4 ply/sport yarn in main shade, white (A); 20 g (1 oz) in each of contrast colours navy (B), turquoise (C) and red (D)
2½ mm, 3 mm, 3¼ mm and 3½ mm/sizes 1, 2, 3, and 4 knitting needles.

Note: When working pattern, carry colour not being used loosely across wrong side of work.

Front
Using A and 3 mm/size 2 needles

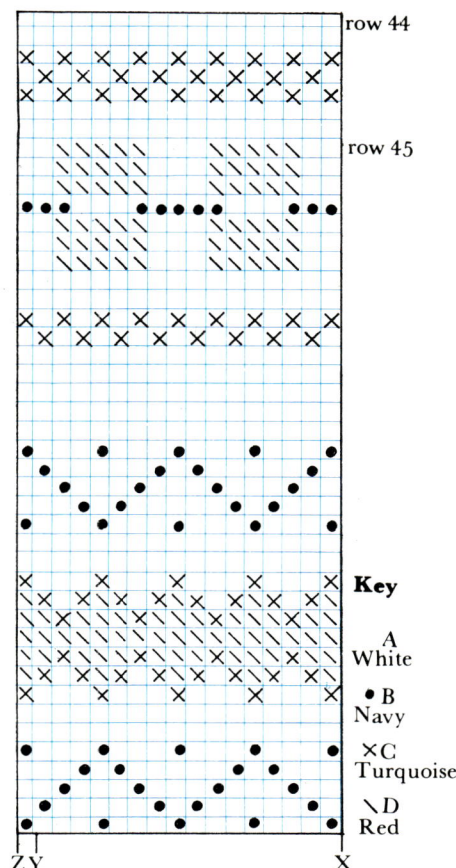

Key

A White

• B Navy

× C Turquoise

\ D Red

cast on 89 [97:105:113] sts. Starting with a K row, work 7 rows st st. K1 row on WS for hemline. Change to 3¼ mm/size 4 needles and K1 row, P1 row. Cont in st st and follow chart for pattern. Rep from X to Y across, end as at Z. Work until row 44 is completed. Turn chart upside down and starting with row 45 follow chart to end.
Change to 3 mm/size 2 needles. Cont in A in st st until piece measures 29 [33:39:46] cm (11½[13:15¼:18]in) or desired length from hem ending with a P row.

Shape armholes: Cont in A in st st, cast off 4 sts at beg of next 2 rows; dec 1 st at both ends of next 6 [7:8:9] rows and of foll alt row 67 [73:79:85] sts. Start yoke patt: *Row 1:* K1 A, (K1, B, K1 A) ending with a P [K:P:K] row. *Row 2:* P1 B, (P1A, P1B) to end. Using A K1 row, P1 row, K1 row. *Row 6:* P3 [2:5:4] A, (P5 C, P3A) until 8 [7:10:9] sts rem, P5 C, P3 [2:5:4] A. *Row 7:* As 6th, knitwise. *Row 8:* As 6th. *Row 9:* K3 [2:5:4] D, (K1 D, K3 A, K4 D) until 8 [7:10:9] sts rem, K1 D, K3 A, K4 [3:6:5] D. Starting with the 8th row, work these patt rows in reverse

225

order, back to and including first row. Cont in A work 1 [3:7:9] rows in st st.

Shape front neck: Next row: K20 [22:24:26] K2 tog, turn. Starting with a P row, work 7 rows in st st for left shoulder, dec 1 st at neck edge on next row and on foll alt rows 3 times. 17 [19:21:23] sts.

Shape shoulders: Cast off 5 [6:7:7] sts at beg of next and foll alt row and 7 [7:7:9] sts at beg of next alt row. Returning to sts still on needle, sl first 23 [25:27:29] sts onto a holder and complete second front shoulder to match first, reversing shapings.

Back

As front, omitting front neck opening, to beg shoulders. 67 [73:79:85] sts. Shape shoulders: cast off 5 [6:7:7] sts at beg of next 4 rows and 7 [7:7:9] sts at beg of foll 2 rows. Leave rem 33 [35:37:39] sts on holder.

Crew neck

Sew right shoulder seam. With RS facing and using 2½ mm/size 1 needles, start at left front shoulder and pick up and K in A 12 sts from each side of neck, and sts from holders at front and back. Work 5 rows K1, P1 rib. P1 row (ridge-row on RS). Work 4 rows in K1, P1 rib. Cast off loosely using a 3½ mm/size 4 needle.

Edgings for side openings (4)

Using A and 3¼ mm/size 3 needles cast on 5 sts and work 10 cm (4 in) in st st. Cast off.

To make up

Press or block work, according to yarn used. Sew left shoulder seam, joining sides of neck ribbing; turn in neck ribbing on ridge-row and hem loosely.

Armbands: With RS facing and using 3 mm/size 2 needles, pick up and K in A 74 [82:90:98] sts round each armhole. Work 2 rows in K1, P1 rib. Cast off in rib. Turn up hem of front and back and catch lightly in position. Sew side opening edgings in place, from hemline for 10 cm (4 in) up each side of front and back; and then sew rem of side seams, joining sides of armbands. Press seams.

Trouser Suit

Sizes

To fit 56 (61:66) cm (22 [24:26] in) chest

Length of pullover: 30 (36:41) cm (12 [14:16] in)

Length of waistcoat/vest: 33 (36:38) cm (13 [14:15] in)

Length of trousers: 58 (63:65) cm (23 [25:25½] in)

Tension/Gauge

7 sts and 9 rows to 2.5 cm (1 in) over st st on 3¼ mm/size 3 needles.

Materials

Pullover: 175 [225:275] g (7 [8:10] oz) of 4 ply/soft yarn in shade A

Waistcoat/vest and trousers: 50 g (2 oz) at double knitting/knitting worsted in shade A, 400 [450:500] g (15 [16:18] oz) in shade B, 150 [175:200] g (6 [7:8] oz) in shade C

3 mm, 3¼ mm and 3½ mm/sizes 2, 3, and 4 knitting needles

Set of 4 double-pointed 3 mm/size 2 needles

4(5) buttons

·7 m (¾ yd) elastic 1·2 cm (½ in) wide.

Pullover back

With 3 mm/size 2 needles and A, cast on 82 [90:98] sts. Work 2.5 cm (1 in) K1, P1 rib. Change to 3¼ mm/size 3 needles and st st. Work straight until back measures 20 [21:23] cm (8 [8¼:9] in) from beg.

Shape armholes: Cast off 5 sts at beg of next 2 rows, then dec 1 st at each end of every alt row until 68 [72:78] sts rem. Work straight until armhole measures 10 [11:13] cm (4 [4¼:5] in).

Shape shoulders: Cast off 7 [7:7] sts at beg of next 4 rows. Cast off 6 [8:9] sts at beg of next 2 rows. Leave rem 28 [28:32] sts on holder.

Front

Work same as back until armhole measures 7 [8:9] cm (2¾ [3¼:3½] in, ending with a P row.

Shape neck: K across 28 [30:32] sts, leaving 12 [12:14] sts on holder. K rem 28 [30:32] sts. Working one side at a time dec 1 st every row at neck edge until 20 [22:23] sts rem. Work straight until piece measures same as back.

Shape shoulders: From arm edge cast off 7 [7:7] sts twice, then 6 [8:9] sts once. Attach yarn to other side of neck and work to correspond.

Sleeves

With 3 mm/size 2 needles and B, cast on 42 [48:54] sts. Work in K1, P1 rib for 2.5 cm (1 in). Change to 3¼ mm/size 3 needles, work in st st and inc 1 st at each end of every 8th row until there are 60 [66:74] sts. Work straight until sleeve measures 24 [26:29] cm (9½ [10¼:11¼] in).

Shape top: Cast off 5 sts at beg of

next 2 rows, then dec 1 st at each end of every alt row until 26 [30:34] rem. Cast off 4 sts at beg of next 4 rows. Cast off rem 10 [14:18] sts. Sew shoulder seams.

Collar

With set of 4 double-pointed needles, pick up and K 100 [106:114] sts round neck including sts from holder.

Work in K1, P1 rib for 8 [9:10] cm (3¼ [3½:4] in). Cast off in rib.

To make up

Press or block work, according to yarn used. Join side and sleeve seams and set in sleeves.

Waistcoat/vest back

With 3¼ mm/size 3 needles and B, cast on 64 [70:76] sts and work in g st for 12 rows. Change to 3½ mm/size 4 needles and st st. At 18 [19:20] cm (7 [7½:8] in) from beg, work first and last 10 [12:12] sts in g st for 2.5 cm (1 in).

Shape armholes: Cast off 5 [6:6] sts at beg of next 2 rows. Then dec 1 st at each end of every alt row 4 [5:6] times working dec inside g st border. 46 [48:52] sts. When armhole measures 8 [9:10] cm (3¼ [3½:4] in) ending with a WS [RS:WS] row, work centre 18 [20:20] sts in g st for 12 rows.

Shape neck: Work 19 [19:21] sts cast off centre 8 [10:10] sts, work rem 19 [19:21] sts. Working one side at a time, dec 1 st at neck edge inside border every row 3 [2:1] times

Shape shoulders: Still keeping a g st border of 5 [6:6] sts, cast off 8 [8:10] sts once, 8 [9:10] sts on second row, still keeping a g st border of 5 [6:6] sts. Attach yarn at neck edge and work other side to correspond.

Left front

With 3¼ mm/size 3 needles and B cast on 28 [32:36] sts and work 12 rows in g st. Change to 3½ mm/size 4 needles and st st keeping 5 sts at front edge in g st. Inc 1 st at end of each K row inside front g st border 11 [12:14] times. 39 [44:50] sts. When side measures 18 [19:20] cm (7 [7½:8] in) from beg work 10 [12:12] sts in g st at side edge for 2.5 cm (1 in).

Shape armholes: Cast off 5 [6:6] sts at armhole edge, then dec 1 st every alt row at side edge 4 [5:5] times, at the same time shaping front by dec 1 st every 3rd row twice, then 1 st every alt row at neck edge inside border until 16 [17:20] st rem. When armhole measures 11 [13:14] cm (4¼ [5:5½] in), shape the shoulder as for back.

Right front

Work as for left front, but reverse shapings and make 4 [4:5] buttonholes in g st border by K2, yo, K2 tog K1.

To make up

Press or block work, according to yarn used. Join side and shoulder seams. Sew on buttons.

Trousers

Make two sections, reversing 1st and 2nd pattern rows and shaping top. With 3¼ mm/size 3 needles and B cast on 100 [108:116] sts. Work in K1, P1 rib for 2.5 cm (1 in). K1 row to form hemline. Starting with a K row work in st st and dec 6 sts evenly across every 12th row 4 times. 76 [84:92] sts. At same time, work 36 [38:42] rows B, 4 rows C, 2 rows B, 4 rows C, 2 rows B, 10 rows A and 2 rows B. Beg patt: Pattern stitch: With C work K1 row, P1 row. *Row 3:* With B, *K1, sl 1 purlwise, rep from * across. *Row 4:* With B, *sl the sl st, P1, rep from * across. These 4 rows make patt. Cont in patt inc 1 st at each end of every 8th row until there are 92 [100:108] sts. When leg measures 46 [48:51] cm (18 [19:20] in) from hemline cast off 6 sts at each end of row. Then dec 1 st at each end of each row every 2.5 cm (1 in) until 76 [84:92] sts rem. When work measures 20 [23:25] cm (8 [9:10] in) from 6 cast-off sts change to A and shape top working in st st. K19 [21:23], purl back: K38 [42:46] purl back. Cont knitting 19 [21:23] more sts each time until all sts are worked off. K1 row on WS to form hemline. Work 2.5 cm (1 in) st st. Cast off.

To make up

Press or block work, according to yarn used. Join leg seams and front and back seams. Insert elastic in top hem, turn up and sew lower hems.

Man's Sweater

Sizes

To fit 96 [102:106] cm (38 [40:42] in) chest
Length: 60 [61:62] cm (23½ [24:24½] in)
Sleeve seam: 47 cm (18½in)

Tension/Gauge

6 sts and 8 rows to 2.5 cm (1 in) over st st on 3½ mm/size 4 needles.

Materials

225 [225:250] g (8 [8:9] oz) of double knitting/knitting worsted in each of shades A and B, 75 g (3 oz) in shade C and 50 g (2 oz) in shade D 3 mm, 3¼ mm, 3½ mm and 4 mm/sizes 2, 3, 4 and 5 knitting needles.

Back

With 3 mm/size 3 needles and B cast on 114 [122:126] sts. Work 5 rows st st. K1 row on WS for hemline. Change to 4 mm/size 5 needles and start check patt: Attach A Row 1 K2 B, 2A, rep from * to last 2 sts, K2 B. *Row 2:* * P2 B, 2A, rep from * to last 2 sts, P2 B. *Row 3:* * K2 A, 2B, rep from * to last 2 sts, K2 A. *Row 4:* * P2 A, 2 B, rep from * to last 2 sts, P2 A. Work 16 more rows in patt. Change to 3½ mm/size 4 needles. Work in st st, 4 rows D, 16 rows C and 4 rows D. Cont in st st and work stripe patt of 2 rows B, 2 rows A, for 52 rows. Work 4 rows D, 16 rows C, 4 rows D.

Shape armholes: Change to stripe patt: Cast off 4 [5:6] sts at beg of next 2 rows. Dec 1 st at beg and end of next and every alt row until 90 [94:96] sts rem. Cont straight until armhole measures 21.5 [22:23] cm (8½ [8¾:9] in), ending with a P row.

Shape shoulders: Cast off 10 [9:9] sts at beg of next 2 rows and 9 [10:10] sts at beg of next 4 rows. Leave rem 34 [36:38] sts on holder.

Front

Work same as back until armhole measures 18 [19:20] cm (7 [7½:8] in), ending with a P row.

Shape neck: K35 [36:37] sts, turn, dec 1st at neck edge on next 5 rows, then on every alt row until 28 [29:29] sts rem, ending with a P row.

Shape shoulders: Cast off 10 [9:9] sts on next row and 9 [10;10] sts on next alt rows. Place centre 20 [22:22] sts on holder. Work other side to correspond.

Upper sleeve

Cuff: With 3¼ mm/size 3 needles and D, cast on 78 [82:86] sts. Work 3 rows st st. K1 row on WS for hemline. Change to 3½ mm/size 4 needles. Cont in st st beg with a K row work 2 rows D, 8 rows C, 2 rows D, * P1 row D on RS.

Change to stripe patt and inc 1 st at beg and end of 5th and every foll 6th row until there are 84 [88:92] sts. Cont straight until work measures 15 cm (6 in) from hemline, ending on a P row.

Shape top: Cast off 3 [3:4] sts at beg of next 2 rows. Dec 1 st at beg and end of next and every alt row till 66 sts rem. Cast off 6 sts at beg of next 6 rows until 30 sts rem. Cast off.

Lower sleeve

With $3\frac{1}{4}$ mm/size 3 needles and B, cast on 54 [54:58] sts. Work hem as for upper sleeve. Change to 4 mm/size 5 needles and check patt, inc at beg and end of 7th and every foll 6th row until there are 78 [82:86] sts. Cast off loosely.

Making up and collar

Press or block work, according to yarn used. Join right shoulder seam. With 3 mm/size 2 needles and A, K 24 [25:25] sts from left shoulder to front holder, K 20 [22:22] sts from holder, K 24 [25:25] sts to shoulder, K 34 [36:38] sts from back holder 102 [108:110] sts. Work in K 1, P 1 rib for 14.5 cm ($5\frac{3}{4}$ in). Change to B and work 2 rows rib. Cast off loosely in rib.

Join left shoulder seam (join collar with flat seam). Set in upper sleeves. Join side and sleeve seams. Turn in and sew cuff hem. Turn up cuff. Join lower sleeve seam. Attach lower sleeve to upper under cuff, so that seam will not show. Fasten down P row * over join, with a running st. Sew cuff to upper sleeve with several back sts. Turn and sew hems.

Dress and Jacket

Sizes

To fit: 81 [86:91:91] cm (32 [34:36:38] in) bust

Dress: Length from top of shoulders 95 [98:100:103] cm ($37\frac{1}{2}$ [$38\frac{1}{2}$:$39\frac{1}{2}$:$40\frac{1}{2}$] in)

Jacket: Length from top of shoulders 60 [61:62:63] cm ($23\frac{1}{2}$[24:$24\frac{1}{2}$:$24\frac{3}{4}$] in)

Sleeve seam: 41cm (16in), all sizes

Tension/Gauge

11 sts and 15 rows to 5 cm (2 in) over st st on 4 mm/size 5 needles.

Materials required

Dress: 350 [350:400:400] g (13 [13:15:15] oz) of Shetland-type double knitting/knitting worsted in main shade (A) and 50 [50:100:100] g (2 [2:4:4] oz each in contrast shades (B and C).

Jacket: 300 [300:350:350] g (11 [11:13:13] oz) in A and 50 g (2 oz) each in B and C.

$3\frac{1}{4}$ mm, $3\frac{1}{2}$ mm and 4 mm/sizes 3, 4, and 5/knitting needles

6 buttons for dress.

Dress back

** With $3\frac{1}{4}$ mm/size 3 needles and A, cast on 140 [146:152:158] sts and work 9 rows st st, starting with a K row.

K 1 row on WS for hemline. Change to 4 mm/size 5 needles. Cont in st st, starting with a K row, and work straight until back measures 10 [11:13:14] cm (4 [$4\frac{1}{4}$:5:$5\frac{1}{2}$] in from hemline, ending with a P row.
Shape as foll:
1st dec row: K8, K2 tog tbl, (K 16 [17:18:19] K2 tog tbl) twice, K48 [50:52:54] K2 tog, (K16 [17:18:19], K2 tog) twice, K8. 134 [140:146:152] sts. Work 15 rows straight.
2nd dec row: K8, K2 tog tbl, (K15[16:17:18], K2 tog tbl) twice, K46 [48:50:52], K2 tog, K15 [16:17:18], K2 tog) twice, K8 128 [134:140:146] sts. Work 15 rows straight.
3rd dec row: K8, K2 tog tbl, (K14 [15:16:17], K2 tog tbl) twice, K44 [46:48:50], K2 tog, (K14 [15:16:17], K2 tog) twice, K8. 122 [128:134:140] sts. Work 15 rows straight.
4th dec row: K8, K2 tog tbl, (K13 [14:15:16], K2 tog tbl) twice, K42 [44:46:48], K2 tog, (K13 [14:15:16], K2 tog) twice, K8. 116 [122:128:134] sts. Work 15 rows straight.
5th dec row: K8, K2 tog tbl, (K12 [13:14:15], K2 tog tbl) twice, K40 [42:44:46] K2 tog, (K12 [13:14:15], K2 tog) twice, K8. 110 [116:122:128] sts. Work 15 rows straight.
6th dec row: K8, K2 tog tbl (K11 [12:13:14], K2 tog tbl) twice, K38 [40:42:44], K2 tog, (K11 [12:13:14] K2 tog) twice K8. 104 [110:116:122] sts. ** Work 15 rows straight.
7th dec row: K8, K2 tog tbl, (K10 [11:12:13] K2 tog tbl) twice, K36 [38:40:42], K2 tog, (K10 [11:12:13], K2 tog) twice, K8. 98 [104:110:116] sts. Work 15 rows straight.
8th dec row: K8, K2 tog tbl, (K9 [10:11:12], K2 tog tbl) twice, K34 [36:38:40], K2 tog, (K9 [10:11:12], K2 tog) twice, K8. 92 [98:104:110] sts. Fasten off A and attach B.
Change to $3\frac{1}{2}$ mm/size 4 needles and P1 row. Work 12 rows K1, P1 rib. Fasten off B and attach C.
Change to $3\frac{1}{4}$ mm/size 3 needles and cont as foll:
Next row: K8, sl 1, K2 tog, psso, K 16 [18:20:22], sl 1, K2 tog, psso, K32 [34:36:38], K3 tog, K16 [18:20:22] K3 tog, K8. 84 [90:96:102] sts. Work 13 rows K1, P1 rib. Fasten off C. Attach A.
Change to $3\frac{1}{2}$ mm/size 4 needles and

cont as foll:
Next row: K8, sl 1, K2 tog, psso, K14 [16:18:20], sl 1, K2 tog, psso, K28 [30:32:34], K3 tog, K14 [16:18:20], K3 tog, K8. 76 [82:88:94] sts. Cont in st st in A and work 7 rows straight, starting with a P row.
Shape sides: Inc 1 st at each end of next and foll 5th row. 80 [86:92:98] sts. Change to 4 mm/size 5 needles and cont inc 1 st at each end of every foll 5th row until there are 94 [100:106:112] sts. Work straight until bodice measures 20 cm (8 in) from end of colour band, ending with a P row.
Shape armholes: Cast off 4 [5:6:7] sts at beg of next 2 rows. Dec 1 st at each end of every row until 68 [72:76:80] sts rem, then on foll 2 alt rows. 64 [68:72:76] sts. Work straight until bodice measures 38 [39:40:41] cm (15 [$15\frac{1}{4}$:$15\frac{3}{4}$:16] in) from end of colour band, ending with a K row.
Shape shoulders and neck: Next row: P 19 [20:21:22], cast off 26 [28:30:32], P to end. Cont on these 19 [20:21:22] sts for first side:
Row 1: Cast off 5 [6:6:6], K to last 2 sts, K2 tog. *Row 2:* P2 tog, P to end. *Row 3:* As first. Work 1 row straight. Cast off rem sts. With RS facing, rejoin yarn to rem sts and K to end. Finish to correspond with first side.

Front

Work as for back from ** to **. 104 [110:116:122] sts. Work 10 rows straight. Divide for front opening:
Next row: P46 [49:52:55] and sl these sts on a spare needle, cast off 12, P to end. Cont on 46 [49:52:55] sts for first side: Work 4 rows straight.
Next row: K8, K2 tog tbl, (K10 [11:12:13] K2 tog tbl) twice, K12 [13:14:15]. 43 [46:49:52] sts. Work 15 rows straight.
Next row: K8, K2 tog tbl, (K9 [10:11:12], K2 tog tbl) twice, K11 [12:13:14]. 40 [43:46:49] sts. Fasten off A and attach B. Change to $3\frac{1}{4}$ mm/size 4 needles and P1 row. Work 12 rows K1, P1 rib. Fasten off B and attach C. Change to $3\frac{1}{4}$ mm/size 3 needles.
Next row: K8, sl 1, K2 tog, psso, K16 [18:20:22], sl 1, K2 tog, psso, K10 [11:12:13]. 36 [39:42:45] sts. Work 13 rows K1, P1 rib. Fasten off C and attach A. Change to $3\frac{1}{2}$ mm/size 4 needles.
Next row: K8, sl 1, K2 tog, psso, K14 [16:18:20], sl 1, K2 tog, psso, K8 [9:10:11]. 32 [35:38:41] sts.
Cont in st st in A and work 7 rows straight, starting with a P row. Inc 1

st at side edge of next and foll 5th row. 34 [37:40:43] sts.

Change to 4 mm/size 5 needles and cont inc 1 st at side edge on every foll 5th row until there are 41 [44:47:50] sts. Work straight until front matches back at side edge, ending with a P row.

Shape armholes: Cast off 4 [5:6:7] sts at beg of next row. Work 1 row straight. Dec 1 st at each end of next row. Dec 1 st at armhole edge on every row, and at the same time dec 1 st at front edge on every foll 4th row until 25 [27:29:31] sts rem. Dec 1 st at armhole edge on foll 2 alt rows and 1 st at front edge on foll 4th row. 22 [24:26:28] sts.

Now keep armhole edge straight and cont dec 1 st at front edge on every 4th row, 2 [3:4:5] times more then on every foll 6th row until 16 [17:18:19] sts rem. Work straight until front matches back at armhole edge, ending with a P row.

Shape shoulders: Cast off 5 [6:6:6] sts at beg of next and fol alt row. Work 1 row. Cast off rem sts. With RS facing, attach A to 46 [49:52:55] sts on spare needle. Work 4 rows straight.

Next row: K12 [13:14:15], K2 tog, (K10 [11:12:13], K2 tog) twice, K8. 43 [46:49:52] sts. Work 15 rows straight.

Next row: K11 [12:13:14], K2 tog, (K9 [10:11:12] K2 tog) twice, K8. 40 [43:46:49] sts. Fasten off A and attach B. Change to 3¼ mm/size 4 needles and P1 row. Work 12 rows K1, P1 rib. Fasten off B and attach C. Change to 3¼ mm/size 3 needles. Next row: K10 [11:1213], K3 tog, K16 [18:20:22], K3 tog, K8. 36 [39:42:45] sts. Work 13 rows K1, P1 rib. Fasten off C and attach A. Change to 3½ mm/size 4 needles. Next row: K8 [9:10:11], K3 tog, K14 [16:18:20]. K3 tog, K8. 32 [35:38:41] sts. Finish to correspond with first side, reversing shaping.

To make up

Press or block work, according to yarn used. Join shoulder seams.

Armhole borders

With RS facing, 3¼ mm/size 3 needles and A, starting at underarm, pick up and K108 [114:120:126] sts all round armhole edge. Work 6 rows K1, P1 rib. Cast off in rib.

Front borders

Right: With 3¼ mm/size 3 needles and B, cast on 166 [170:174:178] sts and work 2 rows K1, P1 rib. Fasten off B, attach C and shape point:

Row 1: K to last 8 sts, turn. *Row 2:* Sl 1, rib to end. *Row 3:* Rib to last 6 sts (thus working 2 sts more than on first row), turn. *Row 4:* As 2nd row. *Row 5:* Rib to last 4 sts, turn. *Row 6:* As 2nd row.

Make buttonholes as foll: *Row 7:* Rib 67 [71:75:79], cast off 3, (rib 14, including st on needle, cast off 3) 5 times, rib 9, turn (thus leaving 2 sts unworked). *Row 8:* (do not sl first st), rib to end, casting on 3 over those cast off. *Row 9:* As 5th row. *Row 10:* As 2nd row. *Row 11:* As 3rd row. *Row 12:* As 2nd row. *Row 13:* In rib as first. *Row 14:* As 2nd row. Fasten off C, attach B and K1 row, then rib 2 rows. Cast off in rib.

Left: with 3¼ mm/size 3 needles and B, cast on 158 [162:166:170] sts and rib 2 rows. Fasten off B, attach C and K1 row, then rib 13 rows. Fasten off C, attach B and K1 row, then rib 2 rows. Cast off in rib. Starting at end of point, i.e. 8 sts up from tip, pin edge of right border to front edge from base of opening round to centre back, with last buttonhole 1·2 cm (½ in) below start of front shaping. Pin left border in position. Join borders neatly at back, then sew in position all round using a flat seam. Sew left border to cast-off sts at centre front. Sew point in position on RS. Join side seams and armhole borders. Fold hem at ridges to WS and sew loosely in position. Press seams. Sew on buttons.

Jacket Back

With 3¼ mm/size 3 needles and A cast on 96 [102:108:114] sts and work 14 rows K1, P1 rib. Change to 4 mm/size 5 needles and st st, starting with a K row, and work until back measures 37 cm (14½ in) ending with RS facing. Place a marker at each end of last row; work 12 more rows.

Shape armholes: Cast off 2 [3:4:5] sts at beg of next 2 rows, then dec 1 st at each end of next and every alt row until 72 [76:80:84] sts rem. Work straight until back measures 60 [61:62:63] cm (23½ [24:24½:25] in), ending with a P row.

Shape shoulders: Cast off 7 [7:8:8] sts at beg of next 4 rows, then 7 [8:7:8] sts at beg of next 2 rows. 30 [32:34:36] sts. Change to 3¼ mm/size 3 needles and K1 row, then rib 3 rows; fasten off A, attach C and K1 row, then rib 2 rows. Fasten off C, attach B and P1 row, then rib 2 rows. Cast off loosely in rib.

Left front

With 3¼ mm/size 3 needles and A, cast on 50 [52:56:58] sts and work 14 rows K1, P1 rib inc 1 st at centre of last row on 2nd and 4th sizes only. 50 [53:56:59] sts. Change to 4 mm/size 5 needles and work in st st until front matches back to markers, ending with a P row.

Shape front: Dec 1 st at end of next and every foll 4th row until 47 [50:53:56] sts rem. Work 3 rows straight, thus ending with a P row. Now keep armhole edge straight and cont dec at front edge on every foll 4th row until 21 [22:23:24] sts rem. Work straight until front matches back at armhole edge, ending with a P row.

Shape armholes: Next row: Cast off 2 [3:4:5], K to last 2 sts, K2 tog. Dec 1 st at armhole edge on every alt row, and at the same time dec 1 st at front edge on every foll 4th row as before until 29 [31:33:35] sts rem.

Shape shoulders: Cast off 7 [7:8:8] sts at beg of next and foll alt row. Work 1 row. Cast off rem sts.

Right front

Work to correspond with left front, reversing shaping.

Sleeves

With 3¼ mm/size 3 needles and B, cast on 44 [46:48:50] sts and work K1, P1 rib for 2 rows; fasten off B, attach C and K1 row, then rib 2 rows. Fasten off C, attach A and P1 row, then work in rib until cuff measures 7·5 cm (3 in) ending with WS facing.

Next row: Rib 2 [3:4:5], M1K, (rib 8, M1K) 5 times, rib 2 [3:4:5]. 50 [52:54:56] sts.

Change to 4 mm/size 5 needles and st st, starting with a K row, shaping sides by inc 1 st at each end of 3rd and every foll 10th [9th:8th:7th] row until there are 68 [72:76:80] sts. Work straight until sleeve seam measures 41 cm (16 in) ending with P row.

Shape top: Cast off 2 [3:4:5] sts at beg of next 2 rows. Dec 1 st at each end of next and every alt row until 46 [42:38:34] sts rem. Work 1 row straight then dec 1 st each end of every foll row until 30 sts rem. Cast off 3 sts at beg of next 2 rows. Cast off rem sts.

To make up

Press or block as for dress.

Left border: With RS facing, 3¼ mm/size 3 needles and A, pick up and K62 [66:70:74] sts from shoulder edge to beg of front shaping and 98 to cast-on edge. 160 [164:168:172] sts. Rib 3 rows. Fasten off A, attach C and K1 row, then rib 2 rows. Fast off C, attach B and P1 row, then rib 2 rows. Cast off in rib.

Right border: Starting at lower edge, work as for left border.

Join shoulder seams, then join borders using a flat seam. Join side and sleeve seams; insert sleeves. Press seams.

Index

Acknowledgements

The Publishers wish to thank the following designers and contributors:
Diana Barr 171; Jan Beaney 20; Margaret Beautemont 125; Fée Canning 43, 110–111, 119 inset, 139; Lydia Cole-Powney 52–56; Roberta Colegate-Stone 156–157; Anne Croft 204, 208; Margaret Darby 96, 109, 130; Lynette de Denne 48 below, 61, 86, 87, 97, 98 below right, 99, 104, 113, 126, 129; Embroiderer's Guild 48 above, 49, 65, 84, 90–91, 92–93, 95, 101, 103, 105, 127, 132–133, 144, 146–151, 155, 158–159, 173, 178, 185, 186–187; Maxine Fitter 206, 207; Morna Grafton 98 above left and right; Audrey Hersch 198; Hobby Horse Ltd, London 209, 211; Valerie Janitch 41, 74, 78, 79, 200, 201; Ann Mary Johnstone 83; Mary Konior 212, 216, 217; Shirley Lane 174, 199; Marilyn Owen 73, 89; Patons and Baldwins Ltd, designs courtesy of 'Stitchcraft' 218–222; Patricia Philpott 71; Frances Rhodes 76–77; Mary Rhodes 120, 121, 123; Jane Simpson 38, 40; Gwyneth Skae 27; Betty Swaddling 21; Lynette Syme 162; Angela Thompson 140–141; Anne Walker 167; Gillian Weaver 24–25; Mary Wolfard 169

The Publishers wish to thank the following organizations and individuals for their kind permission to reproduce the photographs in this book:
Nilson Anthony 66; Theo Bergstrom 135; Camera Press Ltd 44, 46; Phillip Dowell 10–11, 13, 24–25, 80–81, 89, 98 below right, 99, 127, 132–133, 156–157, 158–159; Embroiderer's Guild 186–187; Geoffrey Frosh 131; Michael Holford 8–9 above; J + P Coates Ltd 124; John Ledger 38, 40, 41, 52–59, 70, 71, 74–79, 120–123, 125, 162, 174, 193, 198–201, 202 above, 204–230; Rob Matheson 6–7, 8–9 below, 14, 20, 21, 27, 30–37, 48 above, 49, 50–51, 61, 65, 83, 84, 90–98 above left and right, 100–109, 113–119, 130, 134, 136–155, 169, 173, 178–185; Bryony Nielson 197; PAF International 68, 69, 202 below; Jerry Tubby 43, 48 below, 73, 86, 87, 110–111, 126, 129, 167, 171; Whitbread 62–63